THE 'POURQUOI-PAS?' IN THE ANTARCTIC

Winter Quarters of the Expedition at Petermann Island.

THE VOYAGE OF THE
'POURQUOI-PAS?'

THE JOURNAL OF THE SECOND FRENCH

SOUTH POLAR EXPEDITION, 1908–1910

By

DR. JEAN CHARCOT

English Version by
PHILIP WALSH

WITH A NEW FOREWORD BY
PAUL-ÉMILE VICTOR

Directeur des Expéditions Polaires Françaises
(*Missions Paul-Émile Victor*)

ARCHON BOOKS · HAMDEN, CONN.

First published in French as
Autour du Pole Sud: Expedition du 'Pourquoi-Pas?'
by Flammarion, 1910,
and in English as
The Voyage of the 'Why Not?' in the Antarctic
by Hodder and Stoughton, 1911
Reprinted in 1978 by offset lithography and
republished with the present title in the United Kingdom by
C. Hurst & Co. (Publishers) Ltd., London,
and in the United States of America as an
Archon Book, an imprint of The Shoe String Press, Inc.,
Hamden, Connecticut 06514

© C. Hurst & Co. (Publishers) Ltd., 1978
Foreword to New Impression © Paul-Emile Victor 1978

Library of Congress Cataloging in Publication Data

Charcot, Jean Baptiste Auguste Étienne, 1867-1936.
  The voyage of the Pourquoi-pas? in the Antarctic.

  Translation of Autour Pôle Sud.
  Reprint of the 1911 ed. published by Hodder and
Stoughton, New York and London, under title: The voyage
of the 'Why Not?' in the Antarctic.
  1. Expédition antarctique française, 2d, 1908-1910.
2. Pourquoi-pas (Ship) I. Expédition antarctique
française, 2d, 1908-1910. II. Title.
G850 1908.C4813   1977   919.8'9'04   77-20265
ISBN 0-208-01644-9

Printed in Great Britain

PREFACE

By PAUL-EMILE VICTOR
Directeur des Expeditions Polaires Françaises
(*Missions Paul-Emile Victor*)

CAPTAIN Scott called him the 'polar gentleman'. The two men had met on the slopes of Mont Ventoux, where both went to get into training for the next polar expedition that each was to undertake. It was there that they developed together some pieces of equipment which both were to use later, in particular those nailed soles which were adjusted from underneath like ice crampons, and which saved the life of the Australian Douglas Mawson fifteen years later.

Jean-Baptiste Charcot, doctor of medicine—'Commandant Charcot' as he is known today—was the son of Jean-Martin Charcot, also a medical doctor. The former is known for his expeditions to the Antarctic Peninsula in 1903–5 and 1908–10 and to the Greenland Sea in 1929–36. The latter was a renowned neurologist: specialists from all over the world came to sit at his feet in Paris, and crowned heads were among his patients.

As he told me himself, Jean-Baptiste Charcot, at the age of thirty-five, was 'nothing more than my father's son', a situation which he found unsatisfactory. It was the turn of the century, and at the time three scientific expeditions were being organised for the study of the Antarctic: Adrien de Gerlache's Belgian expedition on board the *Belgica*, the British expedition commanded by the Norwegian Carstens Borchgrevinck on the *Southern Cross*, and W. S. Bruce's Scottish expedition on the *Scotia*.

It was not so much a systematic assault for the purpose of increasing knowledge of the frozen continent, as a spontaneous international effort leading on from a revival of interest in the Poles, which had started with the International Polar Year of 1882–3 and had been nourished by the period of peace, prosperity and general euphoria which the enormous techno-

i

logical and scientific progress in the second half of the nine-teenth century brought about.

Charcot, not yet 'Commandant', felt deeply the absence of France from this international company, and resolved to make it good himself. This led directly to the expedition of the *Français* in 1903–5 along the west coast of the Antarctic Peninsula. The expedition had originally been intended to sail to the Arctic, but when Charcot learned that Nordenskjold's vessel, the *Antarctica*, had disappeared and that there was no news of the Swedish expedition, he cancelled his plan and prepared instead for an expedition to the Antarctic. When Nordenskjold's expedition was rescued by the Argentinians, Charcot decided to carry on the work which de Gerlache had undertaken in the same area five years earlier.

The *Français* set out from Brest on the 1st August 1903. She wintered at Booth-Wandel Island, and then in the summer of 1904–5 sailed along the west coast of the Peninsula. A map was produced which, with corrections made by the *Pourquoi-pas?* expedition three years later, remained the only accurate one for the next quarter of a century. On its return, the *Français*, which had suffered severe damage, was repurchased by Argentina when it arrived in Buenos Aires on the 14th of March 1905. A few months later, it went aground and broke up in the estuary of the River Plate.

Charcot returned to the west coast of the Antarctic Penin-sula in 1908–10 aboard the *Pourquoi-pas?*, which he had ordered from a shipyard at St Malo on returning from his first voyage. It was the most modern and comfortable polar vessel that had been built up to that time. He sailed from Cherbourg on 31 August 1908, and his final port of call before the Antarctic was Punta Arenas, where he put in on 16 December the same year. After following the west coast of the Antarctic Peninsula as closely as possible, he discovered a new territory—Fallieres Land—and then sailed parallel with part of the coast of Alexander I Land, now Alexander I *Island*, which Bellingshausen had discovered some ninety years earlier. The following summer, he discovered Charcot Land (today Charcot Island) which he named after his father. After passing again by Peter I Island, he arrived at Punta

ii

PREFACE

Arenas on 11 February 1910, and returned to Le Havre on 3 June, having explored 3,000 kilometres of unknown coastline. In addition to their survey work and mapping under sail without fixes on land, Charcot's Antarctic expeditions produced an extremely rich harvest of scientific observation in the fields of meteorology, glaciology, geology and, especially, zoology.

Then followed the war of 1914–18, during which for a time Charcot commanded a *cargo-piège* (armed vessel disguised as a merchantman—used by the French, British and German navies in the First World War). After the war he persuaded the French Navy to re-fit and strengthen the *Pourquoi-Pas?*, and between 1926 and 1936 he made regular oceanographic voyages during the summer in the Greenland Sea between Scoresby Sound and Iceland. In 1932, accompanied by the French Navy's polar vessel *Pollux*, he established the French expedition for the Second International Polar Year.

In 1934, when I was embarking at St. Malo on the *Pourquoi-pas?* with three companions for my first Greenland expedition, I saw a blond giant arriving. It was the Australian John Rymill, one-time travelling companion of Gino Watkins, who was preparing an expedition to Graham Land (as the Antarctic Peninsula had been renamed). He had just paid a visit to Charcot, and told me that they had talked at length, poring over Charcot's maps of 1910, which still remained the only ones in existence for that region of the Antarctic.

I myself knew Charcot well, and this I take as my authority for writing this preface. It was largely due to him that I was able to able to organise my first expedition in 1934, among the Angmagssalik Eskimos in east Greenland, an expedition which was to decide my entire future career: I have remained *un polaire* without a break, and today am in charge of French scientific expeditions to both the Arctic and the Antarctic, the *Expeditions Polaires Françaises* which I created in 1947.

Charcot was not one of those head-shaking mandarins who say to the young, 'Prove your ability first and then we shall see'; and then, if success follows, claim it for themselves. I wrote to him for the first time in 1934, asking if he would take me and three companions to East Greenland and drop us off

Suddenly Charcot appeared in a doorway. Although I had never met him, I knew him well by sight. I had made cuttings of newspaper articles about him, and had a collection of photographs of him and his famous ship. He was tall, with a stoop, his hair and goatee beard the colour of pepper and salt, and his moustache yellowed with the English cigarettes which he chain-smoked, but which he inhaled only a few times before throwing them away. His rather large nose balanced his oval face, and together with his beard seemed to make an entity worthy of his piercing dark eyes—lively, sometimes sad, and always with dark circles round them—under his high forehead from which the hair had receded. He was sixty-seven, I was twenty-six.

Charcot glanced round the hall and then came straight over to me. At first it amazed me that he had been able to 'recognise' me, but of course I had forgotten that I was the only person in that place who was under sixty years old.

'I received your letter, *mon petit*,' he said. 'What is the problem?'

I put my request to him as clearly and concisely as I could, and somehow managed not to stammer with emotion. But from the first few words, I felt in a panic, and this certainly showed!

Charcot was standing, and leaned against the heavily moulded side of a doorway. His eyes were fastened upon me, unsmiling.

'So there it is,' I said by way of conclusion. 'I beg to ask you, *Commandant*, if you will take me to Angmagssalik and leave me there for a year to bring back some collections for the museum, and to study the inhabitants . . .'.

'To Angmagssalik?'

'Yes, *Commandant!*'

'But, *mon petit*, you know that I only ever go to Scoresby Sound, which is five hundred kilometres from Angmagssalik!'

iv

PREFACE

'Yes, *Commandant*. . . .'

'Well, you have a nerve!'

He looked at me for a long time without moving—my throat was dry. The old gentlemen still passed by in the hall, talking to each other but for me there was no one else present but this big man with the energetic face. At last I saw a smile come into his eyes, and still looking at me, he said:

'Very well, *mon petit*, I will take you. . . .'

On 16 September 1936, at 5 o'clock in the morning, he was shipwrecked in a fierce gale with his beloved vessel the *Pourquoi-pas?* on the rocks of Akranes, in the Bay of Reykjavik, Iceland. Of the forty-four men on board, only one was saved, a signals petty officer, thanks to whom it was possible to reconstruct what had happened.

I did not hear anything of this until six months later. I was once again in Greenland, after having crossed the ice-cap on foot from west to east with my three companions and teams of dogs—a journey of about 1,000 kilometres at a height of 3,000 metres. At the end of this journey, in August 1936, Charcot had come to collect me at Angmagssalik. He had then left us—my adopted Eskimo family of twenty-five members and myself—at Kangerdlugssuak, 250 kilometres to the north where we were going to build our isolated hut and where I was to live for more than a year, as an Eskimo.

On 10 August I went on board the vessel for the last time to take leave of 'the Pasha', who had decided to sail for Iceland that day. Charcot was writing in his cabin—in front of him were some pages covered with his beautiful regular calligraphy, in the violet ink he always used.

'*Commandant*, I have come to take leave and to thank you.'

He stood up and took my hand in both of his.

'Don't thank me, *mon petit*', he said, 'I have done what I could to help you.' Then, after a silence, he added: 'And you know that I like you very much. . . .'

We were face to face. His eyes did not smile, as at our first meeting two and a half years previously. They looked at me with insistence and with sadness. And after a moment he said:

'If it weren't for my family, I would like best to die at sea. . . .'

Then he looked out a bottle of good wine and another of rum, and thrust them into my pockets.

'*Au revoir, mon petit*,' he said, and suddenly gave me a rough embrace.

I never saw him again.

Charcot was a great and good man.

(*Translated from the French by Adrian Riddiford*)

THE VOYAGE OF THE
'WHY NOT?'
IN THE ANTARCTIC

THE JOURNAL OF THE SECOND FRENCH
SOUTH POLAR EXPEDITION, 1908–1910

By
DR. JEAN CHARCOT

English Version by
PHILIP WALSH

WITH NUMEROUS ILLUSTRATIONS
FROM PHOTOGRAPHS

HODDER AND STOUGHTON

LONDON NEW YORK TORONTO

CONTENTS

v

ILLUSTRATIONS

ILLUSTRATIONS

INTRODUCTION

THE distance between Europe and the Antarctic is the principal cause of the apathy so long shown toward exploration in the latter region, while in the direction of the North Pole, on the contrary, explorations grew more and more numerous.

Recently, however, the South Pole has emerged from darkness. Voyagers and scientific men during the last two centuries have realized that our knowledge of the natural physical conditions of the globe must necessarily remain incomplete as long as there continues so large an unknown zone as that represented by the great white spot covering the southern extremity of the world, twice as vast as the whole of Europe.

The general public, too, has been aroused to a passionate interest in the subject. There is good reason, for there is no other region of which the study is more gratifying to explorers or to the scientific men who give their attention to the observations and collections made by the explorers. Everything there, indeed, is new, much is unexpected, and whoever makes up his mind to go thither is certain of important discoveries to reward his pains.

The circumnavigatory voyages and the expeditions of the Englishmen Cook and Ross, the Russian Bellingshausen, the American Wilkes, the Frenchman Dumont d'Urville, combined with the gallant incursions of the English and American sealers, Biscoe, Morrell, Weddell, Palmer, Pendleton and Balleny, the German Dallmann, and the Norwegians

Larsen and Evensen, narrowed very considerably the limits of the great Terra Incognita which is supposed to exist, and already warranted the view that if the Arctic polar cap is composed of a frozen sea bounded by the northern coasts of Europe, Asia, and America, the Antarctic polar cap, on the other hand, is solid land or at least a vast frozen archipelago surrounded by sea.

A Belgian officer, Commandant de Gerlache, has the credit of spending the first winter amid the Antarctic ices on board the *Belgica* in 1897, his achievement being from all points of view a fine and productive piece of work. It had also the merit of exciting public attention, and undoubtedly it is to his example that we owe the very fruitful pilgrimages of the last few years to the Antarctic. In fact, after the wintering of the Anglo-Norwegian Borchegrevinck Expedition on Ross Land, Europe organized a regular siege of the Antarctic. Beginning with 1902, there were to be seen the English captain, Scott (who had just started out again, having Shackleton with him as a partner) exploring Ross Sea and Victoria Land and making a magnificent raid across the great ice barrier; the German professor, Van Drygalski, on the *Gauss*, wintering in the pack-ice in that difficult sector of the Antarctic Circle which lies south of Kerguelen and discovering new lands there; the Swedish professor Nordenskjöld, accompanied by the Norwegian captain Larsen, wintering under dramatic conditions—but conditions very important for science—east of Graham Land, whence the audacious dash of the Argentine captain Irizar brought him home; the Scottish doctor, Bruce, on board the *Scotia*, discovering Coates Land in Weddell Sea and bringing to a close one of the greatest of surveying campaigns; and finally, in 1904, the little ship *Français*, commanded by me, attempting to verify and continue the discoveries of De Gerlache, while wintering on the west coast of Graham Land.

In connexion with this great joint effort one is pleasantly

struck by the absolute harmony between the heads of the expeditions and the savants who organized them ; and also by the genuinely scientific spirit which animated them all. It is to be hoped that in the conquest of the Antarctic such will always be the case, to the great benefit of universal science. I am sure that in our enlightened age there will be thereby no diminution of the slight glory which explorers are able to shed on their own countries.

In 1908 Sir Ernest Shackleton accomplished his fine and gallant piece of exploration, too well known to all for it to be necessary to dwell on it here, which brought him within 179 kilometres (112 miles) of the Pole. And we on the *Pourquoi-Pas ?* were doing our best—without, however, any desire to challenge comparisons—in the region to the south-west of South America, with results which, thanks to the zeal and energy of my colleagues, the scientific world has been pleased to consider important.

The exploration of the Antarctic, therefore, has started and seems as though it will never cease until the conquest, however arduous and long of accomplishment it may still look, is complete. Captain Scott, indeed, has just set out again for the conquest of the South Pole itself, and we hear of great expeditions preparing in Germany and America. Lastly, the Argentine Republic, which has for several years kept up a permanent observatory on the South Orkneys, is anxious to establish another on the west coast of Graham Land, at the place where we wintered.

The diary of our late expedition forms the subject of my new book ; but I think I ought first of all to explain why I chose as my working-centre this inhospitable region, so unpromising at times and so distant from the actual Pole.

James Ross in 1841, while skirting, in the sector of the Antarctic Circle lying south of Australia, a line of coast trending to the south—called by him Victoria Land—discovered an immense ice-cliff rising absolutely vertical and continuing eastward. This has since been known by the name of the Great Barrier.

Borchegrevinck in 1900 climbed this cliff and ascertained the existence of an ice-plain stretching as far as the eye could reach. Lastly in 1902 the *Discovery* Expedition, skirting the Great Barrier, found King Edward VII Land bounding it on the east, and then, during the course of the winter on Victoria Land, crossed the barrier in a magnificent dash as far as 82° 17′ South latitude. It was quite natural that Shackleton should return to these same regions, staked out by the explorers of his own country ; and it was equally quite natural that, after he had announced his intention of going there, I should abstain from directing my course thither, in spite of the attractions ; for one can sail as far south as 78° and from that point a vast flat plain seems to extend to the earth's axis. But, of necessity, two expeditions of different nationality, with the best intentions in the world and with the best of hearts, could not have avoided coming into rivalry over the glorious prize of the Furthest South ; and, great sporting interest as this rivalry would have had, it could not but have prejudiced completely the observations and perhaps the ultimate results. I must hasten to add, too, that I have no reason for supposing that we should have rivalled the magnificent results attained by my friend Sir Ernest Shackleton ; and therefore the pecuniary sacrifices which my country made would have been entirely wasted.

Besides, the Antarctic is a vast enough field to allow a number of expeditions to work there together with advantage. I resolved to return to the region which I had begun to explore on the *Français* in 1903–1905, i.e. that mountainous projection, due south of Cape Horn, which seems as if it had once been a continuation of America and is improperly known under the general name of Graham Land. There I should be able to continue the researches of the *Français* (themselves considered so valuable) in all branches of science, and to verify, complete, and expand them. To the South Graham Land came to an abrupt end in 67° of latitude. Beyond, Alexander I Land rose amid the ice, scarcely visible and never yet approached. Was it a solitary island or part of a continent? West of it an unknown zone stretched as far as King Edward VII Land. The *Belgica*, carried along by the drift, was able to make some interesting soundings in part of this zone, but the work required continuing as far as possible westward, where nothing had been made out except a small island, reported by Bellingshausen but questioned by some geographers. Had we any right to go on calling by the name of the ' Antarctic Continent ' this portion of our globe where the only indications of land to which we could point were two isolated peaks at a distance from one another?

My exact object was to study in detail and from all points of view as wide a stretch as possible of the Antarctic in this sector of the circle, regardless of latitude. I knew that I had chosen the region where ice confronts the navigator as far north as 61°, where innumerable icebergs dot the sea, and where the coast-line is fringed with high mountains, to all appearance insurmountable. I had no hope therefore of approaching the Pole. Nevertheless, lest any one should cry ' Sour grapes ! ' I must hasten to say that if I had had the chance of stumbling on a road by which I could realise the dream of all Polar explorers I should have made for the Pole enthusiastically and should certainly have spared nothing to reach it.

I had no means of foreseeing, however, what we might discover, and the unknown nature of my undertaking when I made choice of this sector of the circle rendered the organization of the expedition all the more difficult, since it was necessary to be ready for any emergency, and it was impossible, as in the case of an attack on familiar ground, to concentrate one's preparations for a struggle against forces which could not be foreseen.

INTRODUCTION

I had entertained this project of a new expedition even before the end of my former one, and since my return to France, encouraged by the satisfaction the scientists showed with the results I had achieved, I had been looking for the means of realizing my plan. I submitted my programme to the Academy of Sciences, which appointed a committee to consider it and after a favourable examination decided to give its gracious patronage to this new expedition, issuing detailed instructions as to the work which it would like us to undertake. The Museum and the Oceanographical Institute similarly consented to be patrons. With such backers, success was surely inevitable.

Still it took me many long months before I could discern the possibility of raising the necessary funds, though I had no lack either of sympathy or of encouragement. The Paris Press never ceased to raise its powerful voice in my behalf, while devoted friends like MM. Joubin and Rabot, and my own family, too—in spite of the prospect of a long and painful separation—never let me be discouraged.

At last my efforts had a result. I was lucky enough to interest in my work MM. Berteaux, Doumer, and Etienne, who were joined first by MM. J. Dupuy and R. Poincaré, and then by M. Briand, Minister of Public Instruction and M. G. Thomson, Minister of Marine. Soon, after a favourable report had been issued by the Committee on Exploration, I was assured that a handsome grant-in-aid would be included in the Budget for presentation to the Chambers.

On the proposal of M. Doumer, indeed, the Chambers agreed to a vote of 600,000 francs in the Budget of the Ministry of Public Instruction.[1] This proof of confidence on the part of the French Government and the patronage of our great learned societies were to me the finest recompense for the

---

[1] While the expedition was at work in the Antarctic, M. Doumer twice persuaded the Chambers to vote a sum of 50,000 francs, which brought the Government grant up to 700,000 francs.

SOUTH POLAR CHART.
Showing routes of the Charcot (1908–10) and Shackleton (1908–9) Expeditions.

efforts which I had made. To this sum were added later 100,000 francs subscribed by generous donors, including a sum of 10,000 francs from the Geographical Society of Paris and grants from the Museum, the Paris Municipal Council, and the Chambers of Commerce of the big French towns.

The Ministry of Marine put at the disposal of the Expedition three naval officers and promised me 250 tons of coal, the dredging outfit which had already been used on the *Français*, and all the necessary instruments, maps, and documents which could be provided by the Surveying Department and the arsenals.

The Prince of Monaco, whose own labours and great generosity have given such an impulse to surveying work, offered the Expedition a complete oceanographical outfit.

The Museum, the Bureau des Longitudes, the Montsouris Observatory and private observatories, the Meteorological Department, the Agronomic Institute, the Pasteur Institute, and several celebrities in the world of science enriched with loans and gifts our scientific arsenal, already increased by purchases from the funds of the Expedition, until it became one of the richest and completest ever carried by a polar expedition.[1]

Large as was our banking-account in the end—800,000 francs—most South Polar expeditions sent out by other countries have had at their disposal much larger sums, and it is not one of the least of my grounds for pride that we succeeded in organizing ours in so perfect a way at so small an expense, especially when one considers that the ship (which alone cost 400,000 francs) was brought back with the greater part of the equipment in good condition. Account must be taken of the outlay necessary on the wages of the crew for two years, the costly scientific instruments of which I have just

---

[1] When we reached Buenos Aires the Meteorological Department of the Argentine Republic, under the direction of Mr. Davis, lent us still more instruments.

spoken, the food for thirty men for three years, and all the stores required. If I was able to attain so good a result, my thanks are due for the generous interest shown by individuals, including perfect strangers, by the governments of Brazil, the Argentine Republic, and Chili, and also by the great majority of our own purveying firms.

As soon as the scientific staff was definitely constituted, my future colleagues had several months in which to perfect themselves in the duties they would be called upon to perform, while availing themselves of the bounteous hospitality offered them on the yachts of the Prince of Monaco, at the Montsouris and Paris Observatories, at the Meteorological Department, and in the Museum laboratories.

May I be allowed to make special mention here of the excellent relations which have always existed between other Antarctic explorers and myself? Seeking to gain every advantage, I have frequently addressed myself to MM. de Gerlache, Bruce, Scott, Shackleton, Otto Nordenskjöld, and Van Drygalski, and all of them have been kind enough to pour out for my benefit their precious stores of experience.

The ship was not only the most important factor in the Expedition, but also that which demanded attention from the very first. My earliest idea was to try to buy back my old vessel the *Français*, and I caused negotiations to be opened with the Argentine Republic for this purpose. But I learnt that this excellent little ship, renamed the *Austral*, was to be used for the revictualling of the station on the South Orkneys and in the establishment of a new observatory on Wandel Island.[1] Next, with the aid of my friend M. Charles Boyn, ex-Naval Paymaster and now Director of the Agence Générale Maritime, we tried to purchase a whaler, either in

---

[1] In December, 1907, while leaving Buenos Aires on this double duty the *Austral* was wrecked on a shoal in the Rio de da Plata, going down with all the instruments she had on board, while the crew were saved by the French liner *Magellan*.

Scotland or in Norway ; but our search was in vain, for all the vessels offered to us were of ancient build and required considerable alterations. Moreover, our programme involved wintering on board, which made necessary the fitting-up of special accommodation ; and all these alterations and improvements would in the end have brought the price up nearly as high as that of a new boat.

After collecting the needful information in the countries which have concerned themselves most about polar exploration and from the mouths of competent men, we decided with M. Boyn to submit our list of requirements to ' Père ' Gautier, the clever St. Malo shipbuilder, who had been so successful in the matter of the *Français*. My demands were considerable, and all the more difficult to fulfil because of the limitation of my pecuniary means. I wanted, in fact, a very good weather-boat for the navigation of the Antarctic seas, at the same time one powerful enough to resist shock against ice and the grinding which it might have to undergo, fitted with holds capable of taking 250 tons of coal and about 100 tons of food and stores, with comfortable accommodation for the crew of twenty-two and the eight members of the staff, and finally with laboratories.

Père Gautier, with an eye only to the building of a fine boat and the solving of a difficult problem, undertook the job with enthusiasm and presented us with an extremely modest estimate. So the construction of the *Pourquoi-Pas ?*, under the superintendence of M. Boyn, was entrusted to Gautier and Son of St. Malo, and the result proves once more the skill, conscientiousness, and disinterested character of the doyen of French shipbuilders.

The engine had to be strong, powerful, and economical. We chose a compound engine of 450 horse-power built by the firm of Labrosse and Fouché of Nantes, under the superintendence of M. Laubeuf, their head marine engineer.

The *Pourquoi-Pas ?*, commenced in September, 1907,

was launched on May 18, 1908. The robustness of her construction and the care devoted thereto, the simultaneous power and elegance of her lines, were the admiration of all discriminating eyes. Admiral Névy represented the Ministry of Marine at the launch, M. Rabot the Ministry of Public Instruction. My wife as godmother of the vessel, supported by M. Doumer as godfather, broke the customary bottle of Mumm on the stern—and as she broke it at the first attempt a prosperous career was assured in advance for the *Pourquoi-Pas ?*

A few weeks later, when the engine was in its place and the rigging was completed, Monseigneur Riou came to Saint-Malo to baptize the *Pourquoi-Pas ?* as he had formerly baptized the *Français.*

The dimensions of this ship, which obtained the highest character at the Bureau Veritas,[1] were :—

Length at water line	40 metres
Beam	9·20 metres
Depth of keel	5·10 metres
Load water-draught	4·30 metres

Her rigging was that of a three-masted barque, and her masts, sturdy but short, had been selected at heavy expense among the finest specimens in Brest Arsenal. In the case of the wooden scantlings as of the anchors and chains, everything was made about three times as strong as on an ordinary ship of the same tonnage. The powerful ribs were brought very close together, and at the bow as also in the bilge the spaces between the timbers were filled in with chocks of wood. Two very thick plankings covered the ribs, being themselves protected against the wear and tear of the ice by an exterior sheathing. An interior planking, caulked and coal-tarred, made a kind of extra hull inside. The whole vessel, except that the bilge was of elm, was built of the best oak.

On every side she was strengthened by special services.

---

[1] The French ' Lloyd's '—*Trans.*

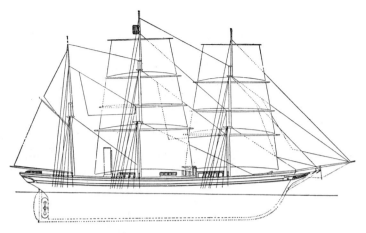

The *Pourquoi-Pas ?*'s Rig.

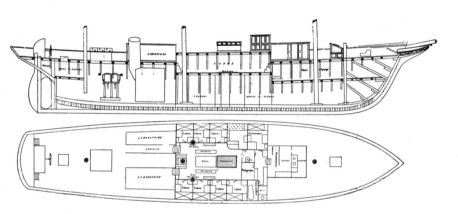

The Plan of the *Pourquoi-Pas ?*

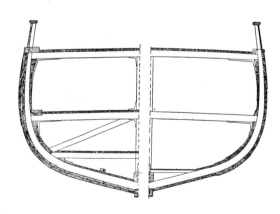

Sections of the *Pourquoi-Pas ?* (to left) and of an Ordinary Boat of
the same Tonnage (to right).

Her bow, which would be called upon to withstand the severest shocks, had been particularly looked after. This was very compactly built and furnished inside with powerful belts, outside with armour-plates and thick galvanized iron sheeting, while its lines were rounded to enable it to ride up over the ice and break it by the weight of the vessel.

Thus the *Pourquoi-Pas ?* was a superb piece of work, of remarkable sturdiness—through which quality alone, as will be seen, she was enabled to escape from the rude ordeal through which she went.

The same care and solidity were shown in erecting the engine as in constructing the hull, and spare parts and repairing-tools were provided in sufficient quantity to allow all the necessary repairs to be executed on board. A steam windlass was furnished by the firm of Libaudière and Mafra of Nantes, which served equally for working the anchor-chains and cables, the dredge-nets and the various fishing-tackle.

The accommodation on board had to meet the necessities of our work and our life in winter-quarters, while providing the maximum of comfort. I believe I may say that the arrangements made gave generally excellent results. Fore-ward, under the deck, were the very spacious quarters for the crew, with eighteen berths, lockers, tables, etc., the height of which between decks was two metres, the same as in all the living-rooms. Behind this and communicating with it was a small ward-room for the subordinate officers, out of which opened the cabins of the skipper and chief engineer and the two-berthed cabin of the quartermaster and second engineer.

In order to give as much space as possible for the stores I had the deck raised over the central portion of the vessel, thus making a poop-deck, on which were placed the quarters of the staff. Out of the big central ward-room opened six cabins, each two metres square, and two others slightly larger. Of these last two, the starboard one was occupied by the second officer, while the port cabin, used by my wife as far as Punta Arenas, communicated with mine ; and in the Antarctic it served at once as bacteriological laboratory, infirmary, and lumber-room. My own cabin opened into the fore passage which gave entrance also to a large photographic laboratory, a bath-room, etc. Below two small ladders, of four steps each, led from the ward-room into the zoological laboratory aft on the starboard side, and on the port side into a passage leading to the after deck, where were the physical science and hydrographic laboratories. These two laboratories were built in the form of a roofing over the deck. By this arrangement it was possible to warm all our apartments with a single stove in the ward-room, which when lighted kept up a constant temperature of from 12 to 14°.

Roofed over on the fore-deck were the cook's galley and offices and a passage which opened to starboard onto a ladderway used in bad weather at sea. This communicated with the poop-deck on the port side by a door easy to block up, only used during our winter-quarters, when the ship had her tarpaulin over her. The accommodation for the staff communicated with the open air both under this fore-roofing and aft. The illumination was provided by a large skylight and by a scuttle in each cabin. Abaft of the engine was a store-room lined with lead, intended for our supplies of spirit, and two sail-stores. On the deck right aft there were kept under cover various appliances, including in particular the surveying apparatus.

The quarters of the crew and of the staff alike, as well as the cook's galley and the laboratories, had a lining of felt two centimetres thick inside the planking. This felt is indispensable to prevent ice forming inside—which would inevitably have occurred without it, however thick the partitions. For the same reason every scrap of metal communicating with the outer air was covered with cork.

The coal-bunkers were three in number, one on either

side of the boiler, and a large central one foreward of the boiler. They held 250 tons of closely stowed coal-briquettes.

The large provision-store had no opening except a hatch in the ward-room, so that nothing could be taken out except under our eyes. Beneath the cabin for the crew were the water-casks, holding 18 tons, and a fairly large hold for the general stores.

I provided each member of the staff with his cabin-furniture, of which the principal items were a folding-bed, a bureau, and a washstand. Every one could arrange these as he pleased, being at liberty also to have made for him all the cupboards and shelves he might consider necessary. Wherever it was possible I had fitted up cupboards and lockers in the ward-room and the alley-ways. In addition to two book-cases in the ward-room a shelf ran round all the cabins, whereon we found room for nearly 3,000 books.

The laboratories were arranged according to the suggestions of those who were to work in them.

Forward of the poop was the steering-department, containing one of the two steering-wheels, the chart-table, and the usual navigating instruments. Lastly, at the top of the mainmast was the distinguishing feature of all polar vessels, the ' crow's-nest ' which is so indispensable for a voyage amid ice. This was reached by a rope-ladder starting from the top-mast cross-trees. Usually the voice is sufficient to convey orders on deck, but to make assurance doubly sure we had installed a ' Le Las ' loud-speaking telephone, which was kindly offered to us by its inventor and which did its work admirably during the whole of the trip.

The *Pourquoi-Pas ?* was the possessor even of a work of art. Father de Guibriant, one of our brave missionaries in China, to whom I had once done a service without knowing it, insisted on offering to our ship the French naval emblem, a magnificent piece of silver and copper work, designed by Comte de Chabannes La Palice and executed by R. Linzeler.

INTRODUCTION

It is worth while to direct particular attention to the lighting arrangements for an expedition called upon to spend several months in the midst of almost total night. I had placed in profusion everywhere, and in particular in each cabin, excellent little slow-burning petroleum-lamps. On the advice of the Marquis De Dion, moreover, I had installed De Dion-Bouton electric lamps, supplied by an eight h.p. motor and accumulators by the same firm. To shelter these from frost they were placed under the fore roofing, against the partition of the various offices heated by the cook's galley. At the outset I decided that our electric lighting must be considered a luxury, only to be used twice a week and on exceptional occasions. As a matter of fact, under the able superintendence of Bongrain, seconded by the ex-torpedo artificer Lerebourg and the motor-engineer Frachat, this installation, hitherto unknown on Polar expeditions, worked constantly for two years, practically without a moment's stop, thus showing the excellence of the motor and the accumulators. I cannot too much insist on the invaluable assistance that it was to us.

In the Polar regions, where for most of the time fresh water can only be obtained by melting down snow or ice, it is necessary to devise practical means of providing it. To this end, I had set up in communication with the kitchen-furnace a great water-butt with a capacity of 250 litres, into which, through a hole pierced in the roof could be thrown lumps of ice as required. Thanks to this plan, we had, without any expense or trouble, as big a water-supply as we needed. As long as the engine-boiler was alight, moreover, a pipe running from it enabled us to melt the ice in the butt rapidly, to feed the water-casks and the boiler itself.

We took a good number of boats, for my previous experience had taught me that, in addition to those requisite for the service of the ship, it might be useful to have others not only to facilitate the various tasks in which we were all engaged, but also for transport over the ice and even for establishing rescue and revictualling-posts. We had a big canoe, a dinghy, two stout whale-boats such as the Norwegian sealers carry (of which one had been on board the *Français* on the former expedition), two small Norwegian boats known by the name of ' prams,' four dories—those flat light vessels used by fishermen on the Newfoundland banks, fitting one into another —two ' Berthon ' boats, and a little folding affair of the ' Williamson ' type. Lastly ' Père ' Gautier built for us a strong picket-boat, specially adapted for work amid ice, with a rounded prow protected by iron plates. This excellent sea-boat was fitted with an eight h.p. De Dion-Bouton motor, which did its duty admirably, in spite of its long and very arduous service and was of great use to the expedition.

In addition to the ordinary instruments and equipment for every long-distance voyage, we took ten ice-saws and the same number of chisels, a dozen small and large ice-anchors and a stock of stakes, ice-hooks, shovels, pickaxes, crowbars, and spades.

The excellent Lucas apparatus, which takes up so little space and yet allows soundings to be taken to the depth of 6,000 metres, was set up on the quarter-deck and was worked at the start by a dynamo, which was afterwards advantage-ously replaced by a small steam-engine. Foreward, on the starboard side, was the steam-bobbin for the steel-wire cable of the dredger, which could be lowered to a depth of 4,000 metres.

I had taken the greatest care in my preparation for our excursions, and making the *Discovery* expedition my model had arranged everything as if for independent groups of three persons each. I had six tents made, each holding three persons, six Nansen kitchens slightly modified by myself, six mess-services, etc., all for three, while the provisions for the excursions of which I shall have occasion to speak later were also divided into portions for three, in such a way that it would only be necessary to empty each into the cooking-pot, thus avoiding labour which would have been painful in a low temperature and after tiring journeys.

The ship's wardrobe was abundant, being chiefly composed of woollen clothes of all kinds and knitted things, while stockings and mittens were to be counted by the hundred. We provided ourselves with lengths of cloth and a sewing-machine. MM. Linzeler, Vimout, and Denian had sent considerable presents to swell the stock on board. In case of our unexpectedly being obliged to winter away from the shelter of our ship, I thought it best to bring reindeer-hide suits and a bed-sack of the same material for every man. We were not called upon to make use of these furs, except the bed-sacks which are so necessary on excursions. Generally speaking, we were comparatively lightly clad, but one indispensable article of clothing was the ' anorak,' a kind of overcoat of pliable but close-fitting canvas, with a hood to it, which went over the ordinary clothes and counteracted the cold admirably by keeping out draughts. For ordinary work a stout mackintosh was sufficient; but on excursions the material known as ' Burberry ' is certainly all that one can desire for lightness and absolute imperviousness to wind and snow.

My previous experience had caused me to give very serious attention to the all-important question of foot-wear, and we took with us a large and varied stock of ordinary boots, of boots of leather with wooden soles (of which a friend, M. Perchot, gave 70 pairs), of sabots fitted with leggings of tarred canvas such as the Icelandic fishermen wear, of strong mountaineering boots, of socks like those of our Mountain Infantry, made for us by one of the regimental tailors, and of *finskoes* and *komagers* from Norway. These last-named, a sort of mocassin of reindeer-hide, well tested on recent expeditions, are the only kind of foot-wear of use on journeys in extreme cold when one is at a distance from the ship. Their drawback

16

is that they get very slippery on hard ice, thus making them really dangerous on glaciers. To remedy this I had made, after the model of those recommended by Captain Scott, a kind of canvas sandal fitted with strong frost-nails, which we could put over them—a very practical invention.

To protect the eyes against snow-ophthalmia I had made some yellow-glassed goggles and masks with cross-shaped slits in them. It will be seen from the story of the Expedition that, thanks to these precautions, we had not a single case of this ophthalmia.

We took a dozen sledges of the type universally adopted on Polar expeditions, several pairs of skis for each man (not only for use on journeys but also for amusement), as well as some toboggans, snow-shoes, and the usual equipments for mountaineering and other excursions, ropes, axes, knapsacks, lanterns, etc. And I must not forget the ' Thermos ' bottles, which are of the greatest assistance in these latitudes, where one suffers almost as much from thirst as in warm countries and where flasks cannot be used.

With regard to all the material coming from Norway, whether clothing and furs or such Polar apparatus as skis, sledges, etc., Mr. Crichton Somerville, a resident in Christiania, was kind enough to devote his care and ability to choosing it or having it made.

The possibility of coming across an ice-plain, such as that which constitutes the Ross Barrier, directed my notice to the advantage of taking some motor-sledges. The Marquis De Dion and M. Bouton, with their usual generosity and their enthusiasm for any new idea, proposed to present the Expedition with the desired vehicles. Captain Scott was interested in the same matter. We decided to make our experiments together, and I shall always remember the pleasant and profitable time which I spent with him and his assistants, Messrs. Skelton and Barnes. The trial took place in mid-winter at Lautaret. We had the assistance of Lieutenant de La Besse, who had long given attention to motor-sledges. General Picquart, Minister of War, put at our disposal during the eight days of the trial ten men from our Alpine garrisons. The results seemed most encouraging. M. Coursier, engineer at the De Dion-Bouton works, who was present, set to work vigorously and thanks to him we were able to take three motor-sledges, on which we built great hopes. Unluckily we never came across, in the region we visited, any surface on which we could use them. MM. de Dion, Bouton, and Coursier must set against this failure the services to the Expedition of the picket-boat and the electric installation.

We carried nearly three years' stock of provisions, and in my selection of these I applied to the leading firms of France, England, Germany, Norway, and America. Owing to the progress of the preserved foods industry, the only real difficulty in provisioning an expedition like ours lies in the necessity of choosing with due regard to variety and space alike. A catalogue of what we placed in our store-rooms would occupy several pages, and I shall simply say that we had almost everything that it was possible to take and that the choice was made with the most scrupulous care, limiting ourselves to the first quality always. The food-products and preserves which can be taken on journeys are nowadays generally familiar, and a description of them would be tedious. I must, however, remark on the convenience and excellent manufacture of all sorts of compressed foods, soup, milk, meats, etc. The same is true of dried vegetables, some of which give remarkable results, especially cabbages and potatoes. In the course of the narrative, however, it will often be necessary to refer to the question of food. Generally we may divide provisions into four classes : those for daily use, those for excursions, those kept for storage-depôts or for emergencies, and, lastly, luxuries.

I shall have occasion later to speak of the provisions for excursions. As for what is placed in the storage-depôts, handy tins of biscuits form the bulk of these ; for in the Antarctic one may always expect to find penguins or seals, which supply excellent fresh meat, as well as fat at need for fuel. It is not too much to say that with biscuits, a knife to kill and cut up animals, and matches to kindle the fat, one can live, at least in most parts of the Antarctic.

Numerous agreeable gifts were made to swell the stores of the Expedition not only in France, but also abroad—at Rio Janeiro, Buenos Aires, and Punta Arenas.

At all places of call, both going and returning, nothing but fresh food was eaten.

In the long run one grows tired of even the best of preserved stuff, especially meats, and it is very probable that the majority of the meals composed exclusively of these, left but an indifferent memory in the minds of the members of the Expedition. Nevertheless, I believe I may say that no expedition was ever better provisioned than ours, as regards both quality and quantity, and that we never ran short of anything on board.

So well stocked with wine was the steward's room that during the whole duration of the voyage the crew were able to have their daily ration and often double. In the ward-room wine was served at discretion to those who drank it and of such good kind that for several weeks I amused myself by having it brought on in bottles with fine green seals, to pretend it was of special quality. But this innocent joke was needless ; for our cellar, thanks to generous givers, was furnished with the best brands, and those who had thus thought of our well-being would have been rewarded could they have seen the pleasure with which we uncorked the noble vintages.

The question of the consumption of alcohol on expeditions has been often discussed and settled in various ways. Personally I consider it neither more nor less dangerous on a Polar expedition than elsewhere, provided that moderation is observed. I even think that rum in certain cases is one of the most useful of medicines ; but from the start I have made a point of waging unrelenting war against the *apéritif*, the great curse of France.

We kept on board an ample stock of antiscorbutics, such as sauerkraut, tomatoes and lime-juice. These combined with vegetables and fruit, either dried or in jam, etc., were evidently more than sufficient to save us from the scurvy that attacked the expeditions of old ; but it will be seen that these ordinary precautions were useless against what one may call modern scurvy—or, more strictly speaking, preserved-food sickness.

Almost as important as the question of the choice of eatables is that of the cases in which they are put up, the good construction of which insures their keeping. I laid down certain requirements in this respect, which unfortunately were not always scrupulously carried out by our French firms. The loss is their own, for if later expeditions discover our store-depôts they will be able to form their judgments on the more or less good state of preservation of the different brands. I desired first of all that everything should be put up in cases easy to handle, of a weight not exceeding 30 kilos, but with many of the goods the need of taking a large quantity and the comparatively small space at our disposal, compelled us to stow them away without their superfluous coverings. These were kept, however, on the storage-depôt provisions. An expedition fortunate enough to have abundant funds would do very well to have its stores put up in ' Venesta ' cases, which are at once strong, water-tight, and light.

Matches—on the usefulness of which I need not insist— were packed in little zinc boxes handy to open and easy to carry on sledges and even in knapsacks.

I pass over in silence the necessities of ordinary life, the thousand little trifles which were nevertheless indispensable for the repair and upkeep of our varied stock or for what we had to make for ourselves, our drugs and our surgical instruments. It turned out that very little had been forgotten, for we never had to want for anything essential.

Coal was of course the sinews of the Expedition. The Minister of Marine gave us at the start 250 tons in briquettes. At Madeira Mr. Gordon-Bennett with his habitual generosity telegraphed spontaneously to his representatives to fill our bunkers at his expense. The Brazilian Government gave us 100 tons when we reached Rio, and on our return filled our bunkers both at Rio and Pernambuco ; and finally on our way back the Chilian Government gave us 70 tons. I had myself sent to Punta Arenas 300 tons of briquettes presented by French mining companies. This important stock the Chilian Government, with great kindness, deposited in its own hulks until our arrival, assisting us then to put on board what we wanted and keeping the remainder until our return. We were thus able to set out with our bunkers absolutely full of coal of the best quality. It will be seen that in the Antarctic we had the opportunity of replenishing them again.

Our numerous spirit-motors necessitated us having on board eleven tons of what is esteemed a most dangerous cargo. We had made for this a lead-lined hold aft, in which the 18-litre cans of Motricine were carefully stored, enclosed two and two in wooden cases. A hand-ventilator supplied air to the bottom of this hold to drive out the dangerous vapours, which are heavier than air. At every change of the watch this ventilator was set working, and thus we managed to carry this risky cargo without any mishap.

As far as the choice of the staff of the *Pourquoi-Pas ?* is concerned, I can only repeat what I said in the case of our former expedition. It is extremely easy in France to find fellow-scientists ready to give up their time, and even to expose their lives, without the slightest hope of recompense. Several of my comrades on the *Français* wished to join this expedition too. One of my fondest hopes would thus have

21

been realized. But Lieutenant Matha, after his long leave of absence, had to make some return for the well-merited confidence placed in him by our naval authorities; and Engineer P. Pléneau had his duties toward the commercial company which had wisely selected him for a difficult enterprise in Siberia and Mongolia. My very friendship for them both obliged me to advise them to renounce this time all ideas of accompanying me. But I was glad to see at my side again my devoted friend and valued collaborator from the first, E. Gourdon.

The staff, as finally constituted, consisted of three naval officers, a geologist, two naturalists, a doctor, and myself. The various departments under our programme were assigned as follows :—

H. Bongrain, sub-lieutenant. Second officer. (Astronomical observations, hydrography, seismography, terrestrial gravitation) ;

J. Rouch, sub-lieutenant. (Meteorology, atmospheric electricity, physical oceanography) ;

R. Godfroy, sub-lieutenant. (Study of tides, atmospheric chemistry) ;

E. Gourdon, D.Sc. (Geology and glaciology) ;

J. Liouville, M.D. (Assistant doctor to the Expedition, zoology) ;

L. Gain, B.Sc. (Zoology and botany) ;

A. Senouque. (Magnetism, actinometry, scientific photography) ;

J.-B. Charcot, head of the Expedition, commander of the *Pourquoi-Pas ?* (Bacteriology).

Apart from their special departments, the naval officers assisted me in the navigation and other duties on board.

I am happy to be able to say that it was thanks to the enthusiasm, energy, and attainments of my colleagues that the Expedition was a success, and my gratitude toward them is all the warmer since they enable me, without laying myself open to a charge of personal vanity, to assert that we succeeded.

I had the same ease in getting together the crew and had to make choice from among 250 applications. Almost all the old crew of the *Français* rejoined me on the *Pourquoi-Pas ?* thus giving me a nucleus of seasoned and devoted men. Chollet had been my navigator for 24 years, Guégen had been on four expeditions with me, Jabet and Libois on three. The new-comers, animated by an excellent spirit, and sailors in the best sense of the term, were spurred on by the example of the veterans to display the same qualities as they.

The crew consisted of —

*Chollet, E., skipper.
*Jabet, boatswain.
*Besnard, assistant boat-
  swain.
*Guégen, J., sailor.
  Hervé,   ,,
  Thomas,   ,,
  Dufrèche,   ,,
  Lerebourgh, ,,
  Aveline,   ,,
  Denais,   ,,
  Nozal,   ,,
  Boland,   ,,

Rosselin, F., chief engineer.
*Poste, second engineer.
*Guégen, F., stoker.
  Monzimet, stoker.
  Lhostis, stoker.
*Libois, stoker and carpenter.
  Frachat, motor engineer.
  Modaine, cook.
*Paumelle, mess steward.
  Van Acken, second steward
    (a Belgian taken on board
    at Punta Arenas, where he
    was living).[1]

It would be difficult to discover a better crew than ours, more energetic, devoted, courageous, patient, and intelligent. All asked but to be allowed to do their best and always went about their work cheerfully and enthusiastically. There was no punishment-book on board, and the need of one was never felt.

---

[1] The names preceded by an asterisk are those of the men who took part in the *Français* Expedition. Boland and Nozal, who signed on as sailors, were mercantile marine cadets. By the terms of their agreements they were treated on board like the other sailors and worked like them, but their very superior training made them most valuable assistants to MM. Bongrain and Rouch, and I thought it right to promote them later to the rank of lieutenant.

INTRODUCTION

As soon as the *Pourquoi-Pas?* was launched, staff and crew set to work on the final preparations and the embarkation and stowage of food and material. In order not to lose time, the stowage was begun at Saint-Malo, while the engine was being put on board and the rigging finished, and was completed at Havre.

THE STAFF BEFORE OUR DEPARTURE.
Bongrain.   Liouville.   Gain.
Gourdon.   Rouch.   Charcot.   Senouque.   Godfroy.

Departure from Havre, August 15, 1908.

FROM HAVRE TO PUNTA ARENAS

Firmly convinced of our sincerity of purpose, the town of Havre showed its goodwill toward us in a touching manner on August 15, 1908. It was in the midst of a sympathetic crowd, collected from far and wide to prove that France is never indifferent to the labours of her sons, that our friends and relations wished us a good journey and all success, while the strains of the ' Marseillaise ' answered the parting salute of the *Pourquoi-Pas ?*

The same day we reached Cherbourg, where the Superintendent of the Dockyard, Admiral Bellue, gave us a warm welcome. His anxiety to aid us in putting on board the coal and material given to us by the Minister of Marine proved once more the interest taken in our work by the naval authorities.

Owing to continued bad weather we were forced to stop at Cherbourg until August 31. Impatient to begin our voyage, we weighed anchor on the first break in the weather, but off the Casquets we were assailed by one of the worst storms of the year, which caused many disasters at sea. The *Pourquoi-Pas ?* early gave proof of those excellent qualities which stood us in such good stead later ; but after battling for twenty-four hours we put into Guernsey to save useless consumption of coal and avoid the necessity of turning back. We left Guernsey again on September 5, to reach Madeira Roads on the 12th. Three days later we set off once more, and on the 22nd we made a twenty-four hours' call at Porto Grande, Saint Vincent.

On October 12 we were at Rio Janeiro, where an unexpected reception awaited us from the people and Government of Brazil and the French colony, headed by our vice-consul, M. Charlat. Baron Rio Branco, Minister of Foreign Affairs, received the whole Expedition at the Itamaraty Palace, and the Minister of Marine, Admiral Alexandrino de Aleucar, did us the great honour of coming on board the *Pourquoi-Pas ?* The entire contents of the arsenal were put at our disposal so generously that, for fear of appearing indiscreet, we dared not express a desire ! Presents and kindnesses were showered on us from all sides by individuals, in addition to the gifts from the Government, while the wife of Captain Barros Cobra (one of the most devoted friends of the Expedition all through) honoured us by sending a special silk flag for the *Pourquoi-Pas ?* embroidered by her own hands.

On the 20th we left the magnificent and flourishing country of Brazil for Buenos Aires. The relations I had kept up with the Argentine Republic since the never-to-be-forgotten reception of the *Français* Expedition, on both the outward and the home voyages, led me to believe that we should be welcomed ; but Argentina was determined to show that she can always do still better. On the motion of Dr. Pinero, the Chambers decided to vote unlimited credit to meet the needs, whatever they might be, of the Expedition. The *Pourquoi-Pas ?* went into dry dock to undergo all the improvements possible. With splendid generosity all materials were provided that she could want. I had the honour of being presented to the President of the Republic by our Minister, M. Thiébault, and the French residents vied with the Argentine people in making our stay at once profitable and pleasant. I met once more my warm and sincere friends, Dr. Fernando Perez and his brother Manuel, Professor Lignières, Colonel Nunez, Dr. Pinero, Admirals Garcia and Barilari, Chief Engineer Sumblad Rosetti, MM. Lainez, Py, Thays, Davis, and Lahille, Father Sola and many others whose friendship had only been increased by lapse of time.

FROM HAVRE TO PUNTA ARENAS

On November 23 we left Buenos Aires, and on December 1 we anchored in the roadstead of Punta Arenas. This was our last place of call in the civilized world, but not the place which showed us the least sympathy. The Chilian Government had put at our disposal all the resources of the town, and the French representative at Santiago, M. Desprez, demonstrated to us by his kindly messages, both as we went and as we came back, that France was watching over us at this distant stage on the way to the lands where we were about to hide ourselves so many long months. The little French colony and the inhabitants of the town feasted us and made much of us, and I hope to be able to show in the following narrative all the good which the Expedition derived from its stay here, and how grateful is the friendship which must bind me henceforward to those of its inhabitants whose names I shall have occasion to mention.

At Punta Arenas my wife, who had bravely accompanied me so far, left me, to return and watch over our home during my absence. This expected and inevitable separation was, nevertheless, a wrench which only our high ideal of duty enabled us to bear with. Certain people may have smiled over the presence of a woman on board during the first part of the journey, and even have found in it an excuse for belittling the grave and serious side of our work. But others —happily the majority—only saw in it a touching proof of love, courage, and interest in the object which I had in view; it is the opinion of these latter for which I care. My own thought was to labour for my country and for the honour of a name made illustrious by my father and rendered still more dear to me by her who, in adopting it as her own, was willing to aid me in sharing its responsibility.

Our First Iceberg.

THE DIARY OF THE EXPEDITION

PART I

THE SUMMER OF 1908–1909

DECEMBER 16, 1908.—In fine calm weather we weigh anchor from Punta Arenas at 9 p.m.   M. Blanchard, the kindly French consul, coming on board on his launch *Laurita* at 8.30, brought with him the Governor, M. Chaigneau ; M. Henkes, one of the Norwegian directors of the Magellan Whaling Company ; M. Grossi, an Italian merchant ; and our fellow-countrymen, MM. Poivre, Beaulier, Detaille and Rocca.   We drank a glass of champagne, and shook with emotion the hands of all these kind-hearted people, now become our friends, and then away we went !   The *Laurita* saluted us with three blasts of her whistle, while her passengers cheered and shouted ' *Vive la France !* '   The crew of the Chilian Government hulk did the same, and at the very end of the roadstead the look-out man standing all alone on a big steamer gave us a loud Godspeed.

December 17.—The night has been calm and clear, but by morning the mountain-tops are wrapped in clouds, and there is a slight southerly breeze, which, however, does not prevent us from making rapid progress.   We leave Magellan Straits for Magdalena Sound and Cockburn Channel, and about 1 in the afternoon we are among the Furies Reefs ; but there is a heavy sea and a strong west wind, and the barometer is falling.   We run the risk by taking this course of

29

losing the hours which we hoped to gain, and worse, if we are caught by a gale forcing us to lie to or run for shelter—especially as our boat is heavy laden and the deck is piled with coal-briquettes, which block the scuppers. We do not hesitate, therefore, to go about and make for Murray Channel, and we thread the Brecknock. Thanks to a very good Chilian map, at 8 p.m. we are able to anchor in the picturesque and well-sheltered little bay of Port Edwards, at the entrance of Whaleboat Sound.

December 18.—At 7 a.m. we are under way, and in spite of fog and rain we easily make Beagle Channel. The weather remains heavy all the morning and it pours with rain, but in the afternoon it clears up finely at times, allowing us to admire the wonderful scenery through which we are passing. The wind blows very strong from the south-west. We pass a small Chilian steamer from Punta Arenas, exchanging salutes, and at 9 p.m. we anchor in Lapataia Bay. The gusts are very strong, but our anchor holds firm.

December 19.—At 3 a.m. we are again on our way. It would have been tempting to touch at Ushuaia, whose houses we could make out and where we were sure to meet again our friends of 1904, with a hearty welcome in store for us. But every stoppage is time lost, and we have to take advantage of the fine season. The gusts are still strong, but soon calm sets in, with very clear weather and an absolutely cloudless sky. A strong current carries us rapidly along through the narrow, picturesque Murray Channel, and soon we make out Orange Bay, the quarters of the Arromanche Mission, where we ourselves stayed with the *Français* in 1904. At midday we are abreast of False Cape Horn, and the swell from the south-west becomes very rough. It increases when at 2 p.m. we pass the real Cape Horn, which in this magnificent summer season has a smiling aspect. There is not a breath of air, and, deprived of the assistance of her sails, our vessel, being overladen above, has a rough shaking. In the evening we pass astern of a big three-masted barque going east, with which we exchange signals. By chance it is a French ship, the *Michelet* of Nantes, which signals to us 'Bon voyage.' At 10 we see on the horizon another three-master going east.

December 20.—Since midnight the wind has been blowing very strong from the north-east, with a storm of snow, the Antarctic's welcome to us. The choppy sea becomes very rough and catches us broadside on. We set our fore top-mast staysail and the two lower topsails, but we are ship-ping water to an extent dangerous for the engines. So at 8 a.m. we let her bear away 25° when all goes well, except for those—and there are many on board—who pay their tribute to sea-sickness. The sea washes in an unpleasant way over the deck and into the ward-room and the cabins.

Next morning the wind falls and it becomes clear and cold, with the thermometer at zero. The evening is calm, but with a very great swell. We brail up generally and head for Smith Island, formerly known to the American sealers as Mount Pisgah Island, but nowadays better called after the man who in 1819 discovered the South Shetlands.

December 22.—At 7 a.m. a cape, which must be part of Smith Island, reveals itself through the mist, and as the weather clears up completely the whole of the imposing snow-covered island appears at a distance of 30 miles. We take Boyd Strait, where we meet our first iceberg, floating in complete isolation, and go a little out of our way so as to skirt it, for the edification of the crew and such of our colleagues to whom the spectacle is new. The swell has ceased, the weather is remarkably clear, and we can distinguish the greater part of the South Shetlands archipelago. Two soundings are taken in Boyd Strait, one giving 2,800 metres, the other 690.

We stand in for Deception Island, and as the narrow entrance of its central haven opens before us we see two little whaleboats, one of which is returning with a whale in tow. The other heads for us. It is the *Raun*, flying the Norwegian

31

flag. Soon we are abreast, the whaler's crew raising cheers in our honour, and the captain offering, in excellent English, to lead the way for us into the centre of the island. Thinking that they were returning from fishing, we accepted the offer, but we learnt afterwards that as a matter of fact these good fellows were going out and insisted on having the honour of piloting us in spite of the loss of time involved.

Although it was expected, yet for those of us who had already visited the Antarctic in 1904 (when we knew that we were the only human beings there) the meeting with vessels quietly carrying on their work in this region had something impressive and almost uncanny about it. This sensation affected us still more strongly when we found ourselves in Deception Island basin, in the midst of a veritable flotilla of boats, all at work as though in some busy Norwegian port. Our pilot brings us up very close to the smooth, precipitous face of the high black cliff on the west side of the passage, and after a sharp turn the whaling-station appears before our eyes, marvellously sheltered in a fairly big bay notched out of the great crater-basin of this weird and picturesque island. We find two three-masters and two steam-vessels, surrounded by several little steam-whalers, this fleet belonging to three different companies. Pieces of whale float about on all sides, and bodies in process of being cut up or waiting their turn lie alongside the various boats. The smell is unbearable.

The captain of the *Raun* asks me to come and visit his little steamer, which I found, despite the trade in which she is engaged, astonishingly clean, and takes me into a little ward-room which is neat, comfortable, and almost elegant, with a fine coal fire burning in a stove. Next we go on board the largest of the steamers, the *Gobernador Bories*, on which is M. Andresen, manager of the Magellan Whaling Company. With great difficulty we make our way amid the bodies of whales and I am taken into a large and extremely clean

32

ward-room, whose furniture is almost luxurious. A parrot, which ought to be feeling very much out of it in the Antarctic, is talking solemnly, and here too there is a fine coal fire in the stove. As on board the *Raun*, my eyes look on this with a little envy, for on the *Pourquoi-Pas ?* we put up with the damp without lighting a fire, so as to economize our coal.

M. Andresen is in bed, but the captain of the *Raun* does not hesitate to go and wake him. I let him do this, for I bring the mail with me and I expect that this unlooked-for surprise will win me pardon for my early visit. M. Andresen shows himself at once a true Norwegian, amiable, cordial, and anxious to be of service to us. I give him the letter from the directors of his company, which I received through the kind intervention of MM. Detaille and Blanchard, asking him to furnish us, if he can, with 30 tons of coal ; and at once he tells me that, in spite of the shortness of fuel, he will make arrangements to satisfy us. So pleased is he at receiving a mail which he did not expect, and which will gladden the whole of the little colony, that he thanks me with an embarrassing gratitude for having taken charge of the letters. Then I leave him to go back to bed, after making an appointment to see him again next day. I bring the captain of the *Raun* back to the *Pourquoi-Pas ?*, where we drink a glass of port together. He makes an admirably turned and sympathetic little speech, wishing us a safe voyage and abundant success, and then returns on board his own ship and sets out at once on his whaling cruise.

The comparatively good anchorages in the bay are occupied by the whalers, and we seek in vain to anchor in deep water with a treacherous holding-ground. The smell, moreover, being really unbearable, we lose no time in moving and making for the further end of the basin, where Pendulum Cove used to be. With difficulty we discover, so to speak, this no longer existing cove, and let fall our anchor at 2 a.m. near the spot where the corvette *Uruguay* anchored in 1905. There has been no night, and the weather is magnificently calm.

I cannot find any document showing who really discovered this island where we are nor who christened it with the name of Deception, most inappropriate in my mind; for it was far from being a deception for us or for the other navigators in this region, who could count on finding here the safe shelter so rare in the Antarctic. It cannot have been discovered by Smith, who only explored the north coast of the South Shetlands in 1819; nor by Bransfield, who, returning with Smith to these regions, some time after, was unable to circumnavigate the islands and considered them part of a continent. I am inclined to think it was known to the Spaniards, or, to be more exact, to the ancestors of the Argentinans. An historical incident, which I, like many others, borrow from the excellent and painstaking works of the learned American explorer Edwin Swift Balch of Philadelphia,[1] probably is to be placed on Deception Island. Mrs. R. Fanning Loper, niece of Captain Nathaniel Brown Palmer, whose share was so great in making known this part of the Antarctic, lent to Mr. E. S. Balch log-books, letters, and various MSS. which had been her uncle's. The following story is noteworthy: 'In 1818 he [Captain Potter] became second mate of the brig *Hersilia*, bound to Cape Horn for seals, Captain James P. Sheffield, master. On this voyage he and a sailor were left upon one of the Falkland Islands to obtain provisions for the brig, while the *Hersilia* went in search of the fabulous Auroras. Soon after the departure of the brig, the *Esprito Santo*, from Buenos Ayres, hove in sight off the island, and " young Nat," as he was then called, piloted her into the harbour, and found that she was bound to a place where there were thousands of seals, but [her captain] refused to divulge the situation. Three days later the *Hersilia* returned, and " young Nat "

---

[1] *Antarctica Addenda*, by Edwin Swift Balch, from the *Journal of the Franklin Institute*, February, 1904.

34

told Captain Sheffield about the *Esprito Santo*, and said he could follow her and find the sealing ground. Captain Sheffield, having great confidence in his second mate, followed his advice, and in a few days discovered the South Shetlands, at that time unknown in the continent of North America. The *Esprito Santo* was anchored there, and the crew was much surprised to see the brig, but their admiration for "young Nat's" skill was so great that they even assisted in loading the *Hersilia*, and [she] returned home with 10,000 of the finest skins.'

Now what makes me suppose that this anchorage was none other than Deception is the fact that in the following summer, 1820-1821, there was at this island a squadron of five American sealers commanded by B. Pendleton, with Palmer as captain of one of them, the sloop *Hero*, and no one seemed astonished at the marvellous shelter for which they apparently unerringly made. This squadron, fitted out at Stonington, Connecticut, then one of the most important whaling centres, was composed of the brigs *Frederick*, Captain B. Pendleton, and *Hersilia*, Captain J. P. Sheffield, the schooners *Express*, Captain E. Williams, and *Free Gift*, Captain F. Dunbar, and the little sloop *Hero*, Captain N. B. Palmer. It was while the flotilla was stopping at Yankee Harbour, afterwards renamed Port Foster, that Pendleton saw, with Palmer, from the top of a peak on the island some land to the west, and sent Palmer reconnoitring on his 40-ton *Hero*. Palmer, who continued his explorations successfully next year, discovered on this excursion either the north coast of Graham Land, close to Trinity, or else the archipelago to which De Gerlache has very rightly given the name, by which it will continue to be known, of Palmer Archipelago. (The *Français* in 1904–1905 made a survey of the north-west coast of this.) E. Fanning [1] says :—

' On the *Hero's* return passage to Yankee Harbour she got becalmed in a thick fog between the South Shetlands and

[1] *Voyages Round the World*, pp. 434–440.

the newly discovered continent, but nearest the former. When this began to clear away, Captain Palmer was surprised to find his little barque between a frigate and sloop of war, and instantly ran up the United States' flag ; the frigate and sloop of war then set the Russian colours. Soon after this a boat was seen pulling from the commodore's ship for the *Hero*, and when alongside the lieutenant presented an invitation from his commodore for Captain Palmer to go on board ; this of course was accepted. These ships he then found were the discovery ships sent out by the Emperor Alexander of Russia. To the commodore's interrogatory if he had any knowledge of those islands then in sight, and what they were, Captain Palmer replied he was well acquainted with them, and that they were the South Shetlands, at the same time making a tender of his services to pilot the ships into a good harbour at Deception Island, the nearest by, where water and refreshments such as the island afforded could be obtained ; he also inform ing the Russian officer that his vessel belonged to a fleet of five sail, out of Stonington, under command of Captain B. Pendleton, and then at anchor in Yankee Harbour, who would most cheerfully render any assistance in his power. The commodore thanked him kindly, " but previous to our being enveloped in the fog," he said, " we had sight of those islands and concluded we had made a discovery, but behold, when the fog lifts, to my great surprise, here is an American vessel in as fine order as if it were but yesterday she had left the United States ; not only this, but her master is ready to pilot my vessels into port ; we must surrender the palm to you Americans," continued he, very flatteringly. His astonish-ment was yet more increased, when Captain Palmer informed him of the existence of an immense extent of land to the south, whose mountains might be seen from the masthead when the fog should clear away entirely.'

Personally I am disposed to think there is nothing im-probable in this tale, especially as the kindly welcome given by the American sealers to a foreign expedition was singularly like that which we enjoyed 87 years later at the hands of Norwegian whalers. Nevertheless, H. R. Mill, while noting that Bellingshausen, when he put into Sydney Harbour in March, 1820, was informed by the Russian consul of W. Smith's discovery of the South Shetlands in 1819, adds that in the account of his arrival at Yaroslav Island (this is the name which he gave to Deception) Bellingshausen only makes slight mention of his meeting with Palmer : ' The American captain Palmer, whom we invited on board, told us of the prodigiously rich harvest of seal-skins which had been made here.' [1] Still, as Fanning says, claiming that Bellingshausen in his admiration for the young captain called the coast visible to the south Palmer Land, this name was adopted in the Russian and English maps published after the return of the Russian ships—a point in favour of the American version.

In any case, it is certain that the sealing flotillas, both American and English, made Deception Island one of their most important centres until the almost complete extermination of the fur-seal in the South Shetlands, and it is more than probable that the little Chilian schooners which continued to come for a few years more to look for the precious booty in this archipelago put in here. Scientific expeditions also came here, apart from Bellingshausen's, which did get so far. In 1829 the *Chanticleer*, commanded by Foster, who was sent out by the British Government to make pendular and magnetic observations, took up its quarters at Pendulum Cove, so named after the pendulum experiments made there between January 9 and March 4 of that year. Foster died as the result of an accident on the return of the expedition, but his narrative was forwarded by Lieutenant Kendall and Dr. Webster, to whom we owe a detailed description of the island. We owe another to the American Lieutenant Johnson, commander of

---

[1] *The Siege of the South Pole*, by Hugh Robert Mill, London, 1905.

the *Sea Gull*, one of the Wilkes Expedition, who stopped there with his ship in 1839.

Dumont d'Urville on the return voyage of his first South Polar Expedition in 1838 passed along the south-west coast of Deception, of which he published an excellent view from the clever pencil of Goupil, an artist on board the *Zélée* and great-uncle of my wife. Lastly, the Argentine corvette *Uruguay*, whose name is universally known through the magnificent way in which she saved the Nordenskjöld Expedition in November, 1903, touched at Deception on January 9, 1905, having been generously sent out by the Argentine Government to look for the *Français*, about whose fate there were fears, happily unfounded.

According to the descriptions of Webster and Johnson, the area of the island, whose centre is 65° 56′ South by 60° 40′ West of Greenwich, is about 50 square kilometres, while its diameter is about 19 kilometres from north to south and 15 kilometres from east to west. In the interior is a great marine lake, very probably produced by the blowing up of a volcano beneath the surface of the sea. This inner basin is almost elliptical in shape, with a diameter of 9 to 10 kilometres and an area of about 22 square kilometres. It communicates with the sea by a very narrow strait, about 180 metres long, on the south-west side of the island. Its depth, which is only 5 or 6 metres at the opening, increases rapidly toward the centre ; according to Kendall, to 177 metres. (It will be seen that a sounding taken by us at the same spot shows a filling up of the basin or else a rise in the level of its bottom.) The inner banks of the island are as a rule flatter than the outer shores. At the entrance of the crater-shaped bay, however, there stands an escarped cliff with perpendicular walls 240 metres high. On the shores are several lakes resembling the ruins of small craters, while others occur on the beach of the island, having no visible communication with the large central basin. Thus Lieutenant Johnson found at the end of the bay a small crater 450 metres in diameter, separated from the main basin by a wall 120 metres thick, rising gradually to the height of 6 metres. Into this lake the wall descended perpendicularly, and its surface-level was the same as that of the main basin.

The descriptions of these explorers do not differ much from what we could have given ourselves, at least as to general lines ; but when one examines Foster's map, which is much the completest and most detailed, one sees that some fairly large modifications of detail have taken place, affecting the small lakes and the heights of the peaks and the shores of the inner basin. Coves have filled in, capes have altered, old lakes have dried up and new ones have formed. But the most important and interesting change—I might even add, the most lamentable—is that which affects Pendulum Cove, which may be said to exist no more. At the time of Foster and the American whalers Pendulum Cove was, as the *Chanticleer's* plan shows, a narrow fjord, shaped like a comma, admirably sheltered, with little depth of water and good holding-ground, making it, in fact, the only really good anchorage in the island. When the *Uruguay* arrived in 1905, Pendulum Cove had disappeared. The fjord had filled in, either through landslips or by upheavals, and there only remained just at the entrance a low crescent-shaped beach, quite close to which the bottom held fairly well. This state of things was what we also found, and the plan which we made differs only in a few insignificant details from that published by our friend Lieutenant Jallour, second in command of the *Uruguay*.

Foster during his stay at Deception saw no volcanic eruptions, but he found on the edge of the basin numerous vents, from which steam was ejected violently, and many hot springs with a temperature as high as 88°. These, too, are the only active volcanic manifestations which we noted. The water of these numerous springs was sulphurous, and had a temperature of 68°. Smiley, the American sealer, who visited

Pendulum Cove in February, 1842, and found there a thermometer left behind by Foster in 1829, reports that ' certainly the island was then undergoing great changes,' that the whole southern shore was actively volcanic—' in flames '—and that he saw ' no less than thirteen eruptions.'

Webster, Johnson, and Dumont d'Urville agree in saying that very little snow settled on Deception, the last-named stating that not only were the shores free from it, but also several of the high peaks. As far as we were concerned, we found a lot, coming down as far as the beach. But it is true that we stopped there in December, while the others paid their visits in March, except Webster ; and he was there from January to March.

The fur-seals, hunted down without mercy or precaution by the American and English sealers, have entirely vanished. This was the cause of the abandonment of Deception for such long years ; but the comparatively new methods employed with so much success in the north in hunting the balaenoptera (rorqual) and the considerable profits assured by this industry, and by the great competition in the northern seas, have restored to this Antarctic island some of its former business.

From the whale-hunter's point of view, there are two sorts of whale, the ' right ' whale and the ' rusher '—a division which coincides with a zoological classification, the former being properly speaking, a balaena (*Balaena Australis* in the southern, *Balaena Groenlandis* in the northern seas), and the others being balaenopteras.

The commercial value of the balaenas is much superior to that of the balaenopteras, not only on account of the quantity and quality of their oil, but also—and perhaps especially—because of the dimensions and quality of their bone, of which the price in the market is high. The bone of the balaenoptera, on the contrary, is very short and of scarcely any use, and the oil which can be extracted from its fat is comparatively scanty. Still, these latter cetaceans having been left alone until recent

40

years, their inferior value is largely compensated for by the numbers of them captured. Hunted without mercy, the right whale, on the other hand, has become very scarce generally. Perhaps it visits the Antarctic, since Ross says he has seen one, and so does Larsen ; but all the other explorers agree in asserting that they have never met one more south than the regions known as Sub-antarctic.

The old-time whalers set out in a boat to ' stick ' their prey by means of a harpoon fastened to a long rope, which uncoiled as the animal fled. They thus had themselves towed by it until, when it was exhausted, they could finish it off with other harpoons. But they only attacked the right whale, which when wounded makes right off, and once dead floats on the surface. They paid no attention to the so-called ' rushers,' which when wounded plunge deep, rush at their foes, or in any case describe a zigzag course, and whose bodies nearly always sink, thus threatening not only the loss of the quarry, but also that of the hunting gear. It is to a Norwegian whaler, Swen Foyn, who died a millionaire through it, that is due the invention of a special weapon, which now makes huge fortunes for some people and enables a vast population of workmen and hardy labourers to live. In the bow of a 40-ton steamer is mounted a cannon, which discharges a harpoon attached to a strong grapnel-rope. When the animal is hit, the two shanks of the harpoon open and explode a small shell. The body is hauled back by means of a steam windlass, fastened alongside, inflated by means of a large trocar communicating with the engine, to prevent it from sinking, and towed to the melting-house. Sometimes, as happened to us at the Faroes and at Deception, a single one of these little boats may be seen coming back with three balaenopteras, sometimes even with six.

The recent Antarctic Expeditions, from De Gerlache's down to that of the *Français*, have certainly done much for this revival of industry in the Antarctic and Sub-Antarctic regions, and I personally claim to have done my small part, though I should have liked to see my fellow-countrymen, severely tested as they have often been in the cod-fisheries, attempting to take advantage of it.

Nevertheless, the bold initiative of my former fellow-explorer, the merchant captain Rallier du Baty, who went to try his luck with his brother and three sailors on a 40-tonner in the Kerguelen Islands, and the praiseworthy persistence of MM. Bossière, the concessionaires of the islands, who recently managed to establish a whaling company in this French archipelago, lead me to hope that one day my exertions will have a result. Perhaps the men who make up the crew of the *Pourquoi-Pas ?* and who have been so vividly impressed by what they have managed to see at Deception may on their return have a good influence over their fishermen comrades. At any rate, since the return of the Nordenskjöld Expedition an Argentine company, having as its managing director the famous and able Norwegian captain Larsen, has established itself in South Georgia and is making huge profits every year. It was three years ago that the chase of the balaenoptera began in our exploration zone ; and in the South Shetlands since our visit one Chilian and two Norwegian companies have set up at Deception, while another has taken as its headquarters Admiralty Bay in George I Land. As far as these whalers are concerned, it has been a pleasure to me to note how useful the *Français* Expedition has been to them in supplementing the discoveries of the *Belgica* ; for we were able, of ourselves, to supply them with the only existing chart of the north-west coast of the Palmer Archipelago, and another of the Bismarck estuary, to guide them to a good anchorage at Port Lockroy and a shelter at Wandel Island, to say nothing of our notes on the numbers and species of balaenopteras, on the movements of the ice-floes, on the winds, etc.

December 23.—In spite of the late hour at which we anchored, every one is up very early to take advantage of the fine weather and set to work. Bongrain is putting up a tent, in which he is going to make observations with the pendulum. Rouch, while continuing his meteorological observations, is undertaking others on the electricity of the atmosphere. God-froy is mapping the contours of our anchorage and making soundings, which differ but little from those of the *Uruguay.* Gourdon is collecting geological specimens. Senouque is busy with magnetism and the measurement of rays, and the zool-ogists, Liouville and Gain, are scouring the neighbourhood, collecting and classifying all they can find. The crew either help in these different observations or are busy with work on board.

As for myself, I am beginning the editing of the reports on the start of the Expedition, which we shall be able to send to France, together with our mail, through the whalers. Every one finds time at intervals to learn ski-ing, gliding down some admirably suitable slopes of deep snow which, at the end of what used to be Pendulum Cove, run down into a little lake covered with ice and snow. The good spirits engendered by this pastime, new to so many of my comrades, causes the valley to ring loudly with merriment.

The cove in which we are anchored has a flat, black beach, bare of snow up to high-water mark, at which point there rises the steam from the spring of hot sulphur-water. At the junction-line of snow and beach there is a regular hedge of whale skeletons, from which, though they are mostly strip-ped of their flesh, there comes a powerful and sickening odour. There is a good deal of offal from the fishery now in progress, and the blue waters of the basin are tinged red with blood. It is clear that there was a whaling station here last year or the year before, for on a large board fixed to two uprights is the legend, ' Sobroan Harbour.' High escarped and snow-clad mountains rise at the end and side of our anchorage, while to the south is a black hill with steep walls, 80 metres in height, on the top of which can be seen the cairn left by the *Uruguay.*

43

Two men go to look for the bottle buried in it. It is broken, but the message is intact. It was meant for the *Français*, which but for her accident would probably have returned via Deception. I was destined therefore after all to receive the message, four years late. This is how it ran (in Spanish) :—

'DECEPTION ISLAND, *January* 8, 1905.

"This day I have visited this bay with the corvette *Uruguay* with the object of getting news of the Expedition under the leadership of Dr. Charcot, and not having succeeded I am going to Wiencke Island to leave a message there.

'(*Signed*) ISMAEL F. GALINDEZ.'

I read this document with emotion. For do I not owe much gratitude to this generous and hospitable people of Argentina, which not only enabled my first expedition, reaching Buenos Ayres in so wretched a state, to set out again under the best possible conditions, sent us a boat to carry our coal to Ushaia, and left a store at Orange Bay for our return, but also, in its anxiety over our absence, despatched the *Uruguay* to look for us?

The *Uruguay*, as we know, after leaving Deception went to Wiencke Island, where we had said we should leave a cairn—as we did, on Casabianca islet in Roosen Channel. Stopped by the ice and overtaken by a north-easterly gale, the Argentine corvette was unable to sail round the island and on her return announced that she had not found our cairn. It was immediately concluded that we had been lost, probably before being able to reach the Antarctic. This was the first news we heard on reaching Puerto Madryn on March 5, 1905.

After breakfast I set out with Liouville on the picket-boat for the whaling station. Just as we leave the anchorage we pass a cliff some 10 metres in height and of singular aspect, black with white spots. It is an ice-cliff with an intermixture of lava and lava-dust, a formation known by the name of fossil ice. About an hour later we reach the whalers' cove

44

With great difficulty—for, in order to let us come alongside, the crew of the *Gobernador Bories* has to move five or six corpses of whales, some of which burst with a report like that of a ·cannon—we arrive at the great factory-ship, where we are received by Captain Stolhani and M. Andresen, our kind friend of the day before.

M. Andresen, with charming courtesy, offers to send me thirty tons of coal on two trips of one of the little steamers, so that the *Pourquoi-Pas ?* need not come alongside the *Gobernador Bories* (necessarily disgusting because of the oil on board) nor stop in unpleasantly close proximity to the whale corpses. So good had been the catch that the coal is beginning to run short ; but a Hamburg collier is expected every day,[1] and if she is late one of the little whalers can go to Punta Arenas with a request for some of the precious fuel to be sent. On my part I ask M. Andresen if I can be of any use to him, when he tells me that Madame Andresen, who accompanies him and is probably the first and only woman that has ever come to the Antarctic, is rather ill, and that a workman on board, one of the cutters-up of the whales, has met with a serious accident. There is no doctor on the station, and the wounded man is coming back on one of the whalers from the Admiralty Bay Station, where they hoped, in vain, to find a doctor. While deploring that the service which we are able to do them is of so melancholy a character, I am happy to be of some use to these excellent people, and immediately Liouville and I examine Mme. Andresen, whose illness is, very fortunately, of a slight nature. It is different with the wounded man. The poor fellow has had four fingers sliced by a steam-chopper, and a regular amputation is essential to save not only his hand, but very probably his life. Liouville puts on a temporary dressing for him, but it is decided to come and operate to-morrow morning.

[1] It will be seen later that this vessel, the *Telephon*, was shipwrecked at the entrance of Admiralty Bay.

I have a long talk with M. Andresen, who gives me some interesting and useful information. There are on Deception Island three whaling companies, one Chilian and two Norwegian ; but apart from some Chilian firemen, the 200 inhabitants of the island are Norwegian. One of the Norwegian companies has as a factory-hulk a steamer of about 2,000 tons, coming from the Falklands, the other has the two three-masters, old sailing vessels which came from the Cape of Good Hope, towed by their little steam launches, while the Magellan Whaling Company, the best equipped, uses as factory-hulk the 3,000-ton steamer on which we are. All these floating factories are supplied by the little iron whale-boats like the *Raun* which piloted us in. These last-named are excellent vessels in spite of their insignificant dimensions, and apparently make light of the terrible seas of these latitudes.

Another company has its headquarters, as I have said, at Admiralty Bay in King George I Land. The catches are so abundant that all these vessels are insufficient, and in the stress of competition they only make use of the most valuable part of the whales' bodies, letting at least 40 per cent. go to waste.

For three years the whale-hunting has lasted here from the end of November to the end of February, when the companies separate, some going to hunt on the Chilian coast or in the Magellan Straits, the others in the waters of the Cape of Good Hope. England, claiming that the South Shetlands, the South Orkneys, and part of Graham Land belong to her equally with the Falklands, compels the whalers to pay her a small royalty, which passes through the hands of the Governor of the Falklands.

M. Andresen tells us that, as regards ice, the summer of 1906–1907 was a bad one, while during the last two summers there has been very little, at least in the region covered by the whale-boats. These vessels, not being built to resist ice-floes, of course avoid them carefully, although they succeed in

46

slipping through them easily enough when they are loose. The end of November, the whole of December, and the beginning of February are as a rule seasons of good weather, the gales to be feared coming from the south-west. I am astonished at this last statement (though I cannot refuse to accept it, since all the whalers on the station whom I have asked have told me the same), because during our two summer campaigns in 1904 and 1904-5 our gales, which were frequent and violent, always came from the north-east,[1] and that in regions not far from Deception Island. The balaenopteras pass this way in considerable numbers during December and January, but begin to go south at the end of the latter month. My hosts therefore listen with the greatest interest to the information which I am able to give them concerning the navigation in February of De Gerlache Strait, so fine a ground for whale hunting, and of Bismarck Estuary, where I do not advise them to go on account of the reefs and ice-floes, and finally concerning Port Lockroy, the only good anchorage which we discovered, and which I recommended from the first as a shelter for whalers, since they can reach it by three separate channels and run no risk of being stopped by floes. On the other hand, I do not commend Port Charcot, on Wandel Island, which cannot hold more than two small boats, or one of medium size, and becomes dangerous with the north-east winds. A visit to Port Lockroy seems their best chance, according to my information, and I think that M. Andresen has decided to put it to the test in February.

After fixing up an appointment on board the *Pourquoi-Pas?* on the next day but one, I bid good-bye to our kind hosts. The anchorage chosen by the whalers has the advantage of being quite close to the entrance of the bay, while

---

[1] It seems as if the whalers' observations were at fault, or we misunderstood them, for on our return to Deception we were able to testify that the frequent gales came from the north-east. M. Andersen must have meant that the gales from the south-west were the only dangerous ones at the anchorage.

providing an excellent shelter from the sea. Its only draw-back lies in its great depth and bad holding-ground. Also, in strong gales the ships sometimes drag their anchors, and one of them, it seems, stranded on the opposite side of the basin. The *Gobernador Bories*, which was probably the first to arrive, is anchored by the stern, quite close to a wide low beach like that at Pendulum Cove, so that she is able by means of a hose to bring straight on board all the fresh water necessary. On the beach is a little granite monument recently erected in memory of M. Andresen's predecessor, who was washed over board last year during a whale hunt.

We return on board to dinner. In my absence the various works have gone on. Gain and Gourdon have been on an excursion, and have met on a neighbouring beach, covered with snow and ice, a herd of 155 seals, Crabbing and Weddell's Seals mixed, who seem to have given them a vocal concert like those which we heard sometimes on the *Français*.

I write my mail until 1 a.m., when I go to look for Bongrain and Boland, who are making a series of pendulum observations in their tent, and take them some cakes and some Mariani wine to warm them.

December 24.—Weather as fine as ever. Liouville goes off to operate on the unfortunate workman, and Gourdon accompanies him to administer the chloroform. They are late in returning, for the operation was a long one ; but both are hopeful of its success. Thus we have been able to do a real service to these good fellows ; for without our aid the patient would have died of gangrene. M. Andresen had quite made up his mind to send him on a whale-boat to Punta Arenas if we had not turned up ; but it is doubtful whether he could have got there in time.

The work begun the previous day starts again. Rouch on the picket-boat has dredged the basin, bringing up an important zoological harvest. He has also taken soundings, and where Foster's chart shows 97 fathoms he has only found 63,

Coaling at Pendulum Cove.

which seems to prove that the filling up is not limited to the shores, but that the crater-shaped basin is also gradually changing. The whalers, too, who have the English chart, have frequently noticed this.

A whale-boat brings us in the morning 16 tons of Newcastle coal stacked loose on deck, and so as not to lose time another brings us 14 tons in the evening. Our men, assisted by the Norwegians, work enthusiastically, and at 6 p.m. our bunkers are full.

I have a long talk with one of the whaling captains, a grave, well educated and intelligent man. He confirms all that M. Andresen and the others told me yesterday, and gives me also some details about whale hunting; among other things, the practical method by which the whalers recognize at a distance the different kinds of balaenopteras. The Hump-back Whale (*Megaptera*), which is of little commercial value, spouts very low and has a protuberance on its back. The Fin Whale (the common *balaenoptera*), which is of medium value, has a fairly large dorsal fin and spouts very high, with a single straight jet. The Blue Whale (or Razor-back), whose value is greater than the two others', has a medium-sized dorsal fin and spouts with a double jet, which looks like a single one of moderate height ending in a plume.

In the evening, when all our work is done, we indulge in ski-ing. At midnight the bell goes full peal, and we keep Christmas Eve. There is a gay Christmas tree covered with knick-knacks and little candles, a present from Mme. Gourdon to the men, who are delighted with it. We for our part have supper and distribute the presents which many of our relatives, with a kindly forethought that arouses in me an emotion I find it hard to hide, intended for us on this chief of all family festivals.

December 25, *Christmas Day.*—The work on shore is finished off and all things put straight on board, while I sort the important mail of the *Pourquoi-Pas?* which the whalers are going to take to Punta Arenas on their return in March. Our news will, therefore, reach France in April. Many things will have happened between now and then, and our letters will only have been written very few days after those we sent from America; but still they will contain news which may perhaps make our absence seem shorter, and will at all events announce not only the happy termination of the first stage of our journey, but also the favourable conditions under which we are setting out.

About 3 o'clock some whaling captains of the Norwegian companies pay a visit to the *Pourquoi-Pas?* Christmas is the only day of the whole season on which they rest. I show them all over the ship, and must confess that I am not a little proud of the flattering appreciation which these experts give to the lines and construction of this vessel, which is in a way my child, and which was so often criticized by those who could speak with no authority. They all tell me that the ice-floes are far fewer this year than previous years; and when I compare this statement with the fact that the ocean-going ships (as we were told in our voyage across, and as is proved too by the broken stem of a German sailer at Rio Janeiro) came across an abundance of floes this winter at considerably more northern latitudes than usual, we may hope that there has been a mild winter, which allowed an almost constant break-up of the ice, or at least a prevalence of favourable winds which drove the floes toward the open sea, and I am prepared to believe this a good augury for our expedition.

Half an hour later M. Andresen arrives with his devoted and amiable wife, now happily recovered from her indisposition. She gives us the best reports on the patient of yesterday. We exchange Christmas greetings, and I am able to present all the Norwegians with picture postcards which my friend Crichton-Somerville sent me from Norway in large quantities, with ' A Merry Christmas and a Happy New Year ' on each of them.

M. Andresen, inexhaustible in kindness and care, tells me that he will do his best to come to Port Lockroy this year and that we may therefore leave a mail there. He assures me, moreover, that in January, 1910, he will certainly come to Port Lockroy and, if the ice permits, as far as Wandel to look for tidings of us. Need I insist on the importance of this generous proposal ? In case of an accident it is to Wandel and Port Lockroy that we shall seek to get. I was keenly reproached over the last expedition for not having made sure of a shelter in emergency. This time the same shall not be said of me. M. Andresen adds that we may be sure also of finding coal at Deception on our return.

We take a glass of champagne and shake hands with genuine emotion, our guests re-embark in their little boat, and we exchange salutes and blasts of the whistle. At 4.45 we weigh anchor. There is a brisk wind from the north-east, but the barometer is rising and the horizon is clear.

Before entering the pass we lessen speed opposite the whaling-station, the Chilian and Norwegian flags dip, the whistles rend the air, and we return the salute of these fine and hospitable people.

At 8 o'clock, with a good north-east breeze, we make for the northern entrance of De Gerlache Strait. The weather is so clear that we can see at the same time Deception, Low Island, and Hoseason, and make out in the south and south-west the high snow-covered lands. About us an innumerable quantity of balaenopteras are plunging.

Our immediate object is to reach Port Lockroy by way of the usually calm and comparatively free waters of the strait so justly named after De Gerlache.

De Gerlache in 1898, expecting to enter what the charts hitherto marked as a bay under the name of Hughes Bay, to his great astonishment found himself in this strait and made a stay there, surveying and making numerous landings. Finally he passed through it and thus reached the Pacific, when he was caught in the ice-pack and stayed until March, 1899, having the honour and glory of being the first man to winter in the Antarctic and bringing back a priceless quantity of notes and observations in the cause of science.

It is beyond discussion that the discovery of this strait belongs to De Gerlache, but it is also incontestable that the numerous American and English sealers, who regularly frequented these regions in the first half of the nineteenth century, knew much more than they told, both of these latitudes and of those visited by the *Français*. They kept silence, either intentionally to choke off competition or through indifference to geographical discoveries, which they were for the most part of the time incapable of appreciating or registering with any semblance of accuracy. It is, further, very probable that Captain W. H. Smiley in 1842 alludes to De Gerlache Strait in his letter to the explorer Wilkes, when he says: ' Many suppose that Palmer Land is a continent and consider that it is the continuation of the land marked out by Wilkes. But this is not the case, for I have sailed *round Palmer Land*.' In any case, in 1874 the German captain Dallmann, of Hamburg, the first to visit this region in a steamship, discovered the south-west entrance of this strait, to which he gave the name of Bismarck Strait. The *Grœnland*, a composite ship, belonged to the German Polar Navigation Company, and was equipped for seal hunting. After touching at Trinity Land, Dallmann made his way along the north-west coast of Palmer Archipelago, and particularly that part of the west coast which is now called Antwerp Island. On January 8 he passed between rocks and reefs at a point which he called Hamburg Haven, and his description of this place agrees remarkably with that given by the *Français* Expedition. He next went south and discovered, in the midst of ' a shoal of rocks which lay in surprising numbers close to the coast,' low islands and rocks level with the water, a vast estuary which he insisted must be a strait and to which he gave the name of Bismarck Strait. The *Grœnland* was then in ' about ' 64° 55′ South latitude. He discovered the archipelago of the Kaiser Wilhelm Islands, of which the principal were Booth, Krogmann, and Petermann Islands, rechristened by the *Belgica* Wandel, Hovgard, and Lund (where we wintered). He indicates plainly the entrance of Roosen Channel—De Gerlache's Neumayer Channel—and the south-west cape of what afterwards was named Wiencke Island. Next, going first north, then north-east, after passing the Paul I reefs, he doubled Cape Grœnland and penetrated into a bay which ought rightly to bear his name. But the ice prevented him from ' penetrating far enough to know whether the bay ended in a strait.' As a matter of fact, there was a channel, which the *Belgica* saw from De Gerlache Strait and named Scholaert Channel. The *Français* used it twice, and surveyed it, rediscovering the two little fjords pointed out by Captain Dallmann. Dallmann, who, it must be remembered, was but a mere sealing captain and, as he confesses himself, had defective chronometers, could scarcely fail to make incorrect observations of longitude. His discoveries were utilized for the first time in A. Petermann's South Polar Chart in 1875 (Stieler's Atlas No. 7, 1894), and then in a chart laid down by L. Frederichsen in 1895 after the German captain's original sketch map. In his over-anxiety to be complete, the last-named geographical expert made the mistake of joining, on the strength of a mere supposition, the entrance of the strait marked by Dallmann with that of an inlet seen by Larsen in 1893–4 on the east coast of Graham Land ; and this is the sole reason for the doubts born later concerning the identification of Bismarck Strait with the Pacific entrance of the strait marked by the *Belgica*.

The *Français* Expedition of 1903–5 settled the question. After touching Smith Island, we surveyed the north-west coast of Palmer Archipelago, so important to navigators in these regions. Then entering the strait from the south-west we sailed down Roosen Channel, discovering Port Lock-roy, Peltier Channel, and Doumer Island. After a detour to the south the *Français* came back to winter at Booth (Wandel) Island, where she stayed nine months. But excursions during this period allowed us not only to complete and extend the survey of this region, but also to prove the non-existence of another supposed strait a little further to the south. During the next summer campaign the *Français* surveyed Scholaert Channel, which joins Dallmann Bay and runs south. A serious grounding of the ship forced her to return in February, all but foundering at Port Lockray. Here the crew had a rest. Next she sailed up De Gerlache Strait again, noting some details for alteration, concerning firstly the channel separating Liège and Brabant Islands, and secondly Hoseason Island, where we were unable to dis-cover the cairn left by Foster, although we landed at the same point as he. In the map drawn by Lieutenant Matha, second in command, we did not trouble ourselves about our own small loss of reputation and the lessening of the area of our discoveries, but were particular to restore all the names given by Dallmann and to render full justice to this modest Hamburg sealing captain. The Germans had done equal justice to the French explorer Bouvet, when in 1899 the *Valdivia* rediscovered the island which bears his name and whose existence had been so long disputed after the voyages of Cook and Ross.

In 1903 the Nordenskjöld Expedition sailed along the northern side of De Gerlache Strait before visiting the coast of Graham Land, and the *Uruguay* when looking for the *Fran-çais* in January, 1905, went as far as the cape at the southern end of Wiencke Island without being able to round the island. Finally, we must note that the celebrated English sealer Biscoe was the first to discover and name in 1832 Mount William, situated on Antwerp Island at the entrance of the strait, and that he landed at a point on the island where we landed in February, 1905.

December 26.—Passing Hoseason Island yesterday Rouch took a sounding. The lead went down to a depth of 1,400 metres without touching the bottom. The temperature at this depth was −0°5.

In the morning we are abreast of Two Hummocks Island, south-west of which in February, 1905, the *Français* found fair shelter from a north-east gale. The weather, like yesterday's, is remarkably fine and clear, and we are sailing over an absolutely smooth sea. We are closer to the coast of Palmer Archipelago, but we can see the opposite shore very distinctly. From time to time we have to avoid a few icebergs and ice-blocks, but they are so scattered that they do not trouble us. There is evidently much less ice than when we were here in 1904 and 1905, and even less, it seems, than when the *Belgica* was here. We came across no marine ice, and no coastal ice-belt or débris of the latter.

Another sounding is taken at the entrance of Scholaert Channel, but an accident to the lead prevents strict accuracy. Apparently the bottom is at about 300 metres.

We enter by the northern end of Roosen Channel, where we have to pass some remains of icebergs piled up very loosely, and soon the superb Mount Français shows up in all its splendid grandeur. Next the approach to Port Lockroy, whose contours are so familiar to us, appears in its turn, and we come abreast of Casabianca Islet, where stands out boldly the long spar with a signal on the top which we set up in 1904, when we left there tidings of ourselves. I go with Gourdon in the dinghy as far as our letter-box, and meanwhile on board they take a sounding of 126 metres and use for the first time the big steam windlass for the dredging-net. It works very well, and the fruitful haul will keep the naturalists busy.

We find our cairn intact and solid, only one of the steel-wire shrouds having broken. The mast is very dry and is

55

covered with a fine white coating, which I mistake at first for a mould similar to what I found on the wooden buildings left by the *Pola* in Jan Mayen Land. A farther examination shows me that it is really down from birds, evidently coming from the numerous neighbouring rookeries. The bottle attached to the mast, containing another phial inside, is unbroken, and we find again the message which we placed in it in February, 1905, as plain and clear as if it had been put there yesterday. It is easy to understand our emotion as we look at it. We substitute for it a temporary note, indicating merely that we are going to spend a day or two at Port Lockroy. This letter-box is cleared very irregularly, and so far we have been the only postmen!

We go on board again and return without difficulty to Port Lockroy, where we let down our anchor close to the spot where the *Français* used to anchor. Nothing seems changed, the rookeries are still inhabited by the penguins, and the gulls are on their solitary little island, where stands an old wine-pump acting as a cairn and indicating the presence of a message like that on Casabianca Islet. The ice-cliff which forms the end wall of the bay has the same appearance as of old, and those of us who took part in the earlier expedition might well think ourselves four years younger! The new-comers land at once and explore the penguins' rookery, which they find just as amusing and interesting as we used to.

In the evening, with snow-shoes on our feet on account of the heavy deposit of snow, Godfroy, Senouque, Jabet and myself ascend to the plateau which runs across the island at the foot of the magnificent peak of Louis-de-Savoie, still wearing its curious ducal crown of ice, to the summit of which Dayné the guide and quartermaster Jabet made their bold climb in 1905. It appears that the snow has increased, altering the formerly level plateau into a huge dome. We see Cape Renard and Wandel Island very distinctly, but fail in our real object, for we wanted chiefly to ascertain whether the passage from here to Wandel Island was free of ice, which was not the case in February, 1904, at the end of December, or in February, 1905. But Doumer Island shuts out the view of the sea.

December 27.—The weather is fine, though a little threatening in the west. Our colleagues are busy with their observations ashore. I have the picket-boat got ready to go to Wandel Island. Obviously the trip is a little risky, for there are 20 miles to cover, 15 in the open sea ; but we ought to be able to see not only whether the way is clear as far as Wandel and whether Port Charcot is blocked as it was in December, 1905, but also the state of the ice to the south and around the island. By using 20 litres of petroleum, of which we have a big supply, we shall save one day's coal and perhaps even more.

At 2 o'clock Godfroy, Gourdon, Besnard, Frachat and myself set off, with our bed-sacks, a tent, and four days' provisions. We take Peltier Channel, which the *Français* discovered, and at the entrance we stop a few minutes to take soundings at the foot of an ice-cliff, which does not rest like its neighbours upon a stratum of rock, but is worn by the swell of the sea as the icebergs are. Close up to the perpendicular face of the cliff we let fall the lead to the depth of 50 metres without touching bottom. Our glaciologist, Gourdon, is going to study this matter with care, for perhaps we have here an ice-barrier in miniature.

All goes well. Even outside the shelter of the channel the picket-boat makes her five knots. The wind blows freshly from the south-west, that is to say a little ahead ; but in hugging the icebergs and islands to escape the wind we are bothered by the chop, which becomes rather pronounced. The floes are few, certainly much fewer than at any time during our last expedition. The wind freshens as we push on, the chop becomes very rough, and we are drenched. Wandel is only two miles away now, and we are already in sight of our big cairn, when our badly protected magneto is flooded and the motor stops. Finally we run up the mast, hoist sail, and try to tack ; but the sea is too heavy, the current is against us, and the ice-blocks compel us to give way, so that we lose the small amount of progress we have made. We drift toward Cape Renard, whose imposing mass towers over us. Should the wind drop, increase, or change, we should find ourselves in a bad plight. To our great regret, when we are so near our goal, we are forced to put about, and now with a quarter-wind we head for Wiencke Island. We fall foul of some floes which bar our way, but we manage to clear them, and after some hours enter Peltier Channel, where we are becalmed. We are resigning ourselves to five miles of sculling in this heavy boat, when our motor, perhaps aware of our curses or with its magneto dry again since we put about, consents to restart work and at 11 p.m. we reach Port Lockroy, frozen to the marrow. We have but partly attained the object of our trip, but if we have secured no information as to the state of the ice south of Wandel, at least we are certain of being able to reach that island without difficulty.

December 28.—The weather is moist and grey, and the low clouds are scarcely higher than the top of the ice cliff. The crew load the large canoe with ice from the bergs to fill up the boiler by means of the specially designed pipe, and all works quickly and well.

Bongrain continues his pendulum observations on Goudier Islet. Rouch and Gourdon go out to dredge and take soundings under the ice cliff where we began last night, and find bottom at 150 metres. Then they look for rock specimens on Casabianca Islet, and hunt the beach for fossils, unfortunately in vain. Gain and Liouville arrange and classify the numerous specimens already gathered. Godfroy examines the atmosphere. I busy myself with various details on board, and get ready the messages and the mail which we are to leave in the cairn for the whalers. If they come this year, there will be some news to go to France. I write what is probably the last letter for a very long time to my dear wife. Thus far this possibility of writing to her, so to speak, daily has given me the illusion of being not so far away from her, but now the separation will seem very real to me. Still I do not yet feel completely cut off from the civilized world in spite of the vast isolation, probably because I am still in regions familiar to me, and perhaps also because of the rapidity and ease with which we have come from Punta Arenas to here.

In 1905 during our stay we captured daily on the line 30 to 50 fish ; to-day we have only got two, though they are of a very good size.

December 29.—Since morning the weather has been clear and calm, with a fine hot sun. While Bongrain was finishing his observations, Gourdon and Senouque measuring the depth of the hollows in the cliff at the foot of which we sounded, and finding it to be 35 metres, and the crew putting all in order for our departure, I went in the picket-boat with Godfroy to change the messages in the two cairns. A number of small floes encumber the entrance to the harbour, but the picket-boat slips through them well until on our return we ground for a long while on the spur of a small ice-block.

At 1.30 we weigh anchor and pass through Peltier Channel without much difficulty, in spite of the numerous floes of fair size which have entered it. Our ship pushes them aside or breaks them with ease, but every time that the shock is a little rough our red paint comes off on the ice, which therefore looks as if it were bleeding beneath our blows.

Abreast of Goetschy Islet, Gourdon gets into a Norwegian boat to look for geological specimens, and Rouch takes a sounding of 90 metres, with a temperature of 0° 1 ; he also uses the drag-net, with some difficulty owing to the narrow space and the presence of ice, but still with very satisfactory results. We pass Doumer Island outside the Channel, the

59

estuary is free, and in this clear weather our chart is sufficient to guide us unhesitatingly to Port Charcot.

Unhappily, at the very moment when we reach the entrance, the famous north-easter, which is so dangerous here, begins to blow. Nevertheless we must make a stay here in order to leave a stock of food. The *Français* was able to spend nine months here—at great risk, it is true, but without serious damage in the end. The *Pourquoi-Pas ?* has 10 more metres in length, and her greater draught of water will not allow her to thrust herself so far into the cove and thus protect herself so well. But to return to Port Lockroy or to keep up steam while sheltering under the island would mean loss of time and waste of coal; for I know no other place in the neighbourhood where we could moor or anchor and put out the fires. Therefore I do not hesitate to enter, and in order to stop our way before the force of the wind we cannon gently off the round stones of Sögen Island and just beach our bows. We run out three ice-anchors to starboard astern, three to port astern, and six from the bows. Finally we stretch across the cove as a bar against the floes some double lengths of steel cable belonging to the drag-nets. As all our moorings are new, I hope that they will hold.

So here I am again at Wandel Island, where for nine months we lived, worked, hoped, sometimes almost despaired and often sorrowed. I am back again under much better conditions, with a ship, equipment, and means which are out of all comparison with those of the former expedition. In addition I have the experience and, what is not so good, four years on to my age. By me I have again Gourdon and eight men from the old crew. Our sympathetic memories go back to our stout little *Français*, whose defective and insufficient engine brought on us so much trouble, and to our beloved comrades, Matha and Pléneau, who would be with me once more, had not inexorable duty kept them away.

Nothing has altered in appearance, and I could believe

Cormorants on their Nests.

that I never left the spot. My eyes are struck by the same familiar objects and the same buildings, my ears catch the same sounds from the rookeries of penguins and cormorants, which give forth the same powerful odour. On the rock where the *Français's* gangway landed is a heap of old, empty and rusty preserved food tins, a pile of stacked bottles, and the head of a seal. ' Victor Hugo Avenue,' of course, is obliterated under a mass of snow, but it would be easy to retrace it.

There is no time, however, for reminiscences, and I climb at once with Gourdon up the height we called Jeanne to survey the neighbourhood and the offing. Our hydrographic signal is still on its cairn, and under a stone I find the little rum bottle in which Dayné enclosed a message on December 25, 1904, when we climbed up together to say good-bye, or rather *au revoir,* to Wandel. The estuary is free of ice save for a few blocks and bergs, but in the offing the floes, if in a loose condition, seem to reach as far as the horizon. On the south side the water is free as far as the Jallour Islets. I am very anxious to try to follow the coast and make my way between it and the Biscoe Islands. Numerous reefs, many hidden under ice, and icebergs beyond number make the journey dangerous ; but it would be of the highest interest. So I make up my mind in any case to push a reconnaissance along this coast. But for the moment there is nothing to do except wait for the end of the north-east gale, and we come down again to visit the familiar spots.

The picket-boat abandoned here in 1904 is in good condition, but is filled with solid ice. Her awning, oars, and planking, from which the paint has come off, are all as white as if they had been frequently and energetically holystoned. The wooden magnetic hut, in which Rey used to work, is absolutely as untouched as if it had just been left, and its stoutness does the greatest honour to its builder, our carpenter Libois. We find in the hut a few objects which were left behind or forgotten, notably a matchbox-stand and on its glazed earthenware base the glass jar containing the report of the Expedition, which I had placed there a few minutes before we left. The stone-built magnetic hut and its observation-stand are also in the same state as when we left, and I find there a few pages of a notebook. As for the portable house, it is almost entirely crushed in under the snow, with all that it contains. It has a strong inclination toward the north, having probably slipped along the ice down the gentle slope in this direction. Its corrugated iron roof has been carried away by the wind, and is now Heaven knows where. Otherwise all that one can see appears to be in a good state. But it would be too long and difficult a job to dig it out entirely. The big cairn on the 60-metre hill which overhangs our cove has suffered no damage. This imposing monument dominates our old station ; the message-box and the leaden plate on which are engraved all the names of the members of the *Français* Expedition are still attached to it.

Happily the north-easter is only blowing now with moderate force. The swell is not very strong, and our ice-anchors and cables alike hold good.

December 30.—A fairly large ice-floe is kept off by the steel-wire hawser. But unfortunately—and this shows that man is never content—I find that for the moment, apart from the blocks and bergs, there is not enough floating ice to protect us, as the *Français* was protected by the blockage of the cove, not only from the swell, but also from dangerous neighbours. We have no time to give up to the heavy labour spent in 1904, when we stretched an anchor-chain across, and I am afraid that in the end the ice-floes will account for our feeble steel-wire hawser.

We scatter over the island, some for exercise, others for work. I go with a few men armed with spades and picks to try to dig out the interior of the portable house. The Christmas tree which we left there the day of our departure comes out in pieces, but we find intact various objects, such as a bread-basket, tins of preserves, desiccated milk, etc.

Some poor penguins had to be killed this evening for the kitchen. Why is man bound to do evil as soon as he visits any place ?

Up to now the north-easter has been blowing with clear weather, but now it is overcast and heavy. The big icefloe which has been toppling over against the hawser passes under it and makes for our ship. We turn it aside and send it along toward the end of the cove.

December 31.—Still the north-easter, accompanied in the morning by a small fine rain. But in the afternoon the sky clears, and the sun comes out. The temperature, which since our arrival in the Antarctic has been about 1 or 2 degrees below zero, is now 2° above.

We open our store-rooms to establish on Wandel Island a depôt containing tins of biscuits, petroleum, a Primus lamp, some tools, and matches. With these and seals, penguins, and cormorants, which never leave the island even in the winter, there will be no danger of immediate death from hunger.

While we are finishing breakfast, the swell increases, and suddenly the helm above our heads begins to move. A great ice-block has broken through the hawser and struck the rudder. Happily there is no damage done, but it is with difficulty that we drive off the aggressor with poles. We are now surrounded by large blocks, which strike against the ship violently and have to be constantly pushed aside. The hawser is stretched across again, but I confess that I have little confidence in its efficacy. I am more anxious than I wish to appear, for injuries to our screw or our rudder, the only ones that I fear, would make us prisoners here, and that would be stupid. This campaign, on which I build such hopes, would then finish before it had well begun. But little by little the sky clears in the direction of Wiencke Island, a favourable sign, as I know well ; and sure enough, toward 8 o'clock in the evening, there is a dead calm. It was high time, for an ice-block all bristling with sharp edges was bearing down on us, and I do not know how we should have been able to defend ourselves against it.

Some of my colleagues are losing nerve, give vent to pessimistic opinions as to the stoutness of the vessel, and insist that we are going to be shut in by the ice-blocks which now choke the cove and would keep us from leaving if we wanted to. It is in vain that I assure them that as soon as it is calm the regular northerly current will quickly clear away all these. Probably their anxiety to see the Expedition on the move makes it difficult for them to bow before a nine months' experience acquired in this locality. To make the time pass, every one goes ashore to practise ski-ing, and I am left on board alone to sort out the little parcels intended for us by our families on the first day of the year.

Guégen, following our old custom, has dug a hole in the snow-hill alongside us, so as to take advantage of the thaw. From this the water flows in abundance, and with a hose stretched along a hawser we are able without fatigue to fill the boiler and the water-casks.

Some of the men take off their skis and search in vain in the snow of Sögen Islet, named after our good dog which died here of old age, to see if they can find his body and that of our pig Toby, who lived eleven months with us and was the delight of all the crew. Kiki and Polaire, two pet dogs presented to us at Buenos Aires, play about over their graves without the slightest respect for their predecessors' memories.

January 1, 1909.—As midnight struck, every bell on board, the foghorns and the phonographs gave forth their sounds in a deafening discord to welcome the New Year. We eat, in accordance with the custom which makes this bring good luck, some fresh grapes which were presented to us for the occasion by M. Blanchard at Punta Arenas. Packed in sawdust, they had already made the journey from Malaga, so that they are

The Magnetic Hut on Wandel Island after Five Years.

of a certain age ; and yet they taste as if they had just been picked.

Chollet, the old companion of all my travels, comes first, as at Port Lockroy in 1905, to shake my hand. Then Libois, the oldest on board, who has also served me long, brings me a very nice letter signed by all the crew. On their part the staff came forward to shake the hands of our brave and devoted helpers. Then, both fore and aft, we wash down with the generous wines of France an abundant supper.

My first thought of the year has been of my own, of my brave and devoted wife, who not merely allowed me to do my duty, but further encouraged and helped me to do it. I told her once to soothe her, on an occasion when she was speaking sadly of anniversaries which we should spend apart, that all days are alike. It is not true, and I did not think so myself. Too many memories of family gatherings, some joyful, others saddened by the vanishing of a loved one, are stirred up by these dates for them to be otherwise than like steps on life's great stair, whereon the mind halts to look back on the way already come, fearing, with the dread of the unknown, to take the next step.

The north-easter has begun to blow afresh, some huge ice-floes come in again, and my night finishes up with the man on the watch, pushing them off and protecting the vessel with fenders. Amid the great solitude, full of the howling of the wind and the sound of the crashing floes, I pray to God on this morning of the first day of the year to give me strength and ability to rise to the height of the task which I have undertaken, of my own free will, with the sole object of being of some use to my country.

About midday the wind dropped. We got the picket-boat quickly into the water, and at 3 o'clock Gourdon, Godfroy, Liouville and myself, slipping through the floes, which have separated a little, make a reconnaisance to the south. Going by way of Salpetrière Bay, among numerous icebergs, we soon

65

reach Hovgard. Here still stands the hydrographic signal
which we set up in 1904, at a little distance from the cleft
between two rocks which served as our home for several weeks.
We search in vain round this island, which we had only seen
before surrounded by an ice-belt, for a shelter for our ship ;
and we push on to Lund (Petermann) Island. We approach
the place where, after months of fruitless effort, we finally
arrived on skis during our previous winter. I climb with
Gourdon to the summit, from which there is a fine and exten-
sive view, while Liouville collects the mosses and lichens which
abound here, defending himself in the meantime against the
attacks of vast numbers of megalestrides, fine, strong chestnut-
coloured birds, which thought that he had designs on their
nests.

Very often, almost every time we land, we have to put up
with the attacks of the megalestris, and its sharp beak and
strong flight justify fear. Still, I must say that never has
any one of us, man or dog, been wounded by them, although
some say that they have been struck on the head. As a rule
every one detests them, but I confess that I have nothing but
admiration for these courageous creatures.

From the peak we see in the offing some floes, close at hand
but of no great extent. Along the coast the water is free as
far as the Jallour Islets ; further on there is a flat ice-pack full
of great clefts. From our observatory we see a fairly big
cove on the east of the island, close to a headland where we
camped twice in succession during our excursion in December,
1904. At that time we dragged our whale boat over the thick
ice at this spot. Now the cove is quite free of ice, and if there
are good enough camping-grounds it will provide our ship
with an excellent shelter, which we must visit. We descend
and get on board the picket-boat, on which during our absence
Godfroy has very ingeniously rigged up a tent with a tarpaulin—no unnecessary precaution, for it is raining in torrents.

There are some shallows at the entrance of the cove, between which the ship will be able to pass; and they will, moreover, stop ice-blocks of deep draught from entering. Altogether this inlet makes an excellent harbour, where two vessels like ours could at need moor, very probably sheltered from all winds, and at any rate from those blowing from between the east-north-east and the south-east, if not from the west. In memory of the date on which we discovered it we laughingly christen it Port Circumcision, its name in future. The great French navigator Bouvet gave the same name, for the same reason, to the remarkable island and cape which he discovered on this day.

As soon as the weather is favourable we shall bring the *Pourquoi-Pas ?* here, and shall find whether we can continue southward along the coast or must, on the other hand, make for the open. My choice would be to advance with successive halts, so as to insure a thorough study of this region. But will ice-floes and reefs permit this, and shall we always find sufficient shelter ? The future will decide.

At 10 p.m. we return on board drenched, and eat with good appetite. At Wandel Island the ice-blocks are still in the same position, and the north-easterly wind is getting up again.

January 2.—The ice anchor which held the hawser across the cove has given way, and already one of the ice-blocks has badly scratched our stern name-board. Certainly Port Charcot is a dangerous place during north-easterly winds, especially for a boat the size of ours. The situation is serious, and it is necessary to come to a decision quickly. A huge ice-block is threatening our stern, which it would soon crush in, another to starboard is knocking against our side, and a third, still more vast, is bearing down on us to port. I have the two last-named firmly fastened to the shore, and, as the first is buttressed up by them, we shall be protected as long as the cables hold.

It is warm and the sun is bright, but the north-easter is

still blowing strong. We shall not be able to get out until there has been a calm of some duration or the wind has changed. Nevertheless, I have all made ready for departure, and I write out the messages to leave in the cairns in French and in English, a language known by all the Norwegians. In the afternoon we suffer the north-easter's worst onset, the weather being very heavy, with violent squalls and blinding snow alternating with sleet or fine rain. For the moment our ice-blocks keep quiet and even protect us against the swell and against other ice, but it is best not to think of what will happen if they recover their freedom of action. The man on the watch has instructions not to leave the stern, and to give warning of the slightest move.

January 3.—At midnight the fall of the barometer ceases, and the wind gradually drops. It snows and rains fast. The ice-blocks astern fall apart slowly, inch by inch. The suspense is terribly unnerving. To set us free a south wind is required, but it continues to blow from the north-east, though weakly. I dare not release our prisoners for fear that the present calm may be deceptive.

At night the snow ceases, but the weather still remains very overcast. I set at liberty the ice-block to port, which is tearing at its cables, and as at 11 o'clock there is a passage just sufficient for the ship I give orders for the fires to be lighted and all cables to be taken up that are not needed to prevent swinging, while I go off to deposit the messages in the cairns.

At 1.30 we begin our move, and just succeed in slipping out, our cove being narrower than my own chart makes it to be. At last we get clear without mishap and make for Lemaire Channel, leaving Cape Renard and False Cape Renard to our left. We have to thread two close-packed belts of broken-up bergs, which give us some pretty hard knocks. The snow is falling in heavy flakes, and abreast of Hovgård we are forced to stop, as we can only see a few metres ahead.

68

Threatening Ice-Blocks.

On the end of the deck the sensation of giddiness produced by the snow falling on the calm black water is very curious. We seem to be rising in a balloon, with the sea and the icebergs plunging rapidly into a bottomless gulf beneath us.

Thanks to a break in the weather, we make Port Circumcision easily and here we moor ourselves firmly with four anchors, almost as if we were alongside a wharf. I believe that there is no risk to our ship here.

January 4.—It is fine and warm, and everybody scatters over the island for the usual researches and observations. We rediscover the locality of our old camps in 1904, and the corned beef tin with the pencil message in it.

I launch the picket-boat and have Godfroy's awning rigged up more securely, for I want to start off this very day and reconnoitre in the neighbourhood of Cape Tuxen and the Berthelot Islands, which are free of ice and ought to give us a good view from their highest point.

At 5 p.m., in beautiful weather, Gourdon, Godfroy and myself set out, and as we only expect to be absent a few hours we only take enough for one meal and the clothes we have on us.

As far as Tuxen the sea is clear, and we sight in passing the cairns, erected in 1904. Beyond the cape there is a wide channel between the land and the ice-fields, which we take. Gourdon and I disembark at the foot of an ice-cliff rising on a base of fallen soil, dominated by the imposing perpendicular wall of green diorite which composes Cape Tuxen. Gourdon collects some zoological specimens, and we spend an hour upon the flat top of the cliff. The Berthelot Islands are surrounded by open water, and the channel appears to continue towards Cape Trois-Perez. The extremely clear weather allows us to make out the wonderful high mountains to the west of this cape. On board once more, we endeavour to penetrate by the channel into the big bay which De Gerlache imagined might be a strait, though it is really the head of an enormous glacier; but we are in the midst of colossal piled-up icebergs and the pack-ice is becoming quite solid. It is, indeed, so thick that very probably it may go through several winters without breaking up. Twice we very narrowly escape considerable danger; for, after we have slipped between an iceberg and the pack, the former bears down upon and all but crushes us. Once the picket-boat is actually wedged in, her ribs crack, and with great difficulty we get away in time, finding for our exit a narrow channel which we only get through by lightening the boat and jumping over the ice, which closes up again as soon as we are gone. It would be absurd to pursue this course, so we make straight for the Berthelot Islands, reaching them soon. Thus, in a few hours we have reached the spot in getting to which we spent six days in 1904 at the cost of great labour, five of us hauling over the ice a boat weighing 850 kilogrammes.

Forthwith we make the long and rather toilsome ascent of the big island to have a look to southward. The whole coast-line is blocked. To take the boat anywhere here would be impossible; but the offing, at a short distance, appears free, so the *Pourquoi-Pas ?* shall try her luck in that direction.

It is 10 p.m. when we get into the picket-boat again, and, judging by the time we took to come, we count on being on board about 1 or 2 a.m. We have a meal of soup, pâté-de-foie-gras, chocolate, jam, and two of our five biscuits—a luxurious repast, which we are destined soon to regret. It is calm, but snow is beginning to fall.

When we reach the edge of the land we seek in vain for an opening. Thick pack-ice is now pressing against the cliff, and in spite of all our efforts we can find no way through. I climb up on to a neighbouring islet to have a look at the ice from a point of vantage; but it is not high enough, so we return to the Berthelot Islands. I climb to the summit of one of these and seem to see in the offing a narrow-winding channel, running to an open space which ought to lead to

Tuxen and clear water. I make a note of the icebergs which choke the channel, and as we have no alternative we make our way into it.

From this moment onward the snow falls constantly, varied with an icy rain. There is no night, and the sun remains hidden in the clouds. These facts, combined with our incessant hard work and the absence of such breaks as a meal, prevent us from knowing, when we chance to look at our watches whether it is night or daytime.

All goes well at the start of the new route, the picket-boat making her way well through the small floes, even climbing over them at times and breaking them up. Godfroy looks after the motor ; I am at the helm, shouting to him in turn, ' Stop,' ' Right ahead,' ' Back her,' or ' Slow ; ' and Gourdon, armed with a boat-hook, pushes off the floes now ahead and now astern. But soon our misery commences. The channel which I noted is closed, while others have opened, ending in lakes from which there is no exit. A biting little west wind alters the position of the ice every minute. We see a channel forming, but to get there we have to cross a large expanse of ice. When this is not too thick the picket-boat, by going alternately full speed ahead and then astern, very slowly cuts a way for herself. But soon this becomes impossible. Then we climb on to the fragile ice and with spade and boat-hooks try to cut a channel. It is a slow and exhausting job. The spade is our best tool, but unhappily it slips from Godfroy's benumbed hands and sinks ! We laugh at the mishap and at the woebegone face of our good friend ; but our already feeble efforts now become almost useless. The ice, moreover, gets so thick that even with the spade we should have been able to do nothing. A large stretch of free water lies ahead of us, but we are completely blocked in.

We stop a few minutes to take a rest, when a penguin coming up through a hole, rises right at our side. We hesitate a moment whether to kill it for food, but none of us are murderously inclined, and we decide to spare it. Like a good fairy anxious to reward us, it turns to the ice, flaps its wings, and suddenly the surface opens, making a wide channel in which the picket-boat floats. We speed along it. But, alas! our joy is of short duration, for though this channel is open the others which we wished to reach close up at the moment when we are about to enter them and regain our freedom!

I have no idea how long our struggle lasts, but I notice that Gourdon whenever he sits down falls asleep, so we moor our boat for a while to the ice, to try to get a little rest. We are beginning to attempt to fix ourselves up, when another channel opens. We push ahead; but it is another fraud, and at last with great difficulty we get to a high reef, where we moor as best we can. I climb to the top of this black and gloomy reef, the home of a couple of megalestrides, which in spite of my protestations that we will do them no harm as long as we are not literally dying of hunger, persist in attacking me. I discover, with aching heart, that the whole conformation of the pack-ice has altered and that we are blocked in fine and snug. There is nothing to do but to wait. One of the planks of the boat is stove in, others are so smashed and damaged by the ice that only a fraction of an inch keeps the water out. It will not bear thinking about.

We want to stretch ourselves out to sleep, but we have scarcely room, and without coverings or change of clothes, wet to our vests, and our socks soaking, we are pierced with cold. We have one tin of beef, and Gourdon finds a few sticks of chocolate, which with two biscuits and a flask of rum constitute all our provisions. With one accord we decide not to touch them for the present.

We settle down as best we can—and best is very bad in the restricted space under the tent, which has holes in several places—and try to sleep; but the frightful coldness of our feet wakes us every minute, and my anxiety to extricate ourselves from this situation makes me rise a dozen times to

The Fight with the Ice at Wandel.

run to the summit of the reef.   After three hours of this game
I notice a channel starting from some thin ice, once over
which we shall be able to get back to the Berthelot Islands,
where there was a cormorant-rookery in 1904.   We may
even find again the practicable channel along the coast.   But
before reaching this thin ice there is a stretch covered by a
pile of icebergs and I cannot see what is in store for us there.
So much the worse ; but we cannot stay here, exposed as we
are to the slightest shock of the ice.   We must act.   I awaken
my comrades, and once more we are off !   After many hardships, detours and shocks, we cross the iceberg-zone and the
thin ice.   There is some open water, to which we have been
long strangers, and we reach the Berthelots.   The cormorants
are still beside an old cairn of ours.   At the last extremity
we could eat these raw, or singed by the aid of our spirit ;
for we have not seen a single seal to provide us with its fat
for fuel, and thus allow us to dry ourselves a little.   To-day
we shall content ourselves with a cake of chocolate and a bis-
cuit divided among the three.   We assert, moreover, that
we are not very hungry—perhaps to make ourselves believe
it.   I climb to the summit of this thickly moss-clad island,
and we decide to go and look again for our old channel along
the coast.   It is still hermetically sealed, and our efforts are
in vain.

We therefore attempt to get back to the Berthelot Islands
to seek for a corner where the picket-boat will be sheltered,
and we can wait ; but in trying to avoid an ice-block we
ground on a rock.   The sea is falling and the boat is already
in a dangerous position.   Our situation is critical ; for the
drop of the tide is about 2 metres, and we are far from land
and our cormorant-isle.   We shore up the boat with the oars
firmly fastened to the mast laid across and resting on the ice-
floe—which fortunately is also aground.   Then, there being
but one tide a day we wait many long hours like this.   My
companions get some snatches of sleep, but I cannot do the

same, my responsibility weighing on me too much. I reproach myself with having dragged them into this adventure without taking more food and clothing, when I am usually so careful. I am anxious not only for them but also for the *Pourquoi-Pas ?* It must be nearly three days since we left, and our comrades on board must be very worried. They will certainly try to succour us, either in boats or in the ship itself; and what risks will they not run, especially in this heavy weather, not to mention the waste of coal!

At last we get afloat and return to our cormorant-rookery, where we decide to wait for a break in the weather or a change of wind. During the hours we spent there I do not know how often I climbed the summit. It is probable that if I added up the climbs made on this wretched trip I should find I have covered more than several thousand metres.

I seem to espy a loosening of the ice along the coast. At any rate the distance to go before reaching open water beyond Cape Tuxen is shortened, so we set out full of hope.

We struggle once more with the ice, making for one rift after another. We seem on the point of gaining ground, when suddenly the motor stops and, in spite of all efforts, amiable encouragements, and harsh words, it is impossible to start it again. While Godfroy takes it to pieces, I use the paddle and with great difficulty we reach the rocky point projecting from the ice-cliff on the coast. Had we not got there we should infallibly have been swept to the end of the bay full of clashing icebergs—and what would have become of our frail boat in that titanic chaos? Even here huge floes pass to and fro according to the movements of the tide, but a lucky eddy seems to protect us.

While the indefatigable Godfroy tries to find a cure for the engine with the help of Gourdon, I make an examination of the rock. I find a few rather rare barnacles and on the summit a solitary megalestris. On my return I hear the

74

comforting sound of the motor which has been so good as to restart work. We take a short rest while waiting for a fresh opportunity to tempt fortune again.

I begin my climbs once more, and about 3 a.m. the ice-floes break away quite sharply from the coast. In a few minutes we are at the foot of the cliff, threading our way as best we can, risking every instant the fall of débris upon our heads, and frequently grounding. Then the motor stops again, and this time there is nothing to be done, the differential is worn out. We have not even the consolation of cursing the poor motor, for it has toiled irreproachably, and the wonder is that it has been able to resist so long the strain to which we have put it. We try to get along with the paddle, oars, and boat-hook, but it is useless, especially as the floes are closing in on us ; and all we can do is to return to our rocky point. It is impossible for us to go back to the Berthelot Islands, and, besides, our comrades would have no chance of finding us there if we could. But, as we cannot stay to perish of hunger and cold and also cannot force others to search for us in the midst of reefs and ice-floes, we decide to abandon the picket-boat and try to reach Cape Tuxen by way of the summit of the ice-cliff. We cannot be sure that this is possible ; but there is nothing else to do, and once we are at the cape, a break in the weather will perhaps make our signals visible from Port Circumcision. Gourdon offers to go alone to Cape Tuxen, but of course I refuse. We reckon that it will take us 8 or 10 hours' tramp in the snow, and we appoint 10 p.m. as our time for setting off.

I am chagrined at being obliged to abandon the picket-boat, which I tested with my wife at Bougival, which M. Doumer christened *Monica*, thus making my infant his god-daughter, and which has served us bravely and faithfully. Although the others do not connect it with such memories as I do, they are also sad over the desertion, and we seek in vain to console ourselves by reckoning up the advantages we shall gain by its absence, the greater room on deck, the decrease in top-weight, etc., etc.

We make up our very light bundles and then, to put strength into ourselves, we open our tin of preserve and eat a little chocolate. I pencil an account of our adventures to leave in the boat, and we wait for the appointed hour, while the snow continues to fall in big, thick flakes. Under the tent on board we look like smugglers preparing to carry out a raid. We joke away, as we have done from the start, but our faces are worn and look serious whenever conversation drops. We are unwilling to confess that we are hungry, and we are even astonished at having been able to do with so little without suffering, but my clothes have become so loose that I tighten my belt in vain ; and my two comrades have since admitted that they were in the same plight.

Ten minutes to 10 ! In a few minutes, we have decided, despite the bad weather, despite the snow falling more heavily than ever, we shall be off, to try our last chance. We have a last look at what we are taking away and another sad glance at what we are leaving. We have our bundles in our hands when suddenly from the direction of Cape Tuxen there comes to us, distinctly and beyond all possibility of doubt, the prolonged whistle of our ship's familiar siren. In an instant we climb the rock and all three of us together shout out with all our might ; and then, conscious that I have a strong voice, I yell thrice in succession loud enough to burst my lungs. They have heard us on board, for the siren answers us with three blasts at intervals, and finally a great joyful-sounding shout from all the crew together reaches our ears. But our distress begins over again and communicates itself to the *Pourquoi-Pas ?*. The fog is dense, the snow is still falling, and how can the ship get here amid the ice-floes and reefs ?

Fortune comes our way, the snow ceases, and through a break in the weather appears a big cloud of black smoke. Soon after we make out hull and masts. How fine she looks, our *Pourquoi-Pas ?*, through the snow and fog, pitching in her struggle with the ice, which she breaks slowly but surely. We admire her with beating hearts. We wave our flag on the end of a boat-hook, and the grand old national ensign rises majestically at the mast-head. The snow hides all up again and then the ship reappears closer at hand, still struggling. Never shall I forget this moving spectacle in so grim a setting.

There is but a little more ice to get through, so we return to the picket-boat, which seems like a long-lost friend, and greedily devour the provisions we have left. With our mouths full we christen our rock Deliverance Point. The ship is now quite close and we can make out the men preparing to launch a boat. But we want to rejoin the ship in proper fashion, by our own efforts. While I hoist the flag astern Godfroy succeeds with a desperate effort in restarting the motor, and we move along rapidly, soon to stop again. So I finish the remaining yards with the paddle, putting all my energy into the work to show them on board that we are not at the end of our strength.

Staff and crew await us at the entry-port in their dripping oilskins. In their faces we can read sincere emotion and joy at their success. I embrace our comrades and shake hands vigorously with all. At this moment my thoughts are not of myself nor of the load off my heart, but of them. What a reception we get ! A good fire, dry clothes and especially dry socks spread out on our bunks, a good supper in readiness for us, and (what pleases us best of all) smiling, happy faces around us.

As I feared, the anxiety on board has been great. At the end of 24 hours, knowing how little we had in the way of provisions, they began to be worried. They hardly knew in what direction we had gone. Rouch set off in a whale-boat with Besnard, Dufrèche, Boland and Hervé, taking bed-sacks and food. They landed first on the Jallour Islands, where they left a cairn and provisions ; then at Cape Tuxen, where they spent the night. They next tried, but in vain, to carry the whale boat over the ice. On their return, Liouville, Gain and Senouque proposed to set out in their turn in the Norwegian boat; but Bongrain decided very wisely to weigh anchor after leaving at Port Circumcision a tent, a dory, some bed-sacks and clothes, provisions in abundance, a stove and a ton of coal.

As they left the cove, a cable fouled the screw, and then the ship grounded rather violently astern; but in spite of the heavy weather and the snow they reached Cape Tuxen, passing through the midst of the reefs without seeing them. Finally they found us. The success of this bold venture does the greatest honour to Bongrain. He was admirably seconded by Rouch, and helped also by all.

We change our clothes and then sit down to table, while I leave to Bongrain, who brought the ship out so well, the task of taking her back. We were gaily describing our adventures, when there came a great shock, the glasses overturned, and the doors of the ward-room banged violently. We have grounded horribly. Probably deceived as to distances by the snow, we have run extremely close to land, and under Cape Tuxen's high black cliff we have stranded ourselves on a rock that is just a-wash. In spite of the engine going immediately astern, the ship will not move. The tide is at its height, and we have already over three inches below our water-line exposed at the bows. All our gaiety vanishes and gloomily we await low tide. Perhaps the ship may then slide off the rock, which stands isolated in the midst of fairly great depths. This hope is shattered, at low tide her bows are exposed 6 feet 9 inches below the water-line, and the rock is just a-wash. The iron stem is bent and broken, the false keel must be ripped for a long way, since large pieces are floating loose on the surface of the water, and there are even fragments of the keel to be seen. Our aft deck is under water.

In fact, we have met with the same accident at the *Fran-çais*; but, if the latter's injury was bad enough to drive us to the pumps night and day, she floated off at once. Now we cannot find out whether we are making water, and in any case we shall be hard put to it to get ourselves off.

All day long we work to lighten the forepart and shift the weight to the stern. Our anchors and chains are secured to the rock, our water-casks emptied, our boats launched and filled with all the heavy weights taken from the forepart which we cannot shift aft. We try in vain to throw out an anchor, but the bottom is rocky and affords no hold whatever.

Need I say what terrible, almost despairing hours I go through? For the moment there is no danger to the crew, the sea is fortunately calm, and it happens that there are no icebergs near us. Land is quite close at hand, and with what we could save from the ship we could winter there under good conditions while waiting to be rescued. Some of us could even try to take a boat to Deception and seek aid from the whalers. But the Expedition would be at an end when barely commenced. All my efforts in organizing it, fitting it out, and bringing it here would be fruitless, and the page which I dreamt of adding to the history of French explorations would never see the light. I am unwilling to believe that we cannot succeed in getting off, if necessary we can empty the ship completely; but in what state will she be? I am already contemplating the possibility—for one must provide for the worst—of returning lamely to Punta Arenas to get our repairs done at any cost, if it swallows up the remains of my private fortune, and making a fresh start. It is not only my honour which is at stake, it is my country's.

At midnight we put the engine full speed astern. The unhappy vessel vibrates as though she wished to shatter herself; but nothing happens. At last, going ahead, we swing a little to starboard, then after waiting a few minutes we go astern with all our might. Violent shocks and alarming sounds of cracking follow. We begin over again, and suddenly with a long grinding noise the ship is off. We are afloat ! What a sigh of relief from every breast, what a shout from every one of us ! We have literally torn the *Pourquoi-Pas ?* from off her fatal rock.

In spite of the terrible weariness for all of these last six days, days without sleep for some, we set to work again packing things back in their places. Anchors and chains are brought smartly on board again, and at 3 a.m. we are ready to start off once more. For the moment the ship is taking in no water (though she will a little later) ; but from now, if I personally cannot afford to forget that we are damaged forward —and badly, to judge by the amount of wood torn off by the shocks and jars given to the ship—and if others probably think about it in silence, we shall all act as if we knew nothing.

To return to Port Circumcision we have to cross some thick drift-ice, made up principally of the débris of icebergs, that is to say, of very compact and hard ice. Once the ship gives a succession of strong rolls. We shall never know whether we touched a shallow, a spur of ice, or perhaps even an unwary whale.[1]

The weather has turned fine again and we have been favoured with a superb sun-rise. For six days we might have forgotten that such a thing existed. Two rather big icebergs block our harbour, which we move out of the way. Then, when the ship is moored, I hoist the colours, congratulate the crew on their courage and spirit, and thank our comrades who came to our aid. Fore and aft we have a lively supper and we go to bed, not to get up again until 1 p.m.

I take back from Petermann Island all that was deposited there for us. Nothing had been forgotten, from medicines to tobacco.

---

[1] When on her return the ship went into dry dock at Monte Video we found a deep scratch, 13 metres long, on the port-side, which may have been done this day. If so, we evidently passed over a point of rock.

The next two days are grey and heavy, with some falls of snow. We spend them in putting straight the ship, which needs it badly, and filling the water-casks. Twin cairns are built, in which we leave documents telling what we have done so far and our plans for the future.

I make several ascents to the summit of the island, by a steep snowy slope, and find that we have few ice-floes to encounter in reaching the open sea, but that our route is strewn with reefs and big icebergs.

On the 12th I climb for the last time to my observatory with Bongrain. The weather is calm and clear. We make a careful note of our direction, and, to save time, from where I am I shout orders for the fires to be got up.

Ninety poor penguins and a seal have to be killed to provide us with a stock of fresh meat. Gain has fastened rings of variously coloured celluloid, such as are used for fowls, round the legs of numerous penguins, both young and old, and of some cormorants. Thus it will perhaps be possible one day to get some certain information about the movements of these birds. Some writers claim, though I do not know upon what observations they found their statements, that the parents do not return to the old rookery a second year, and that it is only inhabited by the young who were hatched there.[1]

At 5 p.m. we begin to weigh anchor, but the ice-blocks force us to manœuvre with care, and it is two hours later before we set out.

The ice that we had to get through was thicker than we supposed. Fragments of the pack, resting against huge bergs, made a barrier which had to be broken by sheer force, and the reefs whose black crests rise up from the white expanse, left us no freedom for manœuvring. Now it is between the perpendicular walls of the icebergs that we are steaming dead slow, but the sea is clear and it is happily fine and calm ;

[1] M. Gain's observations proved, later, that exactly the contrary is the case.

for otherwise we should not have been able to extricate ourselves from our dangerous position. Godfroy is watching
from the crow's-nest the shallows which, owing to the even
surface and transparency of the water, can be very distinctly
made out from that height.

The scenery is superb. The wild and lofty coast, with its
rocks standing out black against the white of the snow and
the blue of the glaciers, is magnificently lighted up, and we see
outlined against the sky the two rounded domes of Le Matin
Mountain—a name which I gave out of gratitude to the newspaper whose generosity made possible my first expedition
and which has never since grudged us its assistance—and a
succession of other summits beyond. At 10 o'clock the sun
sets and the land takes on a delicate rose tint. About us a
number of megapteras are gambolling among the icebergs.
Two of them for over ten minutes have been beating the sea
violently with their tails, which they let fall quite flat, with a
deafening noise. Perhaps it is an amatory demonstration,
for in these movements there is nothing of the agitation or
violence which would be the result, for instance, of an attack
by thrashers, the dreaded enemies of the whales.

At 11 we are able to set off in an open sea. The offing is
completely clear, even of icebergs and, in appearance at least,
of rocks.

We steer to set Victor Hugo Island and round it on the
north, for to the south there is reason to dread the Betbeder
Islands and some reefs on which from the *Français* we saw the
sea breaking with violence.

January 13.—When I go on watch at midnight it is cold,
although the thermometer is only some tenths of a degree
below zero, the blast being penetrating. The swell runs fairly
strong from the south-west. Soon snow falls very thick, completely shutting out the view. But at 3 a.m. the wind blows
strongly from the south-south-west, dispersing the clouds,
and I see Victor Hugo Island very clear to port, as well as

four icebergs and an iceblock. This isolated island, the most northerly of the string known as the Biscoe Islands, is a typical cap-island of medium size, being a segment of a sphere in ice covered with snow. A few reefs, the only black spots in the whole formation, prolong it east and west, as well as another little island of much less dimensions, which apparently is linked to the large one by a line of reefs. It is fairly evident that when Evensen says that he sailed between the land and the most northerly group of the Biscoe Islands it is these of which he is speaking ; for we never saw the sea clear between the others and the land—apart from the question as to whether the reefs allow a passage.

There is a big difference between the present state of the ice and that which we found in 1904 and 1905. In February, 1904, it took us fifteen hours to reach Victor Hugo Island, struggling with all our might in the pack-ice, which already reached as far as the island and which in December, 1905, surrounded it entirely.

We pass the island on the north-west and then steer for Loubet Land. The breeze is fairly strong from the south-west, and the sea choppy and disagreeable. The weather is over-cast, but soon we see very distinctly, lighted up by the ice-blink, the rest of the string of cap-islands, and beyond or between them black masses which look as if they belong to the mainland. The icebergs around us are extremely numerous.

At 1 p.m. we make a big sweep round a mass of table-shaped icebergs, amongst which show up four or five rocky peaks. This neighbourhood is dangerous, for in the very frequent fogs and snowstorms one is constantly running the risk, if one escapes the icebergs, of fouling a reef, whose presence is not always betrayed by breakers. Anyhow, whenever icebergs are seen concentrated round a point, it is wise to keep away from them, for I have noticed that almost invariably they mark out a shoal or a line of reefs. It is a gross error on the part of certain explorers when they say that one can always without fear pass close to icebergs, owing to the enormous base which they have under water ; for a reef often has walls so perpendicular that icebergs rest close up against it. It was through such erroneous reasoning, not based upon experience, that we all but wrecked the *Français* on a reef in Fournier Bay and again in Biscoe Bay and that finally she stranded so seriously on the coast of Adelaide Island. We have had many opportunities of discovering the truth in our navigation of the region in which we now are. I do not mean to say that every group of icebergs necessarily indicates the presence of a reef or a shallow, but unless one is quite in the open sea there is always reason for fear, and it is better to observe caution in their neighbourhood.

The wind is dropping, but the sea remains very rough and we are tossing from side to side. About 4 p.m. a fairly wide opening appears between two of the large cap-shaped islands which, since we left Victor Hugo Island, have followed, one on another, in unbroken succession, even overlapping at times. These two islands are probably those which we marked down on the chart of the *Français* under the names of Rabot and Nansen Islands. The sea appears clear between them, but to reach the strait running between it is necessary to pass between two rows of enormous icebergs of curious shape. One looks like a giant's arm-chair with a back about 40 metres high.

The weather clears and we see the mainland in the shape of a very large bay bounded by high mountains, which we recognize as being Cape Waldeck-Rousseau and Cape Marie. A little floating ice lies across our path, and beyond it is the pack-ice, made up of large and very thick floes.

At 6 o'clock we are in the pack and we could push fairly far into the bay, with careful navigation ; but it is for the south that we want to make, and I am conscious that by pushing on we should lose the benefit of the fine weather, of which we must take the best advantage now, and that we should burn a lot of coal to no particular purpose. We stop, therefore, in the midst of the floes to make a survey of the coast and take a sounding, which gives 400 metres without touching bottom. The weather is splendid, with strong sunshine, but the swell is still very heavy and around us huge fragments of ice collide with a crash, while the sea swirls and eddies between them. A Weddell's Seal lies on a floe sleeping peacefully, with an occasional voluptuous stretch, paying no heed to the rolling and pitching of its couch.

The great inlet at whose entrance we are is situated in 66° 15′ South latitude. Although it does not appear on the English Admiralty charts, it seems to me very probable that it was seen and perhaps even visited by the sealing captain B. Pendleton, of whom we have already spoken in connexion with Deception Island and who commanded the flotilla on which was N. Palmer. J. N. Reynolds indeed says : [1] ' In the northern part of Palmer Land, in latitude 66° 5′ and about 63° west longitude, Captain Pendleton has discovered a bay free from ice, which he entered a long way but without ascertaining its extent southward. In these seas the predominant winds are between west-north-west and west-south-west, and all gales are from the north-east. A gale seldom lasts more than six hours. The fine weather comes from the south-south-west and south-south-east, which does not happen many days in a month.' These last statements prove that Pendleton at least sailed in these regions, although our experience is that even in the good season the north-easterly gales often last more than six hours.

It seems to me only just to give this bay, whose entrance we have definitely marked on the map, the name of Pendleton, which will at all events recall a brave American captain who visited these regions and deserves to have his name commemorated here.

[1] Executive Documents Twenty-third Congress, Second Session : Doc. No. 105, January 27, 1835. 'A Report of J. N. Reynolds in relation to Islands, Reefs, and Shoals in the Pacific Ocean, etc.' New York, September 24, 1828 (quoted by Edwin Swift Balch, *Antarctica*, Philadelphia, 1902).

In manœuvring to get free of the pack, our rudder fouled a big floe badly and one of the strands of the tiller-rope parted. An emergency cable was immediately made, and with the help of poles we got away from the thick floes. During our short stay, however, a quantity of drift-ice, coming from I don't know where, has gathered ahead, and it is not until 10 p.m. that we are clear. We stop for two hours to repair the tiller-rope and take advantage of this forced delay to make a sounding.

On January 14, very early in the morning, we are level with the northernmost point of what in 1905 we named Loubet Land. The weather, which was foggy, has cleared up remarkably, the view is magnificent, and in front of us opens a wide channel leading into a vast bay. To the north the entrance of the strait is bounded by one of the big cap-shaped islands and to the south by the northern extremity of the supposed Loubet Land. I say 'supposed,' since with the help of the clear weather that we are enjoying it seems to me that this Loubet Land is what Biscoe discovered and called Adelaide Island. It was the fog, bad weather, and our accident which prevented us from recognizing it formerly on the *Français*. President Loubet, the sympathetic friend of our earlier expedition, will lose nothing, for his name shall be transferred to land a good deal more important lying to the east of the island.

We were, nevertheless, acting in absolutely good faith when persisting in our error, even after the Expedition's return, with the documentary evidence before our eyes ; and for this reason I went to the London Royal Geographical Society, where with my friend Matha I consulted, to make assurance doubly sure, Biscoe's original journal and the various English charts whereon Adelaide Island is marked according to that navigator's statements. We found on Admiralty chart 1238, published in 1905 and combining all the previous ones, that Adelaide Island is 7 miles from north to south and 8 miles from east to west. It is placed in 67° 15′ South latitude and 68° 21′ longitude west of Greenwich. I do not know why the Admiralty did not accept Biscoe's longitude, which is, as we have said, 69° 26' west of Greenwich. Probably they followed the *Belgica's* erroneous information on the point.

Now our plan of the coast of Loubet Land runs between latitudes 66° 41' and 67° 5' passing through longitude 68° west of Greenwich, which thus leaves Biscoe with full credit for the discovery of the land, whose exact latitude he stated, and assigns to the coast which we sailed along in 1905 an extent of 35 miles, that is to say, at least 27 miles more than was allowed by the earlier navigator. Biscoe, as we shall show more clearly later on, certainly viewed this neighbourhood from a much greater distance than he imagined, which necessarily threw him out in his measurements. He would probably have been very astonished to learn the unexpected details which we are able to give about his discovery, while adding to it considerably. His description of what he could see is quite remarkable in its correctness and must be quoted here in full.

John Biscoe, English sealing captain, whose name deserves to be placed with those of the most famous Antarctic explorers, and who received the gold medal of the Paris Geographical Society, sailed on behalf of the enterprising firm of Enderby Brothers on board the brig *Tula*, accompanied by the cutter *Lively*. In 1831 he discovered Enderby Land. He returned to the Antarctic the following year, starting out from New Zealand. On February 14, 1832, when in 66° 30' S. and 78° 4' W. he came across close groups of icebergs and a quantity of floes. He counted ' not less than four to five hundred icebergs around him.' On February 15, he wrote in his journal : ' On the 15th, strong gales from the southward. Water smooth. Latitude at noon, 67° 01' S., longitude, 71° 48' W. At 5 p.m. saw land bearing east-south-east, which appeared at a great distance— run for it all night with a light breeze from the south-west. At noon our latitude was 67° 15', longitude 69° 29' W. Temperature, air 33° [Fahrenheit], water 33½°, at a depth of 250, no bottom. Barometer 29·30°. This island being the farthest known land to the southward, I have honoured it with the name of H.G.M. Queen Adelaide. It has a most imposing and beautiful appearance, having one very high peak running up into the clouds, and occasionally appears both above and below them ; about one-third of the mountains, which are about 4 miles in extent from north to south, have only a thin scattering of snow over their summits. Toward the base the other two-thirds are buried in a field of snow and ice of the most dazzling brightness. This bed of snow and ice is about 4 miles in extent, sloping gradually down to its termination ; a cliff, 10 or 12 feet high, which is split in every direction for at least 200 or 300 yards from its edge inwards, and which appears to form icebergs, only waiting for some severe gales or other cause to break them adrift and put them in motion. From the great depth of water, I consider this island to have been originally a cluster of perpendicular rocks, and I am thoroughly of opinion that the land I before saw last year, could I have got to it, would have proved to be in the same state as this, and likewise all land found in high southern latitudes.' [1]

This passage in Biscoe's journal proves that he saw very clearly and distinctly the island, or rather the mainland, which we traced and whose surveying we were able to do ; but he was, I repeat, much farther distant than he imagined, probably at least 23 miles off instead of 3. The subsequent narrative of our exploration will prove that otherwise he could not have stated that he had an island in front of him or have assigned to it such modest dimensions as 8 miles, whereas in reality it is 70 miles long ! His distance away is also shown by the height which he gives to the ice-cliffs. I can, indeed, affirm that the average height of these cliffs, which we skirted twice in 1909, and under which at less than a mile's distance we stranded with the *Français* in 1905, is at least 30 metres. They towered above our masts then. Lastly, the soundings which we took at

[1] *The Antarctic Manual* (London : Royal Geographical Society, 1901). ' The Journal of John Biscoe,' p. 331.

over 5 miles from the shore, when compared with Biscoe's sounding, tend equally to prove the case. It is very probable also that Biscoe did not see the highest peaks of Adelaide Island (as happened to us in 1905), and that he saw, ' occasionally, appearing both above and below ' the clouds, the comparatively lower peaks, or that he mistook for the summits the rocky beds beneath them ; for, although the thaw had been considerable during our summer campaign of 1909 the two extraordinary and very lofty peaks which dominate Adelaide Island were covered with a vast mantle of permanent snow, while the spurs, on the other hand, were free of snow, and it is correct to say of them, as seen from the sea, that ' the two-thirds are buried in a field of snow and ice of the most dazzling brightness.'

Now I wish no one to misunderstand the arguments which I think it right to put forward concerning Biscoe's visit or to suppose that I want to criticize him. On the contrary, I have quoted him, before continuing my narrative, because I consider his as the proper basis of my own descriptions, and I profess the sincerest admiration for Biscoe, as for all those who by their energy and doggedness accomplished great things with simple means. It must be remembered, on the one hand, that the methods of observation, as far as the determination of longitude is concerned, were nothing like as exact in 1832 as nowadays and that the value of chronometers then was not to be compared with ours, especially after the long and toilsome voyage which they had to undergo with Biscoe on a vessel of small tonnage, probably unequipped with any one else to look after them except Biscoe himself. And, on the other hand, nothing is so productive of error as the eyesight in polar regions. The least change in the weather alters one's estimates in truly fantastic manner, and all distinction between different levels vanishes. No Polar explorer, I feel sure, will contradict me when I state that it is impossible without a guiding-mark to judge a distance in the Antarctic by the naked eye with any pretence of exactness. I confess that I feel infinitely more pleasure in verifying the correctness of one of my predecessors, whose faith is so good as Biscoe's, than in detecting his errors or proving the incorrectness of his assertions.

From the same point of view, though it is obviously very gratifying to be the first to name a geographical point and to see on the maps designations which recall to one one's own country, I have considered it a point of honour, on this Expedition as on the last, to keep and even restore in the right places the names which my predecessors have given to their discoveries. The various names adopted have always been and will always be the cause of numerous squabbles—and often of violent polemics, for national pride in its narrowest sense here comes on the scene. Nevertheless, as discoveries gradually multiply, the question seems to me more and more easy of solution. At any rate it presents no difficulty in the region where we are, where it is most simple to render unto Caesar the things which are Caesar's. Still, I cannot pass over in silence, after having read Biscoe's own Journal and carefully gone over his ground, the following sentence in H. R. Mill's very interesting book, *The Siege of the South Pole*, p. 162 : ' Graham Land might well be restricted to the southern part south of Adelaide Island.'   Now Biscoe says, precisely, ' this island (Adelaide Island) being the furthest known land to the southward,' and I am not aware that any one ever even claimed, before the *Pourquoi-Pas' ?* voyage, to have seen land *south* of Adelaide Island except Alexander I Land. Further, the land sighted by Biscoe, to which the name of Graham Land has been given, is, as he himself says, *behind* the Biscoe Islands, and seems to me to have the sole right to the name. In this matter the Americans for their part might object and say that Pendleton saw the land before Biscoe, which is probable ; but that captain made the mistake of not describing it and not suggesting any name. In any case, Pendleton Bay is a memorial of his visit to this region.

It seems to me that the name of Palmer Archipelago was

appropriately given by the *Belgica* to the groups of islands situated to the north of De Gerlache Strait and might be extended to Two Hummocks, Christiania, and even Trinity Islands. Then, as indeed the English Admiralty chart calls it, Danco Land will serve as the name of the coast south of De Gerlache Strait, Graham Land extending from 65° to 67° S. latitude. It falls to us now to name the lands discovered by the *Pourquoi-Pas?* south and east of Adelaide Island.

Before the *Français* and the *Pourquoi-Pas?* no one had sighted Adelaide Island since Biscoe except Evensen and De Gerlache. Evensen, who has given no written description of it, merely told me that on November 10, 1893, he sighted what he took to be Adelaide Island and met the first ice-floes, which forced him to divert his course westward. As for De Gerlache, he only writes that on February 16, 1898, after having left the strait on the 13th, and passed on without seeing the Biscoe Islands on account of fog, ' we see land about south-west, doubtless the Adelaide Island, of which Biscoe caught a glimpse.' [1] Lecointe, the Expedition's hydrographer, says in his account [2] that between February 13 and 16, ' we perceived occasionally in the dim distance a land from which we were cut off by ice,' and in the hydrographical section of the scientific report he only devotes the following lines to the place : ' During the night of February 15–16, we sight land to port which seems to be an island, whose location corresponds with that given by Biscoe to Adelaide Island. The higher part of this land is perhaps hidden by the fog. The island presents to us a ridge running from north-east to south-west, the distance separating us from it and the heaviness of the atmosphere preventing us from distinguishing its details.' [3] Moreover, the course, judged entirely by the reckoning on the chart, is probably a little incorrect, since it is impossible that the *Belgica* can have passed within

---

[1] A de Gerlache, *Quinze mois dans l'Antarctique*, p. 161.

[2] G. Lecointe, *Au pays des Manchots*, p. 189.

[3] *Rapports scientifiques de la 'Belgica.' Travaux hydrographiques et Instructives nautiques*, by G. Lecointe, p. 96.

three miles of this coast without running aground and without the staff noticing that they were following a line of cliffs over 30 metres in height.

In any event they were very lucky, for on their course they record, at the same spot where we ran across them and in almost as great numbers, a collection of 85 icebergs. These icebergs, as we were able to assure ourselves, marked a line of most dangerous reefs.

To sum up, since Biscoe's time there has been no definite information.

The bay in front of us is fringed on all sides by high mountains, whose summits are of various shapes. Their bases terminate, as is the case with all others we have seen on Danco and Graham Lands, in ice-cliffs, here and there intersected by steep, rocky outcrops, often forming headlands. Between these headlands huge crevassed glaciers abound, sending down numberless iceblocks. Toward the south in particular, the ice-cliff forms the end of a vast snow-covered terrace coming from the mountains in a gentle undulating slope, out of which rise weird and majestic granite cones, the *nunataks* [1] of Greenland, looking like monolithic nails or teeth of colossal monsters.

Northward a wide channel, though at the present moment choked with floes and icebergs, separates the mainland from the Biscoe Islands, which from this aspect present the same cap-like appearance as when seen from the open sea, their cliffs perhaps higher and more perpendicular and overlapping one another. To the south Adelaide Island, ending in a little cap-shaped island, looks the same, but is vaster and loftier. Near its extremity rises an isolated triangular summit, Vélain Peak, which is to be seen far off at sea, with its three-sided black mass standing out on a white ground. The great cap mounts slowly and gradually toward the south, as far as the imposing mountainous masses which dominate the island and, as we shall see later, form its southern end. Ade-

[1] Insular hills or mountains surrounded by an ice-sheet (Webster).—*Trans.*

laide Island is an enormous skull-cap island, the last of the numerous chain of the Biscoes. But, as the English explorer remarks, it is the only one with mountains on it ; and we may add that its dimensions are such that morphologically it is scarcely one of the group. So too with its coast, as we see distinctly now that our vessel has penetrated some miles into the bay ; there are some very lofty ice-cliffs, like cleavages in the cap, which destroy its regular appearance. It has not, either, the shape of a segment of a circle, a hollow space being cut out of its side. A fjord, roughly comma-shaped, separates it from the land. This being completely blocked with ice, it is impossible to navigate it now ; so also it is equally impossible to say, as the mountains overlap one another, whether at the end of the fjord Adelaide Land joins the mainland and is therefore a peninsula, or whether it is separated from it by a channel, which cannot but be narrow.[1]

Some of the heights which fringe the edge and bottom of the bay seem to be islands. In all cases they are cut off by deep inlets. At the very end rises a rocky mass, whose outline stands out against the sky like that of a crouching lion. It blocks the view on this side and prevents us from discovering whether we are not in the entrance of a strait. However, as we go on a little, from the elevation of the crow's-nest I see a big glacier behind the Lion, looking very much as if it linked up the lateral ridges, and so I feel practically certain that our bay comes to an end there.

In order to proceed farther we have to push aside or avoid some big floes and steam between some very tall icebergs, which literally choke up the bay and its ramifications. Icebergs and iceblocks are decidedly the curse of the region which we have chosen for our expedition. Great or small, they constitute a perpetual danger for the ship, which is never safe from them, whether she be under steam, at rest, or moored

---

[1] This question was settled later by an excursion made during our stay in Marguerite Bay.

alongside a floe or in a cove. Almost always on the move, changing their course with surprising rapidity according to the wind and currents, at times heading opposite ways, they give no opportunity for repose, even in the calmest of weather, and it needs the gift of philosophy and the indifference acquired by habit to have the courage to anchor anywhere. Without risk of exaggeration, I may say that if we had been able to count those which we saw, even during the summer campaign, the figure would easily have mounted to over 10,000. Apart from the danger arising from their bulk, occasionally they break up, setting up great swelling waves which may bring danger too, and scattering over the ice-pack their fragments of blue ice as hard as rocks, against which the ship runs the risk of serious injury, especially when she is steaming in apparent safety amid the much softer floating ice which conceals the dreaded foe.

A short distance off, behind the big floes, we see the coastal pack-ice from which they have broken away.

To loiter in this bay would be an unpardonable mistake in this superb weather, by which we have the chance of profiting. Five clear days are so rare in the Antarctic that one must know how to take advantage of them ; for in a few hours one may accomplish a task absolutely impossible in weather that is merely overcast, and the success of an expedition depends principally on the rapidity with which one can grasp favourable chances. It was for this reason that I insisted on having a comparatively fast ship, and I have had no cause to repent it.

We stay to survey and take a sounding, and then set off again for the open sea and the south of Adelaide Land. But we make a detour to see whether the latter is really an island. We pass alongside a magnificent table iceberg. In the crow's-nest I am just on a level with its top plateau, which a beautiful snowy petrel is skimming in its elegant flight.

From my observatory it seemed as if the Adelaide mountain range united with that of the mainland by a neck of snow, and as if a *nunatak* looking like a Swiss châlet stood in the middle. Later I was bound to recognize that I had been deceived by appearances, as so often happens.

I christen the great bay we have left Matha Bay, in memory of the distinguished Lieutenant Matha, the clever and sympathetic second-in-command of the *Français* Expedition. Though in charge of the hydrographical department, such was his extreme modesty that he never allowed me to give his name to any of our discoveries on that Expedition.

It is 10.30 a.m. when we pass again between the double row of icebergs. We follow the coast-line of Adelaide Land, from which we keep about four or five miles distant. The sea is clear, without trace either of drift ice or floes, but it is crowded with enormous icebergs in the offing, while the coast is bristling with a kind of rampart of ice-blocks, which look very much as if they came from the cliff. Biscoe certainly did not exaggerate when he estimated the icebergs in sight at 500, and there has been no change since his time. So likewise as he remarked, animal life is very scarce. This is a forbidding country, and only at rare intervals does a whale break the silence with its heavy blowing as it appears on the surface for a few moments.

We pass once more, to seaward, the reef where on January 15, 1905—exactly five years and a day ago—we of the *Français* were so justifiably overcome with anxiety and despair at not being able to continue our researches. At that time, to reach where we now are, we should have had to cross by sheer force a thick ice-pack, which only allowed us between it and the coast a channel barely a mile and a half wide. It encouraged in us, nevertheless, the hope of pushing on; and it would assuredly have led us on to the discovery of Matha Bay, but that, in passing between two huge icebergs, whose draught of water persuaded us, in our ignorance, that we were running no risks, we grounded so violently and so seriously damaged our bows that for three months we had to pump 23 hours out of the 24 to keep the ship afloat. What tribulations ensued, caused by an engine with difficulty making 5 knots in dead calm and by constant injuries, while under sail the ship would scarcely steer! And all the time gale of wind followed upon gale, varied by violent snowstorms and dense fogs!

And now what a difference! We have a strong and trustworthy engine, easily making its 8 knots; and even the watches are comfortable, thanks to the wheel-house on the poop and the hitherto prevalent long spells of fine weather. Nevertheless, it is with emotion that we talk to the old crew about our brave little ship on which, with no thought but for the end in view, we struggled so hard and were brought back at last, exhausted, but safe and sound. How sadly we saluted her wreck when we passed it in the River Plate! [1]

It is calm, with a long swell from the west. The peaks above the terrace of ice are swathed in clouds, but the sky shows big blue patches between the north-east and the south, while in the west it is very heavy and violet-black in colour. In honour of our crossing of the Antarctic Circle, the colours are hoisted and double rations served out to the crew.

We pass close to a superb table iceberg of classical regularity of form, measuring 40 metres in height and 2 miles in length. It was here that the *Hertha*, *Belgica*, and *Français* met the pack-ice, and, driven back by it, had to turn away from land. We are the first to penetrate into this region. The Unknown, the Unforeseen are in front of us. How far can we advance?

Biscoe's 8 miles are passed, and yet the coast, with its long and unvarying convexity, continues to make us expect to reach and double a cape, which ever recedes. Our general direction is south-west, till at 8.30 p.m. we are heading S.

---

[1] On the Expedition's return the Argentine Republic asked to buy the *Français* and renamed her the *Austral*. With her rigging altered and her boilers and engine changed she made a voyage to the South Orkneys. Starting out again in the spring of 1907, she was wrecked on the Banco Chico in the River Plate and lost, while her crew were fortunately saved by the French steamer *Magellan*.

Adélie Penguins on the Ice in Marguerite Bay (Adelaide Island in the Background).

30° W. without there being any change in the general aspect
of things, in spite of our 7 knots kept up since 10 o'clock !
The two ends of the great white spherical cap look always the
same distance in front of us and behind, as though the *Pourquoi-Pas ?* were motionless.   Such fantastic navigation would
have been worthy of record in Edgar Allan Poe's *Arthur Gordon
Pym*.

We are making our way, however, for iceberg succeeds on
iceberg.   In the offing, to the west, one of them which is
rather isolated looks to us like a ship seen three-quarter front,
with a smoke-stack and a foremast.   So complete is the
illusion that the crew assert that it is a wreck, and I have to
convince them of their mistake by means of the telescope.

South-west, on the edge of the horizon, and rising toward
the west, there now appears a bright light, which is probably
ice-blink.   In that case we would be navigating between the
mainland and the pack-ice.   In the south and south-east, on
the other hand, the sky has become very gloomy.   The wind
is beginning to blow rather strongly from the south-south-
west, but without raising much of a sea, which confirms my
impression that the pack-ice is not far away on this side.   The
barometer has been dropping constantly since this morning.

A mass of big icebergs blocks our way.   We thread them,
keeping a careful look-out for rocks.   One of them is sculp-
tured in arches and grottoes, while an admirably carved head
stands out from a submarine promontory.

We journey on thus all night, anxiously awaiting the termination of the island-cap.   At length the monotony is temporarily broken by a huge rock, which rises out of the cliff
and stands out very black against the white surface.   There
must be a shallow in the direction of the open sea, for a line of
icebergs stretches out pretty far in continuation of the rock.
Cautiously we make a wide sweep, and we congratulate ourselves on this, for later we found the same icebergs and among

them the tops of rocks just a-wash. Then the cap resume its former appearance.

Towards 11 o'clock there are some magical light effects. The land abeam is sparkling white, while the everfleeing southern point is a metallic green difficult to describe. The southern horizon is golden, sharply outlined against a background of black sky, while the west is purple-red. A few icebergs stand out in deep blue, while others are dyed a brilliant red, as though lighted up by fires inside. We are heading S. 10° W.

At last, toward midnight, a long rocky point runs out of the ice-cliff, and some isolated reefs also appear, in the midst of innumerable icebergs. Our course curves in to S. 40° E., and an enormous black cliff reveals itself, whose summit is plunged in fog. It is almost with a sigh of relief that the officer of the watch and I greet the end of this interminable cap of ice.[1]

January 15.—The termination of the cap is abrupt, with no gradual modification of the slope. A quite small circular cove is hollowed out of the ice-cliff, at the foot of a rocky wall, the perpendicular counterfort of two magnificent peaks, which we are soon to see break through the fog and which are themselves the crown of the mountain range we caught sight of yesterday. This counterfort forms a noble, lofty cape, beyond which there opens a sort of bay or rather gulf, whose end we can scarcely conjecture and whose entrance from where we are seems to have a black-hued island in its centre, rising up quite straight to a height of about 600 metres, with a sawtoothed summit. Another distant cape, certainly a high one, bounds the gulf to the east. Quite a long coast-line follows after this, slightly fog-wrapt, but showing some glacier peaks

---

[1] We give this cape the name of H.M. Queen Alexandra. It seemed to us that this homage was due to the royal spouse of Edward VII, who has taken so much interest in Antarctic expeditions. This cape, situated at the end of Queen Adelaide's Island, marks the extremity of a land discovered by an English sailor and for some years the most southerly land known.

and other rocky headlands. It stretches out of sight south-ward.

I confess to feeling genuine emotion over these lands, on which we are the first to set eyes after the long struggle it has taken me for years to attain my end.

We steer for the entrance of the gulf and our average line is N. 60° E., but we are obliged to turn aside perpetually, for the reefs rise menacingly on all sides. The icebergs are numerous, and big loose ice-floes, evidently recently detached, bar our way.

Since 2 o'clock it has been blowing fairly fresh from the north-west, the sky has had an ugly appearance, and the barometer has been falling in a manner that made me fear a gale, when, almost all of a sudden, the wind falls, the sky becomes remarkably clear and bright over all land within sight, and the sun shines out. Only in the south-west and west do the heavens remain very overcast. Thanks to this unhoped for weather, we shall be able to do in a few hours a considerable amount of surveying.

We know already by a mere glance of the eye that land continues beyond the latitude assigned by Biscoe to Adelaide Island, as there was reason to suppose, though we had not the slightest proof of it until to-day. We see also that it does not take, as was generally indicated (I do not know why), a south-westerly direction ; but, on the contrary, curves inwards, after the great mass of Adelaide Land, first to the south-east and then to S. 20° E. approximately.

We must be about a dozen miles from the coast, and as we gradually approach the floes become more numerous, some rocky points appear, and we advance full slow, keeping a sharp look-out.

The island for which we are making is not in the centre of the bay, as we supposed at first, but is much nearer the western cape, from which it is only divided by a channel 4 miles wide. After undergoing a few rather hard knocks against the stubborn ice, we pass this channel without mishap, and what we took for a bay of moderate extent reveals itself as an enormous inlet, meriting rather the name of a gulf. It is at the present moment choked with thick, flat, coastal pack-ice, touching the northern shore of the island and presenting, from the side on which we are, a front running with a slight concavity to the north, where it joins Adelaide Land about 6 miles away, thus forming a little bay, where it seems to me we ought to be safe. Unfortunately, quite close to the island there are rocks level with the water, and as soon as one goes further away the soundings at once give 80, 100, 250 metres, with a rock bottom. It is therefore impossible to anchor and we have to be content with mooring ourselves to the pack-ice, as near as possible to the island. Great fragments come away from the pack, so that our ice-anchors have to be carried as far as our cables permit, that is to say, about 150 metres; for otherwise we should risk floating away, and whenever the breaking off of the ice was encouraged by the strain on it, we should be obliged to shift our anchors and carry them further forward.

Sledges now replace boats, and on them we transport hawsers and ice-anchors with pickaxes and shovels, to enable the men, once at the desired distance, to bury the anchors and fix them in firmly.

At 5 a.m. we are moored, and almost every one is at work immediately; for I have decided to take full advantage of the fine weather and leave again to-day, as soon as I have examined the offing from the summit of the island and made a note of the land and ice in sight.

I call the gulf Marguerite, after my wife, and the island, Jenny, after Mme. Bongrain.

Jenny Island's southern face has cliffs of great abruptness and perpendicularity, even in their upper two-thirds, which are consequently completely free of snow, which only appears at the base. The crest of the island is extremely jagged crowned with three sharp rocky peaks, which make it look

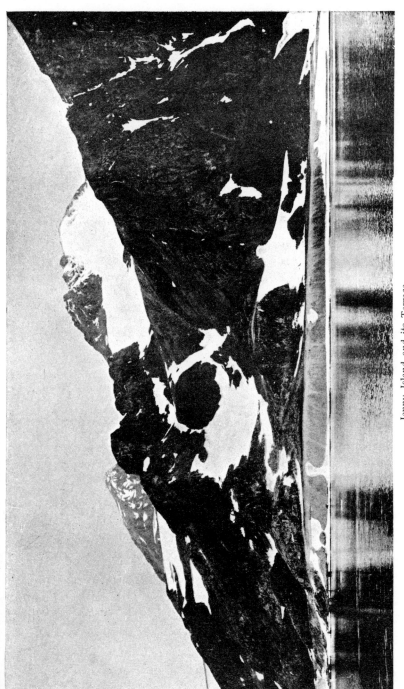

Jenny Island and its Terrace.

from the sea like a seal's tooth. The northern face, on the other hand, is a fairly even slope, rising right up to the summit, formed of rocks much surbedded by frost. Being exposed to the sun, the greater part of it is stripped of snow, which only shows itself in great patches, from which veritable little torrents spring forth. This face generally is slightly concave and in colour is black or reddish. Its juncture with the perpendicular walls of the other sides gives at first sight the impression of a very much damaged crater; but even a superficial examination soon disposes of all ideas about a volcano.

The island is formed entirely of eruptive granitic rocks, seamed with numerous veins. One of its most remarkable peculiarities is found on the west side, in the shape of a great bank of stone rising from the sea to a height of 10 metres, making a vast and perfectly horizontal platform which looks as though it had been patiently and skilfully constructed by navvies. This formation is clearly the remains of an ancient strand.

On the east side are found great heaps of shingle, forming here and there beaches cut up by débris coming down from the mountain, which is perpetually crumbling away, and whose walls rise up, enormous, jagged, ruinous, and tottering.

Opposite the west coast of Jenny Island is the mountainous mass, the kernel, so to speak, of Adelaide Land, from which rise like a superb Alpine scene two peaks, whose elevation is to seem still greater to us when we see it later from the south. They are over 2,000 metres high. Noble glaciers discharge themselves into the sea, and the whole coast, except the promontory itself, is fringed by the usual forbidding ice-cliff of these regions. Further than the eye can see, in an apparently contracting fjord which separates Adelaide Land from the mainland, the pack-ice extends to the north-east, joining on to the pack along the coast running south-east. In Marguerite Bay one can see to the north-east an island surrounded by the ice, resembling Jenny Island, and quite close to Adelaide Land, almost on its edge, an islet formed of a little black cone.   In the background are some black patches which are also islands, reefs, or dependencies of the land.

At 9 a.m. I set out with Godfroy and Gourdon for the crest of the island, whither Gain and Senouque have preceded us.   We have to go quite two kilometres before reaching the shore foot and if last night when the thermometer was 2° below zero the wind was cold and penetrating, now with a brilliant sun in an almost cloudless heaven the heat is really very great.   The ascent, which is all over débris of sharp-angled stones, broken from time to time by patches of snow or ice, is irksome and ruinous to one's boots.

Gulls and megalestrides, in great numbers, swarm around us in defence of their nests.   A glacier clinging to the mountain side forms a little lake, from which gushes a sweetly murmuring torrent, with a cascade elegantly decorated with stalactites glittering in the sun.   We mount, between two of the peaks, to a crest of about 450 metres high, which abruptly makes an acute angle with the perpendicular north wall of the island and the slope which we have just climbed.   The view is magnificent, and allows us to see in detail these lands virgin as yet from all human gaze.   But it is the open sea which especially interests me for the moment.   The ice in the sea, blocks and floes, is fairly abundant but possible to get through.   The reefs are very numerous, forming an oblique line which stretches very far into the offing, and vary in dimensions from rocky points to islets.   About 45 miles to the south-east I seem to see the pack-ice running to join the coastal ice.   Not a trace of Alexander I Land ; and yet later we are to see it very plainly even from the foot of the island, in apparently much less clear weather.   It was, therefore, hidden to-day in an evidently local fog, melting into the dark sky of the west and south-east.   This proves, once more, how all statements in the Antarctic are subject to error.   In this beautiful weather, which allowed us to see other lands at a considerable distance,

Alexander Land, though large and but a few miles off, was invisible, without anything to make us suspect the limitation of our view. We might, therefore, with the best faith in the world, have squarely asserted, on our return, that to the south-west there was no land within the limit of sight from an elevation of 450 metres.

The heat has merely increased during our ascent, and, after toiling through the now soft, thick snow of the pack-ice, we return on board all of a perspiration. It is 1° below zero in the shade, but it is so fine in the sun that after a tub of cold water on the bridge two of us stop a good half hour completely undressed, drying ourselves in the kindly rays.

At 2.30 we get under way, and use the drag-net for 250 metres. During this time Gourdon goes off in the dinghy to build a cairn upon the strange platform on the west shore. We pick him up as we steam out, and make for the south-west, passing alongside two small rocky isles separated from Jenny Island by a channel 3 miles wide. It is still very fine and clear. We have not yet had the slightest glimpse of Alexander I Land, but the continuation of Loubet Land, to which we give the name of the President of to-day, M. Fallières, is magnificently lit up. This land seems chiefly composed of conical rocky masses, standing out in great black triangles against the glaciers which they separate. It seems also cut up by deep bays, while there are islets running out into the sea, many of them curiously shaped. After a series of triangular peaks comes a remarkable cape, very red in colour and looking like a great broken-down and toppling tower.

The ice about us, floes, blocks, and débris of blocks, is fairly abundant, and the rocks and islets being numerous we have to proceed slowly and with great precautions.

Snow is beginning to fall thickly, and by shutting out the view complicates matters. It is curious to notice that during the short cessations of the snowfall the wind comes in small gusts from the south-east, while the snowflakes come from the north-west, that is to say, against the wind.

At midnight the ship is covered with snow, and the sky is very overcast, except to the south, where during a rift we distinctly see high land, which cannot be other than Alexander I Land. We have just passed a long line of reefs, and we are on the edge of the belt formed of very dense pack-ice, with numerous bergs scattered over it. From the masthead I make out a vast channel, which, at a distance of some miles from us, runs into the open sea to the east and appears to penetrate obliquely a fair distance into the ice. We reach this channel, and make use of it. A pretty fresh breeze rises from the south-east, soon bringing along with it very clear weather. We must take advantage of this unhoped-for luck in these regions, and we go ahead as rapidly as we are allowed by an ice-pack getting thicker and thicker.

Alexander I Land, seen by us at a distance and from a direction never before known, stands out very distinctly, lit up and gilded by the sun's rays. All the southern coast of Fallières Land also shows up, outlined against a blue sky which could scarcely hide anything from us. Between it and Alexander I Land are two comparatively small islands with rounded summits. Then, quite close to Alexander I Land, is what I first take for a big mountainous island, but what we are later to discover to be a part of Alexander I Land itself.

This land has the same characteristics as Graham Land. The aspect of its mountains is identical with that of Adelaide Land's, and here again, on the side at which we are looking, the base is formed by an enormous terrace of rounded snow, the ice-cliffs being already visible from the crow's-nest. The summits are lofty, and form a jagged crest. The two extremities east and west end in rocky promontories, which look, from where we are, as if they plunged straight into the sea. Between Alexander I Land and the islands to the east of it the pack-ice stretches to the limit of vision, as also between

On the Summit of Jenny Island.

the islands and the most southerly point of Fallières Land. The same is the case in the west, where the ice bounds the horizon, its monotony only broken by numerous great icebergs.

The pack before us is becoming more and more dense and solid. We still keep on, but with difficulty. The floes are enormous in extent and height, some being more than 2 metres above the level of the sea. We have to push or drag off the big ones, break up the little ones, and manœuvre every minute. There is not a moment's rest for the helmsman or the engineers. The jars are sometimes alarming, but we proceed along metre by metre. Numerous soundings are taken, giving a rocky bottom and depths varying very abruptly between 108 and 477 metres.

At 11 o'clock we are about 15 miles from the cliff, when the pack-ice becomes quite solid, made up of big, closely crowded floes resting on their sides and apparently forced up into hummocks. From the height of the crow's-nest I can see no channel, no break in the continuity allowing us to hope for further advance. We must needs stop, therefore. Taking advantage of a small space of open water, we dredge over 144 metres. Numerous surveys are made, based on observations under the best conditions. To the photographs taken by all our cameras I cannot resist my desire to add one of the ship herself, so I go off in a canoe to take her from a neighbouring floe. Animal life is scanty ; two or three seals, a few penguins, and that is all.

We stay here part of the day, but without being able to get any nearer. By an exceptional chance we have been able to penetrate into this vast hollow, hitherto closed against all-comers by impenetrable ice. To avoid turning back, I thought for a moment of stopping where we are and awaiting events ; but a little reflection made me abandon this idea. We have, from the point reached in this beautiful unhoped-for weather, noted down everything possible. The state of the ice hardly permits us to reckon now on advancing much farther in a direction that will allow us to record important new details, and a landing on the ice-terrace could only be effected with the greatest difficulty. Moreover, its exploration would only be interesting with several weeks before us —which would be impossible with the ship afloat and the chances so many of our not being able to return on board by a fixed date or even near it. Further, there is the risk of being carried away by the drift ice far from a region so interesting to study as this, and of being blocked in and compelled to winter to no purpose on a moving icefield ; or again, since the coast is close at hand, of being crushed by the pressure which, to judge from the condition of the ice, must be tremendous if bad weather sets in. I consider it preferable, therefore, from all points of view, to try to push toward the east, where beyond the pack-ice we have come through there is to be seen some open water ; and, if we can find no way out on that side, to return to Marguerite Bay, where Jenny Island makes a magnificent observatory from which to watch for a favourable opportunity of proceeding in one direction or another. Thus, too, we shall best save coal, our sinews of war.

But to reach the open water is no light task. The ice has closed against us and a long, painful and irksome job is before us. At the mast-head, from which I am looking for the most navigable channels, I am shaken by the vibrations from the bumps we get, in spite of all precautions, and I cannot help reflecting that we are navigating thus with our bows perhaps seriously injured. Still all seems to hold good, the engine does its duty, and only three pump-valves are broken.

In the evening the ice becomes so solid and close-packed that we cannot move. At the end of some hours there is a relaxation and we start off again, pushing the ice slowly before us. So we get to the edge of the pack, pass through some drift-ice, and at last are in free water.

We try to make eastward and aim for Fallières Land, but

soon our path is blocked by ice still more solid than that in front of Alexander I Land, and we only get back to Marguerite Bay after having to go through another long struggle with the ice, which had blocked the entry to our cove since we left it.

It is 6 a.m., and the appearance of the heavens is now threatening. But during the whole of this excursion we have enjoyed the best weather imaginable, and never for an instant have we ceased to see at once with great clearness Alexander I Land, the whole of the coast with the cape which we look on as the southern extremity of Fallières Land, and Adelaide Land, whose two magnificent peaks rise up in the air in pointed spires on the top of domes of Byzantine style. Such weather is almost indispensable for the navigation of this reef- and iceberg-infested region, and I confess that I do not very well see how one would survive a gale and thick weather.

We are now already in a position to take back precise information concerning the lands south of Adelaide Island, where the present maps are blank, and concerning Alexander I Land, which up to now has only been seen at very great distances and always from the same side and has seemed rather like a land of legend.

Bellingshausen, coming from the east on January 21, 1821, discovered Peter I Island and coasting along the pack-ice saw at a distance of about 40 miles, surrounded by ' impassable ' ice, a great land stretching far toward the south-west, to which he gave the name of Alexander I and of which he published an excellent coast-view. He was then obliged by the ice to turn north-west.

When later, thanks to Biscoe, Graham Land could be vaguely outlined as far as Adelaide Island, the geographers considered it one of the important Antarctic problems to ascertain whether the land discovered by Bellingshausen was or was not a prolongation of this Graham Land. The three glimpses of Alexander I Land from Bellingshausen's time to that of the *Pourquoi-Pas ?* Expedition added no information to supplement the Russian navigator's description, which still remained much the most complete.

The Norwegian sealing captain Evensen, on November 20, 1893, reached latitude 69° 10′ S. by longitude 76° 12′ west of Greenwich. The following days, especially November 22, as he sailed north, he sighted Alexander I Land surrounded by impassable ice. Unfortunately, though the estimable and kindly Evensen is a daring and skilful captain, geographical questions seem to interest him very little, for he gave no details of his voyage, and when I went to see him at Sandefjord all that I could get out of him about Alexander I Land was : ' Very high and fine mountains, plenty of icebergs ! '

On February 16, 1898, the *Belgica* Expedition (apparently unaware of Evensen's voyage) saw Alexander I Land for a few hours, but the various members are not agreed in their accounts. De Gerlache contents himself with writing that on February 16 at 4 o'clock this land ' looked superb with its mighty glaciers scarcely divided from one another by a few darker peaks, standing out yellowish-white against the deep blue of the sky.' [1]

Lecointe says : ' We only sight Alexander I Land at a great distance, without being able to form even an approximate idea of what the distance is ' [2]—which does not prevent him, however, from publishing a view of the coast of this land and a map, in which are clearly traced the contours of the coasts, mountains, and valleys. I must hasten to add that view and map alike agree as little with the descriptions of Arc-

---

[1] De Gerlache, *Quinze Mois dans l'Antarctique,* p. 162.

[2] Lecointe, *Rapport scientifique de la ' Belgica.'* *Travaux hydrographiques,* p. 98. In his narrative, *Au pays des Manchots,* p. 189, the same author says : ' On February 16, we sighted Alexander Land, discovered in 1821 by Bellingshausen. We are so far away that we cannot even judge the distance.' A view of the coast and a map are reproduced in the two works quoted and also among the maps of the *Belgica* Expedition.

Ice-Floes off Alexander I. Land.

towski, a member of the Expedition, and of Bellingshausen as with that which we are in a position to write.

The *Belgica's* doctor, F. A. Cook, for his part, does not hesitate to give, with a lavish display of figures and measurements, a detailed description (totally different from Lecointe's) of what he called the ' Alexander Islands.' But herein he is tripped up by his comrade Arctowski, who gives a fourth varying description while confessing that ' we took no measurement and have little to add to Bellingshausen's description.' [1] What Arctowski says on the subject, moreover, (I will quote it later) is so correct as to accord ill with the published statements of his two colleagues. Congratulations are due to this savant for having been the only one to give information of any value, refusing to stray outside the bounds of honest observation.

On board the *Français* on January 11 and 13, 1905, we ourselves sighted Alexander I Land at a distance of over 60 miles. Solid pack-ice made our efforts to approach it unavailing. We promised ourselves we would not rest there, and we have kept our word ; for three years later we have reached a point which no one succeeded in attaining before, after crossing ice always described by the same epithet ' impassable.'

Until the arrival of the *Pourquoi-Pas ?* in 1909, therefore, there had been no advance made since 1821, and as we have got to so favourable a spot we must do our best to profit by it. Accordingly I should like to find a place where the ship will be in comparative safety, and where we may perhaps winter, or at least stay a while, without burning coal as we are doing now. So much am I exercised over this question that scarcely are we moored alongside the ice when—though it is 48 hours since I last slept—I take my skis and, leaving every one on board slumbering except the man on watch,

---

[1] Henryk Arctowski, *Antarctic Manual*, 1901. ' Exploration of Antarctic Lands,' pp. 495-6.

cross the strip of pack-ice which rests on the island and divides the gulf in two. Arriving on the other side, I put off my skis and take a long walk round the island, now over a beach with pebbly slopes, now amid débris of fantastic shape, now over snow-banks. Unfortunately my observations are not of a reassuring character. On this side also the ice presents a big concavity, which is much less sheltered and stretches wider than the cove in which lies the *Pourquoi-Pas?* The bottom is rocky and dangerous along the island; and finally the bay is full of icebergs. The island itself provides no cove in which to shelter from icebergs, nor any reefs to which to moor. This discovery worries me much, but I do not wish to abandon hope before searching and sounding afresh all round the ship.

There are plenty of seals on the ice, both Crabbing and Weddell's. A few megalestrides make for me shrieking, as if I were planning to injure their nestlings; and, lastly, four or five Adélie Penguins, destitute of all fear, come up to me and chatter away. I ask the penguins where their rookery is, but the rascals pretend not to understand, and it is no use my hunting for it, I cannot discover it. But we part none the less good friends.

In the afternoon every one is busy with his own work. The men go to collect ice from the bergs, which we convert into water for the boiler. Gourdon, Senouque and Gain proceed over the ice to explore the black cone to the north-east of our cove. Deceived as to the distance (as constantly happens here), they do not return until late in the evening.

The north-west wind has sprung up strong. Most fortunately we are no longer in the pack-ice about Alexander I Land nor among the reefs. We are, or at least I imagine so, in comparative safety and are burning the minimum amount of coal necessary to keep up steam for half an hour, whether for working the ropes by winch or for starting the engine in case we should go adrift or an iceberg should bear down on us—which is scarcely to be feared with the wind now blowing.

Next day the north-westerly to northerly wind is still strong, but the ice seems to hold good, and we have four hawsers out, three in front, with the anchor of one of them 100 metres away, and the fourth astern.

We fit up one of our motor-sledges, and in the evening we are able to try it. The motor at first gives us some difficulty, then it starts away and succeeds in carrying its five passengers gaily enough ; but it must undergo some modification of detail before anything serious can be attempted with it. I realize that the whole will not be in working order until after numerous trials and changes, which will be made during our winter season. Besides, I look on these automobile sledges in the light of a first experiment for future expeditions, and I only really depend on the hand-sledges.

January 19.—The wind has been very strong all night and has increased still more this morning. The pack around us is breaking away in great slabs. An ice-anchor is carried still further than the others ; but the rifts multiply. I give orders to put back on board all our material that is lying about, to dismantle the motor sledge, and to make up the fires. With the wind from the northern quarter we have evidently nothing to fear from the sea, but without the engine being under steam, if our ice-anchors should fail or, worse still, if a huge fragment of the pack should break away, carrying us with it, we should be ashore in a few minutes.

About 11 o'clock the motor sledge was in danger, a big rift having opened close by it ; but happily it was not completely dismantled and the motor was persuaded to start off at once, so it made good its own escape, coming back gaily with its chauffeur. With the help of the windlass and some ice-anchors we were able to bring together two sections of the pack over which it passed and to hoist it on board again without mishap.

At 2 o'clock we must needs set off to look for a better shelter and some firmer ice at the end of the north-westerly cove.

A cable's length from an ice-cliff and quite close to a superb glacier, with a frontage all chaotic and slashed with crevasses, we are somewhat sheltered from the wind and do not feel any chop. One or 2 miles from us rises the half-rocky, half-snowy cone, goal of one of yesterday's excursions, surrounded by the pack-ice, which joins on to the glacier and whose bounds are marked by a line of hummocks and crevasses. Two soundings, taken not far apart, give 66 and 97 metres, with a bottom of liquid green mud. So there is no anchorage, and we must keep our fires alight and content ourselves with ice-anchors.

The clear weather allows us to see distinctly Alexander I Land and the end-region of Fallières Land.

The wind is strong, but it is curious to notice that we have not yet experienced one of those great north-easterly gales which made our two summer campaigns of 1904 and 1905 so unpleasant and difficult, not to say dangerous. Except at Wandel, where the wind, however, blew with comparatively little force and where for one day there was a drizzle of snow, the winds of this region have not been really violent and have been accompanied always by clear weather. Either we are enjoying an exceptional summer or previously we experienced two very bad ones.

The sunset this evening has been very fine, touching up with a fairy pink the crenellated tops of our glacier. Quite close to us an iceberg of tabular shape is stranded, barely detached from the cliff. The place can be seen which it occupied evidently but a short while ago. It is interesting for glaciological examination, and Gourdon begins at once to measure it and take soundings at its foot. If it were to go adrift we should see for the first time a table-berg as comparatively small as this coming from an ice-cliff. Up to now, indeed, all the many cliffs near which we have stayed have

Glacier Face in Marguerite Bay.

been cleft, thus launching on the sea large quantities of fragments of small dimensions or giving birth to ice-blocks dangerous to the ship but tiny compared with the icebergs to be met in such numbers, which must come from formations after the style of the great Ross Barrier.

January 20.—The wind having grown much milder, the barometer showing a tendency to rise, and the weather being clear, we set off with the intention of following the coast and in the vague hope of finding winter quarters. We get away from the pack-ice without difficulty, for a southerly current prevails which seems permanent. We stop abreast of Jenny Island, where Senouque goes to fetch the stand of his theodolite, which he left behind. Meanwhile, we make a long dredge, which promises work for Liouville and Gain.

But the snow begins to fall heavily and the wind strengthens again. As we have no reason for hazarding ourselves in the midst of rocks in this weather, we return to our mooring-place and eat, to console ourselves, an excellent dinner consisting of soup made from Brussel sprouts, of seal *à la Saint-Hubert*, and of purée of peas. This menu was much appreciated. On the other hand, six Antarctic prawns, which the zoologists had handed over to the cook, were not at all a success.

At 10 p.m. it is still snowing, and the entrance of the bay, the neighbouring peaks, and Jenny Island are completely blotted out, while, curiously enough, through the falling snow can be seen the much more distant Fallières Land lighted up very clearly.

I have a fit of the blues, not so much on account of the delay caused to our plans by the bad weather as because of my anxiety concerning winter quarters, which I should so much have liked to find here ; and also because of the report presented to me on the coal supply. Evidently our daily consumption, when we are moored, is small, but when day is added to day, in the end the total is considerable.

At 11 p.m. I am distracted from my sombre reflections by an occurrence which convinces me of the danger of our present situation. We were, as before, 300 or 400 metres from the iceberg detached from the cliff, which Gourdon had been examining at intervals. I was writing in my cabin when a noise like a big explosion of fireworks, accompanied and followed by a loud rumbling, brought me in a few strides on deck just in time to see the magnificent spectacle of the iceberg splitting open and capsizing. Enormous spurs of glaucous hue jump out of the water, and even rocks are uplifted as if by a submarine mine; the sea boils fiercely and in a few seconds its surface far and wide is covered by débris of all sizes. The iceberg has lost a good third of its bulk. The sea was at its height at the time of the occurrence, and it is probable that the mass of ice, being almost afloat, first rolled, then slipped on the ledge where it was resting, and finally lost its balance. This seems to prove once more that table-bergs are very rarely, if ever, formed from these high, narrow cliffs, whose base is bathed by comparatively shallow waters.

We thought the spectacle at an end, when the same phenomenon was repeated a second and a third time. But we see the largest fragment left, about 15 metres above the water, come rolling straight toward us—fortunately driving quantities of débris before it. By good luck the engine is ready and we go astern at the first word, while we pay out the hawsers to their fullest extent. The mass of débris, striking our stern first, makes it swing, so that the iceberg, continuing on its terrible way, finds the ship already on the move and, instead of striking her full amidships or in the stern, touches her comparatively lightly on the port side. Our poor dinghy, which was on the port side, is crushed between the *Pourquoi-Pas?* and the berg and hurled on to the ice, as flat as a pancake. We may think ourselves lucky to have escaped the same fate.

Gently we move away, without touching the remains of

the iceberg, for fear of upsetting its very doubtful stability, which would be disastrous this time, and proceed to moor ourselves further off. A huge block of ice from the berg remains wedged between the bobstay and the stem, where it will long be ; but we have suffered no injury and have escaped with the dinghy smashed and one hawser cut by the only man who lost his head, using his knife instead of merely paying out as I ordered.

Thanks to the ingenuity and skill of Libois, aided by Chollet, by the end of a week the fragments of the dinghy were built into a boat perhaps a little stronger than before the accident.

January 21.—Although the wind is still blowing a little from the north-east, I decide to go out, after taking a series of soundings, and begin the search for an anchorage. Unfortunately we find nowhere good, and in spots close to Jenny Island, which are sheltered a little from the winds of the open, we get a depth of 97 metres, with a rocky bottom. At 1 o'clock we pass to the south of the island between it and the two large rocky islets, looking in vain for a little cove.

Soon we are on the other side of the island, and although we have behind us still the gusts of the north-easter, with nothing to protect us from it, we cross a zone of complete calm. We make for the opposite coast, and the breeze springs up again freshly, but this time from the east-south-east, bringing with it very clear weather and a blue sky. So we steam southward along this magnificent coastline of high mountains, some black, some red, with weird outlines, intersected by glaciers and high peaks. Big fjords ran into it, islands project from it. There would certainly be good winter anchorages there, but unhappily an ice-belt a dozen miles broad separates us from it and fills up all the inlets.

As I expected, with the prevailing wind some fairly big slabs break away and drift seaward, leaving a channel through which we can go full steam ahead. We skirt the edge of the ice at a distance of a few metres, so that in spite of the growing wind we have no sea. We stop frequently to survey, for the weather is remarkably clear and we see not only Alexander I Land but the whole coast as far as the terminal cape, which seems to be on a big island. We are able to correct certain errors made by ourselves on the previous days, and in this way we recognize that what we took for a big island to the east is part of the land itself, while, on the other hand, some more small islands appear very far to the south. At each stoppage for surveying Rouch takes a sounding.

About 7 p.m. the ice-pack curves to the west away from the coast, and brings us upon a collection of icebegs. To go farther becomes absolutely impossible. We moor ourselves to the pack, which I have been examining from the crow's-nest, and on which I am going to take a turn with Gourdon. This pack is at least 5 or 6 metres thick, the lower section being very hard, while the upper layer of snow is melting and one sinks to the knees in the pickle. It is very flat and has comparatively few icebergs toward the open sea. Close to the land, on the other hand, it contains some table-bergs of so vast a size that we mistook them at first for an ice-terrace. These table-bergs, like some quite close to us, have their walls hollowed out into cells separated by kinds of pillars, which give them a curious aspect.

Will the pack-ice break entirely loose this winter? At the moment the pieces coming away are insignificant in size, and not a crack nor a stretch of water betrays that disintegration is in progress. Only a few big blue patches show that the heat of the sun is melting the upper layer of snow. Moreover, the considerable quantity of ice driven by the prevailing wind down the little channel in which we are will come back at the first change of the wind and prevent a strong swell, the chief agent in a breakup, from having its effect. These reflections worry me, for I am thinking of nothing but our winter quarters.

Before starting off again we dredge for about 200 metres.

Unfortunately the windlass gets damaged, which makes it a long task bringing back the net. This injury is tiresome, for until it is completely repaired the windlass will be no use for our cables, and little even for our hawsers.

During the night, after making all possible observations and assuring ourselves that we could not get any farther, we go back the same way we came, so as not to get blocked in our channel. Arriving next morning south of Jenny Island we find the wind blowing again very strongly from the north-east, but as the weather is clear I decide to return to Alexander I Land and to go close up to it if, as I hope, yesterday's wind has scattered the ice a little ; if not, to examine it from the south-west side.

We go ahead full steam, with the wind behind, heading due south-west. The ice does not trouble us ; but at the end of 2 hours we are in the midst of a jumble of rocks, through which we pass untouched, I don't know how. Only 4 hours later do we meet the dense pack-ice, into which we plunge straightway, beginning afresh the old struggle to make a few miles to the south ; but Alexander I Land is before us, in all its mass, and the toil which we are inflicting on ourselves is worth while.

Slowly and with difficulty we approach, the big icebergs taking their part in the affair to bar our way and force us to make many detours. We push aside the floes, one by one, winning our way hardly ; but we do advance, and from the crow's-nest it looks as if a fairly big stretch of open water bathed the foot of the ice-cliff. At last we get there and cross this kind of big lake, sounding frequently and finding bottom varying considerably between 66 and 180 metres. Less than 2 miles from the cliff we are stopped by some enormous coastal ice-floes standing 1 metre 60 above the water, separated from one another by large crevasses, but so closely packed that the ship cannot get through them. The floes are too big for us to push aside, and join on to a coastal ice-belt which stops at the cliff-foot. Dragging a Norwegian boat along with us and jumping or crossing from floe to floe, we could certainly get there, but the risks to be run and the time which would be taken, with the ship meanwhile in a position which might at any moment become dangerous, would not be compensated for by the interest of the trip. We can see very distinctly the configuration of this ice-cliff ; once we got there we should require a regular expedition, and perhaps even then might not end by surmounting the perpendicular wall, full of crevasses and 30 metres high. Should we succeed in this climb, we should still have to cross an enormous ice-cap of 15 or 16 miles, covered by thick glacier snow, to reach the perpendicular mountain-walls rising above it, whose details we can see admirably from here. There would be no use in all this unless we could leave the ship for several days, or rather several weeks. At the foot of the cliff we cannot see even a rock ; only, just in front of us, two little islands stand out, scarcely higher than the cliff, and like it covered by a thick and even layer of ice. So I shall not run after the vain glory of actually touching the cliff of a land which we have had the fortune of being the first to reach, when we should learn nothing more by doing so. By taking advantage of the fine weather which we continue to enjoy we shall be able to accomplish some much more useful work.

The north-east wind has given place, as it did yesterday, to a nice south-east breeze, bringing an absolutely clear sky, which allows us to get all our guiding-points from the extremity of the continental land to the peaks of Adelaide Land, whose snows are magnificently tinted by the sun a dull old gold. All the cameras on board are at work incessantly, while Bongrain gets through a long and thorough piece of surveying work. When this is finished it is time for us to be off, for the big floes have treacherously surrounded us, and it is with difficulty that we get clear enough to make a dredge of 180 metres. Apart from zoological specimens, we secure thus a bucketful of small and medium-sized stones, some of which are generously given by our geologist to the crew, anxious to have souvenirs of this land of which they have been talking so long.

From here we see Alexander I Land almost from the same quarter as before; but, being so near, we easily supplement our previous information and can confirm what we noted previously. To the north this island is composed of an enormous ice-cap, like that on Adelaide Land, but much bigger and more irregular in contour. Some high scarped and clear-cut mountains, with jagged summits, make a range running east and west, with the same general characteristics as the Adelaide Land mountains. The aspect of the country must be most repulsive and inhospitable.

As usual, there is very little animal life. A very few seals are asleep on the floes, and there are two snowy petrels, two megalestrides, and five or six Adélie Penguins. As for whales it is long since we have seen any.

After making the circuit of our little lake (which is narrowing every minute), and vainly seeking a ready way out, we plunge boldly into the pack, steering at first north-west to take advantage of the south-east breeze, which helps us along well. At 9.30 p.m. we are clear and are skirting the drift on the edge of the pack-ice, trying to approach Alexander I Land from the west. The drift compels us to steer roughly westward at first, and then south-west. We keep our eyes on the land, and still see the mountains rising out of the ice-cap, which looks like a segment of a circle. Soon we espy a new range, this time running north and south, but rising, like the other, out of the cap. Apparently only the western end of the range descends straight into the sea, or at least stands upon a very thin portion of the cap. We soon recognize what Bellingshausen drew with such care; but he must still have been further away than he imagined. Of Lecointe's plan, although he drew it so boldly, we can recognize nothing, in spite of the best of wills. But Arctowski's description atones for this.[1]

At 10.30 p.m. the ice permits us to steer S. 20° W., true, which takes us into a great indentation in the pack, of which we cannot yet see the end. There is a good deal of drift-ice and some ice-blocks ; but this does not prevent us from going full steam ahead.

The portion of the pack we are leaving to port, whose direction is west-north-west, is marked out by ten big table-bergs, very close together and almost identical in shape and dimensions, looking like a string of gigantic railway carriages painted with Ripolin. Through a mist one might easily take this line of icebergs for an ice-wall. Numerous very big table-bergs are to be seen everywhere, evenly scattered ; and, although I have no right to affirm this, I feel convinced that there must be an ice-wall, perhaps south of Alexander I Land. The solid eastern part of the pack, after some 20 miles, runs into the coastal ice starting from the foot of the cliffs of Alexander I Land. The scene is magnificently lighted up by the sun, which all but touches the horizon.

The night—if one may use this term at the present season —is lovely and calm. We now see the east coast, and it is possible to plot out the whole island as follows, it seems to me. Upon a great segment of a sphere in snow there rests a letter T formed by two mountain ranges, the shorter running east and west, the larger practically north and south. The former is the higher, with a very steep northern face. The latter, whose face nearest to us is quite mild, after its junction

---

[1] It seems interesting to quote the preciser passages of Arctowski's description (*Rapports scientifiques de la ' Belgica.'* *Géologie*, p. 42) : ' Alexander Land, which lies to the south has some very high peaks rising majestically above a mountainous mass stretching in the direction north to south and fading away dimly on the horizon. In front of us is a cape, the extremity of a range running from east to west, making the northern coast of this land. . . . Further to the south the mountains appear to decrease in importance, and their outline is gentle. . . . It is to be noted that here, too, there is very plainly marked an ice-plain sloping very gently toward the sea, and in this plain the numerous glaciers coming down from the mountains lose themselves.'

with the short range decreases in height gradually toward
the south. Several little spurs run out from this range, and
almost at its southern extremity (which looks to us like a
cone) appear two little mounds rising up from a black-hued
plateau.

A sounding gives a depth of 326 metres. Half an hour
later, at a distance of only 12 miles from the shore, we get
574 metres, with a bottom of mud and small stones ; so that
here as everywhere else in this region the depths are very
varying. At midnight, when we have reached the most
southerly angle of the big indentation in the pack, we are
stopped by the ice. From the crow's-nest I perceive with
regret that this pack, which is made up of thick floes all but
soldered on to one another, is practically impassable, and
that we should consume all the rest of our coal in struggling
on a few miles, without learning much more ; for in this clear
weather (which cannot last for ever) we can see to a very
considerable distance.

After what we must look upon as the terminal cape there
is no more land to be seen ; everywhere the pack-ice stretches
to the horizon under a very clear sky. Alas ! why cannot
we push further south ? And yet, have we the right to complain when we have attained a point not attained before, and
seen what no one has seen previously ?

While we are surveying the north-western arm of the pack
closes slowly up toward us. We must make haste to be off,
or we are in danger of being caught in the same fix as the
Belgica or of being crushed against the coastal belt by the
first westerly gale. So we set off again ; but we have been
on our way an hour when a mirage deceives me into thinking
that a channel has just opened to the south. We put about
immediately and return on our tracks to discover my error,
after almost running into an iceberg and meeting with some
hard knocks against the floes, which awaken my companions,
to whom I had promised a quiet passage. It was time to

leave our bay, for the ice was drifting rapidly from the west, and the row of ten table-bergs approaching the eastern pack-ice left us but a narrow channel, which must have closed up soon after we got away.

The pack extends out of sight north-west and west. If we tried to turn that way we should certainly risk being obliged to go far northward and, even if we could make south again within sight of Alexander I Land, we might see it at such a distance that we could add nothing to Bellingshausen's description. I therefore prefer to return to Marguerite Bay to find out what is happening there, and to decide whether it is possible to winter there or whether we may hope, after the break-up of the pack, to seek favourable quarters elsewhere.

The weather continues very clear, and enables us to see all our country distinctly ; but the wind has risen very fresh and strong in the south-east. We take surveys and soundings and, after nearly grazing a rock flush with the water, of which the only warning is a lucky eddy seen a few moments before we are on it, we take our usual channel. At 10 o'clock we are moored to the pack-ice under Jenny Island. The weather is truly unparalleled in its clearness and purity of atmosphere, and the sky is without a cloud. The wind has fallen, and the sun's heat is considerable. One is reminded of a very fine winter's day at Nice.

It is settled that Bongrain, Gain and Boland shall start to-morrow night on a two days' trip in the north-east fjord, to try to discover whether Adelaide Land is an island or joins on to the mainland.

January 24.—Although to-day is Sunday, as the wind coming from the south and south-west is not likely to bother us, I dismount the windlass for repairs without loss of time. It is a difficult job, but is carried through successfully, and in two days' time the windlass will again be fit for work.

At 8.30 p.m., in calm and delightful weather, Bongrain, Gain and Boland set off. I have advised them to travel for

choice at night, to avoid snow-blindness and also to benefit
by the freezing of the snow ; for by noon the sun causes one
to sink in up to the knees.   They take with them five days'
food.   The wheel of an old bicycle, which I forgot to put
ashore when we started, fitted to the back of the sledge is
converted into an excellent cyclometer.

January 25.—It is calm and a little foggy, and a small
fine rain—a very rare thing in these latitudes—is falling un-
ceasingly.   We are all working on board with the utmost
zeal.   The windlass is almost in its place again, the picket
boat is repaired and the dinghy in the process of repair.   The
excellent fresh water procurable in abundance on shore is
collected in all our boats and thus we fill up our boiler and
water-casks without any expenditure of fuel.

Great slabs of our ice-pack, which were broken off by the
swell from the recent gale, are drifting away on the southerly
current, and thus the strip dividing us from the eastern side of
the bay, full of icebergs, is growing rapidly thinner—which is
rather alarming.

At last we have seen two more whales, one in the west, the
other in the east of the bay.   Moreover, Hervé found yesterday
in the north of the island, among some débris 8 metres above
water-level, a huge fragment of whale-bone.   We have found
no more, but this practically suffices to prove a comparatively
recent upheaval of the ground.

Gourdon has come across an Antarctic Penguin.   We have
seen none since Wandel Island, and I think they must be rare
so far south.   Lastly, 18 fine fish have been caught in the
trammel-net.

January 26.—I awake to find the ship dressed, the crew
having wished to celebrate the anniversary of my wedding.
They have made a mistake of two days, but I do not unde-
ceive the good fellows, for I am touched by this spontaneous
attention on their part.

Starting out early on skis, I was anxious to assure myself

as to the condition of the pack. The narrow strip which separates us from the eastern part of the bay and protects us against the icebergs collected there and those enclosed in the strip itself is in a parlous state. Undermined by the swell attacking it on both sides, it shows big rifts and big pools of water. Many seals are sleeping on the ice. I amuse myself by approaching them without disturbing them, and then striking my skis with my staff. In every case the sleeper opens one eye with a blink, then the other, and looks without the least astonishment on the strange apparition which I must present. If I do not move, it stretches itself out, seeks a comfortable position, and goes off to sleep again. At the side of a large mother seal, however, there is a young one asleep. I begin my game again, whereon the mother shows the utmost indifference; but her little one, on the other hand, is terribly scared and tries to escape, showing its teeth and snorting. I noticed that this young seal had three great scars in the caudal region, one of them almost circular and like those found, one might almost say invariably, on adults. The cause is disputed, some attributing the wounds to the struggles among the seals at the courting season. In that case the young one now before me must be extremely precocious. It is very probable that there are various reasons for these wounds, some evidently being from the attacks of thrashers and even of sea-leopards.

A fine rain never ceases falling, like what they call the *crachin* at Brest; and this goes on until 3 in the afternoon. At this moment the sun comes out, but almost simultaneously a tempest of wind springs up from the north-west. I had hoped that, owing to the narrowness of the bay, wind coming from the western regions could not stir up a dangerous sea here. But I was strangely deceived, for in a very short time it is so high that the deck is covered with spray. Great pieces of the pack break off and dash violently against our stern and rudder, threatening us with most serious damage. Every one sets to work with poles and oars to push off the blocks of ice, and after 2 hours' struggle we succeed in guiding past us the most dangerous pieces.

The ship, however, continues to pound heavily against the pack until the débris of floes and bergs, accumulating little by little around us, make a barrier of some 40 metres, which completely checks the swell. The ship only moves now under the influence of the heavy blasts. Our usual enemy, the ice, has once again become our protecting friend. It was high time, for our strength was beginning to fail.

The sea breaks violently on the edge of this barrier, and the spectacle is magnificent. It must be fearful outside. The whole entrance of the bay is covered by a great black shroud, and the high mountains facing us are as though wrapped in a thick layer of grey wool. This shroud has formed very rapidly, for the sky was quite blue when the storm began. From time to time scraps of cloud break away from it and scud off with startling speed. At the end of the fjord, on the other hand, to the north-east the weather is admirably clear.

A huge ice-block, some 10 metres high, has just broken through the ice athwart us ; but fortunately has been stopped about 15 metres off us by some big floes, which I trust it cannot shift. But the future is not at all promising. I really do not see how we can hope to wait here until the sea calms down around us. Not to speak of other possibilities, it is certain that if what has just happened had taken place at a season when there were some hours of night, however short, it would have been impossible for us to protect our ship and its stern would have been shattered.

At 11 p.m. the wind's violence increases, the mist invades our bay, and behind the peaks of Jenny Island huge clouds roll, looking like great solid masses. The mountains to the north-east, east, and south-east can still be seen, but are as though enveloped in a weird and terrible steel-blue atmosphere. The whole sea is tinged with yellow from the diatoms which covered the rocks and ice, but have now been washed off and broken up by the storm.

At last, toward midnight, the barometer, which had fallen considerably, goes up a little, while the wind only blows in great gusts interspersed with periods of complete calm. Then the gusts steadily decrease in intensity, and toward 2 o'clock the high wind gives place to a mild breeze.

At 3 a.m. the man on watch announces to me that Bongrain, Gain and Boland are to be seen on the pack. I give orders for supper to be prepared for them, and go to meet them with Godfroy. They have got on very well, without any mishap, and are much astonished to hear that we have experienced bad weather, having themselves had only fine and calm. This does not surprise me much. Indeed, it is very common in the fjord regions, and I have noticed it myself in Iceland and the Faroes.

Helped by a good smooth ice surface for the sledge, especially on the journey out, they travelled about 60 kilometres. Gain and Boland climbed to the summit of a little island in a narrow fjord full of icebergs, which they said seemed from their rounded shapes to have been there several years. They are certain that it was a strait in front of them, but they would have required several more days to settle the question outright. Still, thanks to the surveys, and sketches of the coast which they made, it was possible for us later to recognize from Matha Bay that their supposition was well based. Adelaide Land is therefore an island still, but is very close to the mainland and is of a size of which there was no suspicion up to now.

There being a complete calm to-day, the floating ice carried by the southerly current is going out of our bay. The weather is grey and soft, and almost all the mountains are enveloped in low clouds, which hide them from our sight. Our situation here worries me extremely, and, although I have no exaggerated fears for the safety of the ship as long as we have our fires up and continual daylight, I think it necessary to take all precautions for a possible rapid abandonment of her. I make out accordingly lists of clothing to be put in every man's bag, while I map out for each one his special post and duty, so that in case of accident we may still have not only the prime necessities but also the means of carrying on some scientific work and of either trying to get back to Deception Island or waiting rescue in some place more easy of access than where we are to an expedition in search of us. But I do not want to make these desperate preparations so soon after our recent alarm, for fear they should have a demoralizing influence on the spirits of some of the crew, and I keep in reserve the task of breaking the news to them in fine weather and almost in a joking way.

Bongrain came to me this evening to communicate to me his anxiety about the situation we were in, and to ask me if I did not think we ought to be off quickly. I answered him that, alas! I only too fully shared his apprehensions, but that I wished to hold on here as long as possible, so that the ice might perhaps unblock for us a place on the coast where we could find shelter. Moreover, to go out in heavy and threatening weather, as now, would not be desirable. We could not risk leaving before ascertaining the route to be taken by climbing to the summit of the island in clear weather. I was still hoping against hope, I must confess, to see one of the coast fjords unlock so that we might winter in it. I should be content with very little, if it were only a deep cleft in the coastal pack-ice to shelter us from the icebergs and allow us to be frozen in.

During the night the wind has begun to blow again from the same direction, not with great strength, but bringing along some huge ice-blocks, some of which by their size almost deserve the name of bergs. One of them which alarms me particularly gets stranded in a shallow close to the western point of the island. There is no lack of dangerous neighbours, and their number cannot grow less, for just opposite to us is the factory for ice-blocks and at the foot of the glaciers a big reserve seems to be only waiting for a favourable opportunity to bear down upon us.

I spend the greater part of the night upon deck, which enables me to espy a rat which, the reverse of timid, is calmly wandering astern, generally in the neighbourhood of the laboratory, where there are some birds waiting to be stuffed. The poor little beast is pretty, but still I must give orders for its destruction, for another of its kind has been seen, and as they may be of different sexes the ship might quickly be populated and our provisions, nets, and furs damaged in the same way as happened on the *Français*. But if I must have rats exterminated, I set myself absolutely against the totally unnecessary destruction of the megalestrides, which come in great numbers to feed on the remains of the seals left on the ice. My defence of them brings down on me the wrath of the sportsmen, but I do not give way ; for, apart from all other considerations, in our present circumstances it is certain that if any accident forced us to abandon the ship we should be very glad to use as food these same birds, whose bodies at present are left to rot on the ice. We must kill what is necessary for our collections and our kitchen, but I will always oppose killing for the mere pleasure of destruction.

There is a lot of ice around us, but a big floe, about a kilometre and a half in length, lies parallel with the ship, so that we are protected to seaward, and the fairly strong south-west wind which is blowing does not alarm me. The weather is heavy and especially black to the south. It is snowing fast.

All spend the day in work, the staff continuing their observations. Advantage is taken of the lull to take the engine to pieces quickly, and the crew finish both the repair of the dinghy and the putting together of a number of sledges, so as to be prepared for every emergency.

While Bongrain was returning from his observations with

Boland, an Adélie Penguin jumped on the ice, holding in its beak a very big fish. Boland seized on it, and the fish, of a kind new to us, is now in a bottle ; but the easily comprehensible anger of the poor penguin was comic. In a perfect fury it accompanied the robber right back to the ship, protesting energetically.

I have examined afresh the strip of pack-ice to which we are moored. It is rapidly diminishing in extent, which does not tend to ease my fears.

January 29.—At 3 a.m. the man on watch comes to tell me that an iceberg is bearing down on us. Happily he is exaggerating ; but nevertheless it is with great difficulty that the whole of the crew succeeds in sheering off and turning astern a very big ice-block. Half an hour later the wind begins to blow very hard from the south-west, unfortunately driving toward the end of the bay all the small ice and the floes which served to protect us.

At 1 p.m. a real iceberg this time, which I thought firmly stranded some distance away from us, begins to move. To salve my conscience, I have the fires made up ; but, with our bows wedged in an indentation in the pack, we could have made but a little way astern, even if the wind allowed us. We get ready with all the poles and thick planks on board, not so much to try to sheer off the enormous mass as to seek at least to break the shock. With majestic menace the berg bears down on us slowly, slanting across our stern, and thus blocking our one chance of manœuvring. All the poles are waiting when, about 10 metres away from us, as if in pity it gently changes its course and contents itself with crashing into the ice a little astern of us. So we excavate in the pack a little basin, which we close with big floes moored by ice-anchors in order to protect our rudder and screw. While this work is in progress I search for a better place for the ship nearer to land. I come back with my mind made up, at the first lull, to draw closer to the island, and put the ship into an opening in the ice where it should be better sheltered. At 5 in the afternoon the wind drops almost of a sudden; but an hour later, when we are about to start moving it begins to blow harder than ever, veering to the north-west, raising up immediately a stormy sea, which makes us bang violently against the thick pack-ice. The berg which frightened us so much this morning during the little lull had gone seaward, but again it bears down on us, and with anxious hearts we get ready to receive it. The same providential intervention, however, causes it to make a manœuvre identical with that of this morning, but in the contrary direction, and after coming still nearer to us it passes this time ahead of us and ranges up to the pack at the very place where I had decided to moor the *Pourquoi-Pas ?* The crew now ask me to moor the berg itself with ice-anchors to prevent it coming back, and although this device may be puerile with such a mass I let them adopt it, in order to encourage their inventive zeal. Shortly after the monster capsized and broke up, covering a vast area with ice-blocks in the course of a few moments. This was the end of its career, after warning us of the danger of our position.

The whole day is spent in watching the ice-blocks and pushing off those that approach us. The blows we receive are formidable, and their frequency makes them dangerous even for so stout a vessel as ours. My cabin writing-desk, which is fixed to a beam, receives such jars that everything in it is upset and I can write no longer. Still, what I most fear is a collision.

Except that the mountains of Adelaide Land are wrapped in a pall of heavy clouds, the weather is very clear, especially in the east and north-east. In the offing, that is to say, to the south, the sky is black, bordered on the horizon with a luminous band of gold, probably due to ice-blink.

January 30.—At midnight the wind suddenly dropped. The thermometer recorded 2° below zero and went down to 6° below, to rise again by noon to + 8°, thus giving us on the same day the minimum and maximum readings of our present visit to the Antarctic. At 10 a.m. the weather was fine and clear, and I took advantage of it to climb with Gourdon to the summit of the island. What we saw was not cheerful. While the little strip separating our vessel from the bay full of icebergs is rapidly diminishing and is even on the point of vanishing, on the other hand the coastal pack does not seem to have changed since we first saw it, and still stretches some 8 or 10 miles.

The situation therefore is most grave, and the moment is one of those when the responsibility of the head of an expedition is truly agonizing. If our expedition were merely one of adventure, aiming simply at beating the record or accomplishing a sporting feat, I would gladly take the risk (although the result would almost certainly, and very quickly, be a wintering on land and a retreat full of incident, like that of the *Tegethoff* Expedition) and would stay here, burning the last ton of coal. But I must not forget the pecuniary sacrifices made by my country at the request of the Académie des Sciences, and that what is expected of us above all is scientific discoveries. Our equipment of instruments is very fine, and to make use of it we require safe and serviceable winter quarters. Now here we have no anchorage and no chance of mooring ourselves to the shore, against which the first gale of wind would infallibly dash us. As the strip of pack-ice which protects us from bad weather from the eastern quarter and the numerous big icebergs is on the point of breaking up, even if we escape from the latter we should be obliged to skirt the edge of the pack, thus going further and further away from the island on which alone we could establish observatories ; and I have every reason to believe that we could not long keep up the struggle necessary for the security of our vessel. The bad weather we have encountered is nothing in comparison with what we shall have to encounter in the coming months. Yet these few hours of continual toil and struggle have already wearied out a hardy and enthusiastic crew, and I know by experience that gales of from fifteen days to a month in duration are not exceptional here. Lastly, it is still possible to struggle by daylight, but at night this becomes an absolute impossibility, and we have already seen our first two stars, which herald the coming of the night hours. On the other hand, our stock of coal is gradually being exhausted. Now we must reckon on two months at least, perhaps three, either before the coast unlocks to allow us to seek for possible shelter or before we can hope to be shut in by the ice. I believe that every serious explorer would decide with me that, under our present conditions, my duty is not to risk an adventure with the majority of chances in favour of the loss of the ship and, in any case, of our having to winter in such a situation that we should lose all the profit of our labours.

It was a great, almost a desperate, blow to me to have to leave this region where, with more luck, we might have accomplished such interesting work, and where I hoped to make important sledging excursions. It was with anguish of heart that I made up my mind ; but really I did not think I had the right to cause the Expedition to run such big risks any longer. I thought it best, however, to call together my companions on the staff, and, explaining the position to them, I asked their advice. They answered that we must start as soon as possible to look for winter quarters in Matha Bay and, if we cannot find them there, return to Port Circumcision.

I hesitated also about leaving a station on shore ; but, apart from the fact that we had not the necessary installation, in view of the difficulty of landing to do so, I would not have ventured to undertake the responsibility without joining the party myself—and, on the other hand, I did not think I ought to quit the ship.

I decided therefore to leave as soon as possible. From the top of the island we had seen the offing full of ice. At all costs it was necessary to escape being frozen up at sea, and

132

Embarking in the Norwegian Boat in Matha Bay.

risking a winter which would have to be spent like the *Belgica's* in an almost identical region. Our summer campaign had been more fruitful than we could have hoped, since we had surveyed a considerable extent of new coast south of Adelaide Land, reached Alexander I Land, corrected the charts, and discovered a big bay north of Adelaide Land while making during our voyage numerous soundings, drags, and observations of all kinds. It was absolutely necessary now, if we were to make sure of our winter's work, to run no danger, by attempting too much, of cutting off our retreat and compromising the future of the Expedition, compelling ourselves to renounce all ideas of winter quarters and return to Cape Horn—which would be disastrous. After wintering we could still hope, with the coal we should have left, to have a profitable campaign on the high sea, more adventurous in character and freer from anxiety about finding a favourable spot for winter quarters and the prosecution of the important work entrusted to us.

We leave on the terrace of Jenny Island a cairn with a message in it, and at 10.30 p.m. we get under weigh. It is with a heavy heart that I depart ; and yet I ought to rejoice at the fine weather which allows the Expedition to escape from this dangerous spot.

A very small breeze from the south-south-west is blowing, and a few big floes coming from the bay force us to make detours. At midnight we begin to round the cap of Adelaide Land, keeping a good distance away to escape the reefs at the southern end, which stretch out very far, marked at the present moment by numerous big icebergs.

The weather is very clear, and all the lands are in sight, standing out against a magnificent orange sky. Only the high peaks of Adelaide Land are wrapped in light woolly clouds. Toward 1 a.m. we reach the edge of the pack-ice, which is very thick to the south, loose enough to the west, but thicker again along the land. There is just a channel for us, but we still have to pick our way to escape the thick and frequently big floes. With the ice in this condition we should have had the greatest difficulty in making Marguerite Bay when we first arrived, and I do not think we could have reached Alexander I Land. I continue to believe, therefore, that we had the benefit of a rather exceptional state of things.

A little before 3 o'clock the sun rises, and the light effects become wonderful. Some of the icebergs are purple in hue, others violet, others look like masses of molten iron, while some are blue or a dazzling silvery white. The whole pack is tinted pink, and it is difficult to imagine anything at once more beautiful and more fantastic. We soon came upon a great collection of icebergs stretching out in a line as far as the big black rock we noticed when we came, which breaks the monotony of the cap. There are over 240 icy monsters, and in the middle of them, more than 15 miles in the offing, can be seen numerous reefs. The pack-ice forces us to steam between land and reefs, skirting the line of icebergs, but happily without any mishap to our keel.

The wind, without altering in strength, veers from south-south-west to south-west, and then to west-south-west. The sea becomes clear and we pursue our journey to Matha Bay, taking soundings every four hours. At 6 p.m. we notice the double row of monstrous icebergs which seem always to mark out on either side the entrance to Matha Bay, one row resting on the shallows of Adelaide Land, the other on those of the Biscoe Islands. We recognize some by their strange shapes as having been seen by us, almost in the same places, on our first attempt to penetrate into the bay.

This bay now seems very generally free of ice and we head for the end, toward the big promontory which we called on account of its form the Lion, behind which we hope to find a large inlet.

Accordingly we leave on our right the big comma-shaped channel, formed by the ice-cap and a large mountainous islet, which we resolve to explore later. It is dull and grey and a strong east-south-east wind is rising, while in the north-east and east the sky is overcast and threatening. The floes, ice-blocks, and débris of the latter are becoming close-packed, and we make our way slowly ; but at last we double the Lion and penetrate into a big bay of clear water leading us right up to the coastal pack-ice, which fills up a fjord of large extent. We moor ourselves firmly to the pack, which divides us from a picturesque crevassed glacier.

The night is windy, but we are well sheltered from the present direction of the wind and from the sea, and toward 9 a.m. a calm returns and the day declares itself magnificently clear. Every one starts energetically to work, and it is not until about 3 o'clock, after a good dredge, that we are ready to start again.

The coast is wonderful with its fine tall mountains of weird aspect, but all the inlets are choked with the thick pack-ice, and at one single point stands an island ending in a rocky promontory, in place of the everlasting ice-cliff. A little beyond this promontory there is a low rocky island, for which we head in the hope of finding there a cove in which we can anchor for the winter.

We embark in the Norwegian boat, and find on the reef an imposing rookery of Adélie Penguins and some magnificent striated rocks, but absolutely nothing of service to our ship ; no cove, no anchorage, considerable depths of water, which allow the already approaching icebergs to come close to the islet, and not even a shelter against the swell of the open sea, which we feel a little in spite of the calm weather following the land breezes.

We cross the bay and, after making sure that the pack-ice closes up all the windings on both sides alike, we enter the channel behind the cap of Adelaide Land. Big icebergs, enormous floes more than 2 metres above water-level, and ice promontories which look as if freshly broken away from the coast, block our way, proving to us once more how inhospitable is this region and how unfavourable to a stay of any kind.

Gain and Boland recognize at the end of the channel we are threading some peaks which they saw during their excursion on the other side. So Adelaide Land is really an island, though the strait which separates it from the land we named after President Loubet is always very narrow and grows smaller as it goes on.

After a few stops for surveying, we are brought up at midnight by the pack which surrounds part of Adelaide Land, the islet opposite it, and two conical black islets which appear to the south. This pack joins straight on to that which we found all round Matha Bay.

The swell makes itself felt pretty strongly, the sky is overcast from the north-west to the north-east, and icebergs and thick floes are making their way into our channel. Unfortunately we have nothing to do here, and to idle about would be unwise, to say nothing of the useless expenditure of coal. Between the Biscoe Islands and the land the scene is literally choked with ice. We must make up our minds, therefore, to return to Petermann Island ; and, this being the only decision to which we can come, the sooner we are there to commence our observations and economize our coal, the better. Further, there is already a certain amount of night, and experience has taught me only too well the great difficulties which may befall one on this coast through the sudden movements of the ice, the gales, and the reefs. I cannot lose time and risk spending long days on the high sea without an opportunity of attaining our object, to finish up perhaps by missing it altogether. The line of reefs separating us from Petermann Island cannot be crossed from the sea side except in broad daylight, and in weather that is at least moderately good. On the *Français* we were kept over a week at sea partly by a gale, partly by fog, and it was only by a rather risky decision that we were

Rock Formation in Matla Bay.

able to regain Wandel, taking advantage of a few hours of
moonlight.

At 4 a.m. we come out of Matha Bay, rival swells from the
south-west, north-west, and north-east setting up a most
unpleasant cross-chop, and causing the ship to pitch and toss
wildly. The wind blows fairly strong from the north-east,
accompanied by a hurricane of snow crystals, painful to the
eyes and obstructive to the view, which is so much wanted in
the midst of a sea strewn with fragments of icebergs. Happily this state of affairs does not last long, and I confess that
I am agreeably surprised ; for never on my previous campaign
did we experience north-east winds which did not end in gales
and blow generally for several days, at least for a dozen hours.

From noon onward the weather turns quite fine, the sky
only remaining a little overcast in the north. All day long we
coast the Biscoe Islands, which form, as it were, an uninter-
rupted line of big, little, and medium-sized caps, all monoton-
ously alike and overlapping one another. They can scarcely
be counted, and it would be a tedious task to attempt to do
so ; but it may be said that they begin with Victor Hugo
Island and end with Adelaide Land.

Biscoe discovered these islands after Adelaide Land, and
this is how he speaks of them in his diary : ' On the 17th and
18th [of February] passed several small islands of exactly the
same appearance as Adelaide Island. This range lays west-
south-west and east-north-east, and had no mountains on
their tops, but a complete field of snow and ice perfectly
smooth except their edges. I could plainly see a tier of
very high mountains in the background, which had a grand
appearance.

' *February* 19.—At 4 p.m. I sent the boat to an island,
which appeared to join the mainland, and some naked rocks
lying off the mouth of a considerable entrance. I had great
hopes of finding seal in them. At 10 a.m. the boat returned,
not having found anything alive on the island, but having

pulled quite round what Mr. White informed me was an excellent harbour for shelter, although a rocky bottom. I have named this Pitt's Island, from the great likeness of an iceberg to that statesman in a sitting posture, and which for some time I took to be a rock. This island has many bays in it; the centre part of the west side, latitude 65° 20′ S., longitude 66° 38′ W., by good sights [and] chronometers.' [1]

Biscoe says nothing more about these islands, and I confess that I do not understand why the English Admiralty chart places Pitt Island in 65° 40′ W. instead of 66° 38′ W., and why it adorns it with three mountainous peaks standing in a triangle, about which Biscoe has not a word.

Before our time these islands were not mentioned again except by Evensen, who coasted along them going south, and in running back passed between the two most northerly, that is to say, very probably south of Victor Hugo Island, as we did on several occasions.

As for the *Belgica*, she saw none of them, and De Gerlache writes : [2] ' We pass, without seeing them, the position of the Biscoe Islands as marked on the Admiralty chart. It is true that the weather is rather overcast, and that we may have left them a few miles to one side or the other of our course.'

On the *Français* we vainly sought for Pitt Island at the place indicated by Biscoe, and in despair we gave this name to a big cap-shaped island in 65° 28′ S. latitude and 66° W. longitude (Greenwich) ; but in spite of all our efforts it was impossible for us to get through the ice, which always cut us off, and to rediscover the bay which Lieutenant White entered.

At 6 p.m. we are abreast of Victor Hugo Island, but shortly before midnight the lack of light forces us to stop. The ship is in a fairly dense pack, in the midst of icebergs. About 2.30 we start again with the greatest precautions, as the reefs are

---

[1] *Antarctic Manual*, p. 332.
[2] *Quinze mois dans l'Antarctique*, p. 168.

hidden by floes ; but at last we recognize our former bearings, and at 5 o'clock we enter Port Circumcision. When the ship is barely moored, I have stretched provisionally across the entrance three double iron-wire hawsers to prevent the intrusion of ice-blocks.

PART II
AUTUMN, WINTER, AND SPRING, 1909

IT is here, therefore, that we must winter, and I confess that it is a genuine disappointment to me. In spite of having tried to persuade myself that there was small chance of finding a shelter elsewhere, I had still nourished hopes ; and our discovery of Marguerite Bay and the apparently favourable situation of Jenny Island seemed at first to be a realization of these hopes. But if it is difficult to console oneself for not wintering further south, at least one must admit the advantages of our present situation.

The ship appears to be safe, the shape of the island is favourable to the establishment of our observatories, and the neighbourhood of Wandel will permit us, by comparison with the observations of four years ago, to form some precise ideas of the physical and biological conditions of this region. Very often during our winter stay at Wandel we asked ourselves whether, exposed as we were at the opening of the vast passage formed by De Gerlache Strait, this local influence did not cause some modifications of the general conditions. Here it will be easy for us to find this out.

From another point of view it seemed to us also in 1904 that the difficulty of exploration, caused by the frequent shifting of the pack-ice, ceased with Petermann (Lund) Island. We are justified, therefore, in hoping to be able to make excursions along the coast, and the configuration of the glacier situated right in front of our haven seems favourable to our penetration even on to the mainland.

140

Penguin Rookery on Petermann Island.

Lastly, and this consideration must not be despised, there is on Petermann Island a well populated penguin rookery, which promises us in the autumn and spring material both for study and for food ; not only fresh meat but also eggs, when it pleases these good birds to provide them for us. And there is also the amusement to be derived from them.

Our kingdom is about 2 kilometres at its greatest length, and the island is divided into two sections united by an isthmus of a little more than 200 metres broad, which separates two picturesque fjords with generally steep cliffs. The northern section is a big ice-cap, 127 metres high, with scarped walls, terminating to the north-west in an outcrop of huge rocks. The only possible passage by land between the north and south sections is a very steep slope, tiring to climb whether covered with soft snow or when the latter is blown off by the wind and leaves uncovered a frozen surface.

We are on the southern section, which is also composed of an ice-cap, about 50 metres in height, with fairly gentle slopes descending to the shore on the south-east, north, and south-east. In the last-named quarter are fine, picturesque rocks, crowned by penguin rookeries. Port Circumcision is a notch in the south-east coast, and its generally flat surroundings are favourable to our winter establishment. The whole is dominated by a clump of rocks 35 metres high on ' Megalestris Hill.' Lastly, there is a group of little islands to the south-west.

The influence of the persistent north-east winds makes itself felt in the configuration of the two masses of Petermann Island as in all the neighbouring region. The rocks to the north-east are swept by the wind, which accumulates more and more snow on the south-west side, where the coast is formed by the sheer wall of a high ice-cliff with a snow-cornice towering over it. Port Circumcision, the entrance to which is made rather difficult for a ship as big as ours by huge lumpy rocks, is a cove running north and south. The end of the cove and its eastern face are precipitous walls of ice, 7 or 8 metres high, rising on a base of rock. On the east the rocky face is rather lower. The depth increases rather abruptly toward the sea end, so that, as was the case with the *Français* at Wandel, I deem it necessary to turn the stern toward the entrance, in deeper water, in order to prevent pounding due to the swell damaging the screw and rudder, the 'Achilles' heels' of all Polar vessels. If we turned the ship the other way, our draught of water astern would not allow us to force her sufficiently into the cove for her to be well protected and well moored.

We begin to establish ourselves immediately, which is no light task; for, apart from the scientific programme (the carrying out of which necessitates a rather complicated organization), if we wish to take full advantage of our excellent position, we must also provide for the safety of the ship, and render as comfortable as possible the life of the thirty men who make up the Expedition.

Our observations will gain a lot by beginning as soon as possible. So we set on foot simultaneously all the organizing work, and our little corner becomes like a veritable ant-hill in its activity. The building material is carried to the chosen spots either by sledge or by boat. Senouque erects on flat ground at a good distance from all other buildings, so as to withdraw his magnetic needles from the influence of iron and steel, a wooden hut with double walls, covered with tarred canvas, in which to instal his apparatus for the registration of terrestrial magnetism.

Rouch builds a little hut of planks to contain his apparatus for the study of atmospheric electricity. Close to the ship and on an elevation of 35 metres, which for some reason or other has been christened 'Megalestris Hill' he puts up a shelter for the meteorological instruments, using as supports the iron network uprights presented by the Prince of Monaco.

Bongrain requires two huts, one for the seismograph, the

other for the transit instrument and its accessories. The first hut is quickly run up. It is a small portable affair of ' Venesta,' i.e. of panels of specially prepared wood fibre, the lightness and strength of which make them of the greatest use in Polar exploration. The other hut is made of planks covered with tarred canvas.

In all these buildings the great difficulty is to level the ground by removing or fetching rocks, and the task is particularly laborious through these being almost always soldered together by a thick layer of ice. Then it is necessary to consolidate the whole affair by heaping still more rocks round the base and stretching solid iron-wire shrouds over the roof ; for our huts must withstand the violent and continual attacks of Antarctic tempests.

In turning up the ground for the foundations of the future magnetic hut we found some seal bones, some of which showed curious pathological deformities.

While the little village springs up in this hitherto desert place, there is the greatest activity on board. First the ship has to be suitably moored, with a wealth of precautions which is all the greater because, safe as our haven appears, we do not yet know what might happen with strong winds coming from various points of the compass. The entrance is 85 metres across. Here we set up two barriers of steel wire to prevent the ice-blocks from coming in, and with ten hawsers we fix the ship in its place. Hawsers to act as barriers are secured to land with ice-anchors firmly driven into the ice, or, better still, into interstices of the rocks where the conformation of the ground permits of this. Last of all, I decide to twist the ship's two anchor-chains round suitably situated rocks. On the port side this is comparatively simple, for the rock which must serve as a bitt is right ahead and almost flush with the water ; but the rock to starboard is about 40 metres off and 10 metres high. To accomplish the job it is necessary to plan out a whole system of tackle and coils ; and yet in half a day the two heavy chains are in their places, to all appearance firmly laced about their rocks. The firmness of the starboard chain is of particular importance, for it will have to bear the brunt of the north-east blasts, which are the most frequent and violent in this region.

The top-gallant yards are unrigged, lowered, and then placed parallel to one another and fastened together with planks, thus making a broad gangway between the ship and the land. To facilitate communications, a path is cut in the rock cornice at the end of this gangway.

By means of bamboos serving as telegraph poles, we carry wires to the various observatories, which are then lighted by the electric installation on board ; and this is certainly one of our most useful and pleasing innovations. It will be easy at any time to have a good light by which to read the instruments, a luxury impossible to appreciate too highly. During the wintering of the *Français* one of our greatest preoccupations and greatest troubles was precisely this question of illumination. We used to set out, equipped with what we considered our best lantern, protecting it with care against the wind ; and just as we were about to use it, a gust would blow it out. As it was no use thinking of taking matches in the storm and snow, we must needs return on board to relight the lantern, and before accomplishing our object we often had to make the journey three or four times over. Also, by means of a microphonic communication Bongrain (whose practical turn of mind knows how to apply itself to such installations) is able to transmit the time on board to the transit instrument without carrying the chronometers across.

While the sailors unreeve the ropes, and dry and unbend the sails, the engineers and stokers look to the boiler and take the engine to pieces for the winter. Then the ship is covered fore and aft with huge awnings held in place by a solid framework. In this way the whole after-deck makes an enclosed saloon, lighted by day through windows pierced in the awning,

One of the Meteorological Shelters in Autumn.

The same Shelter in Spring.

and at night by two electric lamps. On the starboard side this saloon forms an annexe to the biological laboratory, on the port side and aft a vast workshop in which are set up various benches, the lathe, the drill, etc., etc. Here, too, are erected the two washing machines, in which once a week ice is to be melted for washing our linen, using seal's fat as fuel. Foreward the awning also makes a big saloon adjoining the crew's berths ; a roofing of planks covered with tarred canvas forms a lateral prolongation of the roof of the cook's galley. Only the central poop remains uncovered, and for this I get the sailmakers to construct a little tent to protect the ward-room skylight, easy to put on and off according to the weather.

All the boats are hauled up on shore, ready to be launched when required, except the picket-boat, which we keep temporarily afloat, firmly moored in a little cove where she seems safe. In one of the dories hauled ashore on a headland away from the ship and covered up, we put the explosives.

Our 10 tons of spirit are disembarked in their turn, and sheltered under canvas. It is with great relief that I see the ship for a time cleared of its dangerous cargo.

Finally Gourdon, who has done me the very great service of undertaking the important but thankless job of commissariat officer, with the care which he devotes to everything superintends the getting on shore of the cases of provisions, which he has put under an imposing building, with a roof formed of oars supporting a tent. Against this provision store we place skis and sledges, spare oars, etc.

Beside these arrangements, which require time and labour, a whole series of minor operations are in progress. Godfroy has set working his two tide registers, and puts up a gauge with marks easy to read from the ship. Rouch with runners from the sledges constructs a little erection of tropical appearance, singularly out of harmony with the snow, over the ground thermometers, which are buried in the ice. Gourdon, Gain and Liouville help me to set up on the summit of the island a cairn with a weathercock, which can be read from on board with the aid of field glasses. Thus the island bristles with odd-looking buildings, whose upkeep, alteration and improvement are our perpetual occupation.

All this setting in order of our winter quarters has taken nearly a month. I have thought it necessary to describe the general scheme for the better comprehension of what is to follow, before resuming my personal journal of daily events. The latter, I hope, will give the reader who wishes to realize our life of alternate activity and monotony a better picture than he could gather from long dissertations of our existence in winter quarters, with the illusions and disillusions, the achievements and mistakes which are the lot of Polar explorers whose one anxiety is to accomplish the task which they have undertaken.

The weather during this period has been characterized by strong gales, generally from the north-east, by snow, and by overcast skies. We cannot, therefore, but be glad that we are already in winter quarters and have commenced our series of observations.

On board the *Français* we kept afloat until March 5 in weather pretty much like this, and the experience left me, as well as my comrades of the period, the memory of a brave but very laborious struggle, rendered still more unpleasant by the long nights spent amid icebergs and reefs. We have had the luck this time of escaping this by arriving early in the Antarctic, and we have nothing to regret, for we could have done no useful work at sea.

Since our arrival here, up to the end of the month, we have had only four fine days, and, as will be seen afterwards, we took full advantage of them.

February 7.—Last night the weather was calm and wonderful, with some splendid effects of soft light, tinting the scenery in the tenderest of hues. Nearly all of us went out after dinner to indulge in tobogganing or ski-ing, and we

146

spent a good hour amusing ourselves with a penguin which refused to leave us. We stuck on his head now a cap, now a mitten, and nothing could have been funnier than this grotesquely muffled creature running along the snow and trying to free himself from his cumbrous head-dress. What was most curious, he seemed himself to be delighted with the game, coming back to us, stretching out his head, and evincing great satisfaction.

To-day it is still fine, and the sun is so bright that I took the opportunity of having a bath on deck.

The island is becoming quite picturesque with its little houses of various shapes. The seismograph hut (which reminds me of my garden at Neuilly, where I set it up experimentally) is especially pretty, leaning against a rock, with its little pointed roof and the telegraph posts joining it to the ship. The atmospheric electricity hut is less graceful in shape, but has its note of gaiety, nevertheless, for to strengthen its walls we have covered them with the zinc signs of the kindly purveyors who gave them to us with their goods ; and these familiar pictures recall memories of all the corners of France in which our eyes have looked at them.

February 8.—Jabet, whose duty it is every morning to inform me of the weather, announces to me to-day : ' Calm, no clouds.' We launch a whale-boat at once, and Gourdon, Godfroy, Gain, three of the crew, and myself set off. The weather is like yesterday's, fine and cloudless. It is so warm that, even sitting still at the tiller, I cannot stand my coat, while the rowers are in a perspiration with only their shirts on. Passing close to icebergs of strange and graceful shape, we reach without difficulty the first of the Argentine Islands, and after climbing to its summit we proceed to that which lies most to the south.

This very picturesque group of islands is composed of rocks of various colours, grey, red, or black, sometimes even green through the thick covering of moss upon them. Our

147

excursion is also enlivened by the fairly abundant animal life we came across. There are a lot of gulls and megalestrides, perhaps more than we have ever seen together before. On the floes the penguins gaze at us gravely, while the terns with their deafening cries pass overhead, and a cormorant cuts through air with its heavy flight, making straight for its object without a pause.

On the last island we find what we were looking for, a fine view over Cape Trois-Perez. It looks as if this cape were the end of a mountain range isolated from those in the background. But is it a deep fjord lying south of it, a strait making one more island, or a mere valley choked by a glacier, as is so often the case ? It is only by making the long excursion later that we can solve this question.

We lunch merrily, like canoeists on a holiday, close to a little cascade of fresh water ; but just as we are leaving we find that our rudder has disappeared, and we shall never know either how or where it went. We replace it easily enough with a plank nailed to a boat-hook.

Scarcely an hour later, thanks to the free water, we are back on board, although during the *Français* Expedition the same journey took thirty hours of hard work. It is true that all that time we had to drag this same whale-boat over the ice.

In the harbour we see the ship moving alternately ahead and astern. The underset has become formidable in this nook, securely closed in though it seems to be. One of the iron-wire hawsers from the stern has broken in consequence of the sudden strains caused by this perpetual movement. I try, with a certain amount of success, to set things right by hanging here and there by ropes from the new hawsers ballasted buckets reaching into the water, which stop too sharp pulls by the elastic resistance they afford.

Next day, as the weather continues fine, I take the whale-boat with three men to Wandel, where I wish to deposit a message telling where we are. We find on our way a lot of

Penguins' Tracks at Whaleboat Point.

The Huts for the Transit Instrument and the Seismograph.

Sending up a Meteorological Balloon.

icebergs and some masses of accumulated ice, which are often tiresome to get through.

A whale in some shallows is engaged in an interesting operation. It is evidently trying to discover whether there is enough water for it, and for over five minutes it feels its way, sinking a little, coming up again, and finally, finding what it wants, makes its usual plunge.

Having reached the headland east of Hovgard, we rest for a few minutes at this spot where we used to camp four years ago. It gives me great pleasure to recognize these little corners connected with the memories of the hard but cheerfully endured struggle of our former Expedition. At Wandel we moor at ' Whaleboat Point,' which used to serve us as a landing-place, and I proceed to take my message to the magnetic hut. Thanks to the astonishingly fine and warm weather, the rocks are more uncovered than they ever used to be, and the ice-cliffs are crumbling away noisily, covering the sea with their débris.

I cannot get used to the idea that Wandel is uninhabited. In spite of myself, I look for the familiar outline of the masts of the little *Français*, and I should be in no way astonished to see a human being coming toward me. I put down the indifferent, and as it seems to me affected, air of the penguins to their having been accustomed to see me before. It is certain, at least as far as I am concerned that, if ' every separa- tion, even the most looked-forward- to, has its grief,' a coming back, on the other hand, has its sweetness. This impression of a persistence of life at our old winter quarters is so strong that their nearness to Petermann robs this station of its feeling of isolation for me, and I am very frequently obliged to make an effort to convince myself that we are really all alone in the Antarctic.

On our way back we land at Hovgard, in a big hollow where a considerable fall of the ice-cliffs has left bare the rocks covered with enormous barnacles. The delighted men paddle about laughing in the icy water, picking these up and filling the boat with them.

A great black pall rises to seaward, with a north-west breeze, and in the evening the sky is completely covered except in the south-east, where a big blue gash lights up the mountain-tops fantastically. An enormous iceberg has come to a stop at the northern point of our haven. It is 65 metres high, more than double our mast. If such monsters, however, are dangerous neighbours when they capsize, the slight depth in which we are and the narrowness of the pass remove all fears of a collision. Our barrier appears to hold good and up to now only ice-blocks of a small size, and consequently harmless, have succeeded in getting past them.

February 16.—During these last few days the weather has been bad, the wind blowing more or less strongly from between north and east-north-east. It is dull and grey, with a fine snow and sometimes even rain, which was unknown to us on the first expedition. From time to time the wind drops for several hours, and the snow falls in big silent flakes. The temperature keeps generally above zero, and it is difficult to imagine anything more disagreeable than this muggy, humid weather, which seems likely to last, for the barometer has fallen this morning to 723 mm.

This does not prevent us from busying ourselves with the work and observations already started, and continuing our installations, which is the most important duty of the moment. But we must not think of excursions, and I watch the days growing shorter with regret.

Rouch having no hut suitable for them has had to content himself with fixing up the registering vane and anemometer on board ; but the ship is too sheltered and the information given is necessarily inadequate. So I decide to go to Wandel Island as soon as I can, to take down the house we left there four years ago. Put together again here, it will make a magnificent observatory.

In any case, the bad weather has been turned to profit, since I have had the excursion tents put up to test their strength. The experiment has been a perfect success, for these frail-looking structures have victoriously resisted the assaults of wind and snow. I had them made of green silk to avoid eye-strain, from which we suffered so much on our previous expedition during our summer excursions in perpetual daylight. This colour of theirs shows up pleasantly against the white snow. The arrangement I have adopted seems a good one. The tent is in the shape of a gendarme's cap, big enough for three persons. The uprights are simply made of four long ski-poles, joined two and two at their top-ends and passed through a big hem in the silk. This spreads out on all sides and stretches horizontally over the ground in such a way that it can be covered over with snow, which not only keeps the tent in place by its weight, but also prevents the air from penetrating into the interior. The poles, which go but a little way into the snow, being stopped by a ring bound round with thread, are fastened by cords to two ice-axes driven firmly in, and the opening is formed of a canvas bag, which can be tied up either inside or out with a cord. In an intense cold such as we expected these tents, which are the lightest and least cumbersome one could imagine, when once folded up, would leave nothing to be desired, I believe ; but in this half-melted snow it would be better perhaps to replace the silk with some thicker material, such as Burberry.

Chollet and two of the crew have taken a boat round the island. He found very few seals, and this discovery is annoying, for we want fat to economize the coal, with which I am very miserly, and I wished to lay up before the winter a good stock of meat. The poor penguins will be the first to suffer for this, since we must sacrifice some hundreds of them. I detest these massacres, however indispensable they are in our position, and they grieve me all the more because the birds here are so gentle and inoffensive.

The penguins, if a subject of most absorbing study to Gain, are a perpetual distraction for us. There is, on a rock rising out of the snow a few metres from the ship, a colony of country-folk (for this is the name I give to a few couples living separate and isolated from the big rookeries) which gives us special delight. It is composed of three couples with their young and a mad penguin, which indulges in extraordinary contortions and on which the others look with a kind of indulgent pity. The men always call him the ' loony.' He often acts as nurse to the little ones when the parents are away looking for food. The young have as yet no down except on their heads, where it forms a little cap which gives them a comic appearance. They rather rouse our pity, these little birds, so lacking in gaiety, and already as grave and dignified as their parents.

Many other young penguins belonging to the big rookery have already lost their down, which has been replaced by fine blue-black feathers ; but they have as yet no white circle round the iris. This and their size and the bluish colour of their plumage are all that distinguish them from their elders. The latter take them to their bath, but the underset is strong around the rocks on account of the bad weather, and the sea breaks with considerable force, so that they have great difficulty in entering the water and coming out again. Some of the old ones even have had rough shocks in trying to be too clever, and it is a wonder that they come through their adventures without being injured. We spend hours watching these birds with their human ways. The other day I witnessed a scene which has often been repeated since. A mamma penguin coming back from fishing was assailed by her two starving youngsters ; but, probably in order to make them take exercise, she tried to avoid them, forcing them to run and stopping from time to time to disgorge a beakful for them. Then she would start off again, holding out her beak to the little ones without opening it, making feints, but always finishing up by distributing her doles between the two with the greatest fairness.

Toward noon to-day the wind changes and blows smartly from the south-west, bringing clear weather with it. I take advantage of this to be off at once in the picket-boat with Gain and four men to Wandel, where we arrive without difficulty, after meeting innumerable icebergs but seeing no marine ice.

As we discovered on our recent visits, the house which I had had built of small panels, each one metre long, to facilitate transport, is, except for the roof having been blown off, in perfect condition, in spite of the attacks of the wind and the pressure of the snow. It is easy to take the upper section to pieces, the screws coming apart readily. But a complicated task awaits us over the completely buried lower section, for we have to cut into the ice to get the panels out, and soon we get down to the water. The only way to get rid of this is to dig a long channel, a tedious job; still, before the end of the day a good part of the house is already taken down and put on board the picket-boat. Before we start back I climb as far as the cairn, where I find four penguins in process of moulting. At this period of their existence these poor birds, separating into little groups and apparently hiding themselves away, have a curious, suffering look about them, probably due to the fact that, as they do not go into the sea during the moult, they deprive themselves of food. They seem so ashamed at being surprised by me in their retirement that I am tempted to apologise to them for my indiscreet visit.

During my absence Gourdon and Senouque have been in the Norwegian boat as far as the glacier on Danco Land, opposite our anchorage, and they bring back the good news that it is easy to land there.

Rouch is upset, and we torment him unmercifully, for he has just discovered, in setting the sunlight-register to work for the first time, that the instrument, which he bought at the last moment, is for the northern hemisphere. We are clever enough on board to alter the apparatus as wanted and to make use of it. But evidently the big instrument makers are not yet accustomed to South Polar expeditions.

February 17.—The weather is magnificent, like yesterday's, but the wind is blowing fresh from the north-east, and we must make haste, for this bodes no good. I set off, therefore, for Wandel with Liouville in the morning. We worked hard taking the house to pieces, under a sun so hot that we stripped to our shirts and turned up our sleeves.

Water bothers us more and more, but this time more than two-thirds of the building is taken down and put on board. As we gradually cleared the interior of ice, we discovered all that we left there four years ago, most of it in good condition. The barrel containing 160 litres of alcohol, 5° below proof, which will be very useful to our naturalists, is got out, and we find in the middle of a pile of rubbish, boxes of preserved food and milk, some glass-ware, a bread-basket, and finally, the little Simpson-Strickland engine of the picket-boat which we had to abandon. This engine is now encased in a huge block of ice. Later on, on board, when the ice was melted, this engine was in perfect condition; so much so that as we were dissatisfied with the electric motor which worked the Lucas sounder, we fitted some piping to communicate with the boiler, and practically without the necessity of repairs, this engine enabled us to take soundings of great depth during the whole of the rest of our campaign.

Just as Gain did yesterday, Liouville brings back from his trip an interesting harvest. On our way back we land on a big floe to kill a sea-leopard, more than three metres long. The poor brute defends itself bravely, but the revolver soon accounts for it. It is a magnificent specimen for the Museum that we tow back, but its death leaves a painful impression on my mind. It is strange that the men of the crew, who are brave fellows, kind and good to the animals which they keep

A Sea Leopard.

A Crabbing Seal.

A Sea Leopard.

on board, take pleasure in these slaughters and get excited over them. It is true that the sportsmen who kill without necessity, purely for pleasure, give a bad example to the lower classes. Moreover, no amount of reasoning succeeds in subduing this instinct, a relic of barbarism, which makes men, even the best of them in their ordinary lives, believe that by taking part in this useless exercise they are proving their courage. Bongrain, for his part, has succeeded in killing a Weddell's Seal, so that we are provided with fat and meat for some time, and our collection is getting gradually richer. We now only need a Ross's Seal to complete the series of Antarctic Seals ; but we can scarcely hope to get one of these until the summer campaign on the southern ice-pack.

There are four kinds of Antarctic seals, and, without giving a detailed description, which belongs to the Natural History department, I may mention some of their particularly distinctive characteristics.

Weddell's Seal (*Leptonychotes Weddelli*), or false sea-leopard, is spotted sometimes with white, sometimes with yellow, on a yellowish or grey ground. It is slenderer than the Crabbing Seal, generally larger in size, and with its head proportionately smaller. The teeth are of medium size and the dentition is simple.

The Sea-leopard (*Hydrurga Leptonyx*) is the king of Antarctic seals. It is dark grey, flecked with yellow spots of a very large size. Its head, which is distinctly separated from the body and at the end of a slender neck, is long, and the powerful jaw is remarkable for its large teeth, of which the molars have a peculiar arrangement as regards their points. They are three in number, placed in a line parallel to the elongated axis of the jaw, the tops of the two small lateral points curving in towards the central one, which is large and very sharp. The animal, as a whole, gives a fine impression of supple force and strength.

The Crabbing Seal, or Dumont d'Urville's Seal (*Lobodon*

Carcinophaga), has fur varying from olive-brown to silvery-white, sprinkled sometimes with large patches of a yellowish colour. Its size and proportions are intermediate between those of Weddell's and Ross's Seals. It is more heavy and thick-set than the former, and less than the latter. The molars are characteristic, small compared with those of the sea-leopard ; they consist of a central point, a smaller point in front, and two or three others behind. The principal point has a bulbous crown, and all have a tendency to curve backward.

As for Ross's Seal (*Ommatophoca Rossi*), the coloration is generally olive in the dorsal region, shading off gradually to dark olive in the abdominal region, with places that are lighter and yellowish on the neck and breast. The body is like a spindle-shaped bag, with very small limbs. The neck is thick, shaped like a large round purse under the chin. The head is short and big, the eyes prominent, and the flippers are considerably smaller than is the case with other seals. The dentition is very feeble.

All these animals are harmless to man, from whom they do not fly, not having learned to know him. However, I think it would be better not to trust too much in the sea-leopard, which is of the right size and disposition to defend itself in case of necessity. The most numerous seals around us in our winter quarters are the Crabbing and Weddell's Seals, sometimes in single specimens, sometimes collected in groups, even of more than one species. We have seen a fair number of sea-leopards, but always by themselves. As for Fur Seals, which used formerly to exist in abundance, at least in the South Shetlands, the great commercial value of their skins has caused their probably complete extinction. In any case, we have never met any, and the whalers of Deception Island, who are well placed for seeing and meeting them, have never come across any.

February 21.—Except for a short, sudden gale from the

south-west, which only lasted for a few hours, the wind blows persistently from the north-east, with the usual concomitants of a drizzle of snow, or even rain, and a high temperature. The thermometer has risen to $+8°$, and the thaw is so strong that one hears as it were the noise of a regular torrent all over our island, while on the mountain there are great crashes and rumblings of avalanches. The snow is everywhere coloured green and red by diatoms, and one might almost say that white snow is the exception. Usually it is pink, but in consequence of the abundance of unicellular algae in places it turns to scarlet ; as for the green snow, its colour is so intense that it gives the impression, at a distance, of regular prairies. Some rocks, which certainly have not seen daylight for many years, are uncovered, and if in the neighbourhood of the coast icebergs are numerous, they are very few in the offing, and not a fragment of marine ice is to be seen.

We have descended, by way of a snow-ravine, on to some rocks which enable one to see the end of the southern fjord. On the ice-cliff, which has been laid bare by the thaw, we can see numerous streaky layers, looking like carpet flower-beds. The diatoms cause this brilliant coloration of red, green, and brown.

The sea must be very heavy in the open, for the swell makes itself felt everywhere, and the *Pourquoi-Pas ?* is rocked in its haven in such a way as to make me fear for its moorings and for the gangway. Evidently this is an exceptional autumn, and I do not know whether we ought to feel confident or anxious about the future. For the present, the weather is eminently disagreeable, and the sea's freedom from ice is of no value to us, since with the persistent storms and the continual snow or fog we cannot take advantage of it, and we should all prefer dry cold and the view of a good ice-pack.

February 22.—Godfroy, Gain and Liouville, with five men, set off in the picket-boat, towing the dinghy, to fetch what remains of the portable house. They return at 6.30,

bringing back all that I had left. The day's fine weather has
not stopped the thaw, and our island becomes dirtier and
dirtier. All that has been thrown overboard appears again
on the surface, giving an ugly appearance to the picture.
There are whales about us in considerable number, and the
sound of their powerful blowing is heard on the air every
moment. As the whalers very rightly suppose, they go
southward at the end of February.

February 23, Shrove Tuesday.—Without troubling about
the Carnival, the men have been at work since morning, and
under the direction of Gourdon, are stacking on land the cases
of provisions. At lunchtime Liouville appears with his
beard shaved off, wearing Austrian whiskers, with his nose
painted red and his head covered with a tropical helmet.
Then Gourdon and Gain disguise themselves in their turn,
showing a strong preference for white clothes and tropical
head-gear. The mess steward turns out in a most extraordinary garb, and the cook is disguised as the chef in
a big hotel. This is the signal for a general masquerade,
very merry, though simple. The crew are content with
turning up their trouser-legs and displaying superb red under-
clothing, which, with their blue knitted vests and sealers'
boots and caps, makes a lovely uniform. Bongrain adds
to his already respectable height by adorning his head-dress
with the only feather on board, and carries in his hand an
enormous pole. Then every one gets hold of a gun and the
troop goes through evolutions on the island, while Liouville
uses a clarionet as a bugle and Lerebourg accompanies him
on a tin box as a drum, and Gourdon, harnessed to a sledge,
represents the ambulance service. The greatest merriment
prevails, and the rest of the day is treated as a holiday. In
spite of the north-east wind, we have been spared snow in
the afternoon, but in the evening it begins to fall again, so
that we do not lack confetti, fortunately clean. Dinner in-
cludes pancakes, well washed down, and Gourdon brings

158

Shrove Tuesday Masquerade.

Shrove Tuesday Parade.

out of the hold a tin box, labelled ' For Shrove Tuesday,' containing some excellent honey, which a member of his family
kindly presented before we started from home.

February 28.—The weather is worse than it has ever been.
Yesterday rain was coming down in torrents ; to-day the wind
blows from the north-east, with formidable gusts from
the east-north-east, which lift up regular whirlwinds of spray
in the channel. Through the violence of these gusts, which
catch her broadside on, the ship moves from her moorings.
However, we are protected here by the ice-cliff, which is
almost as high as our tops. If this were not so, where should
we be ? One of our hawsers breaks, and the day is spent in
attending to them and increasing them. Those to starboard
astern are made threefold, supplementary tackle is fastened
about the rock, and the forward chain is hauled taut.

In spite of all these precautions, the ship from time to
time meets with more shocks against the rock to port. Happily
we know she is stout, but nevertheless we could do without
these continual blows ; for one calm day, when the water
was particularly transparent, we were able to see that the
summer campaign had not only brought the serious injury
to the stem, but had also left numerous traces on the sheathing
and also on the hull itself.

Off Berthelot Island, there is a very pretty effect of light.
The land stands out brilliantly illuminated, so that the smallest
details can be made out, in an atmosphere of metallic blue,
whilst elsewhere everything is wrapped in mist and fog.

Our first month in winter quarters is at an end, and no
one has wasted his time. Not only have we established ourselves, but every one's work is well under way and organized
in a fashion that seems satisfactory. Boland is attached
to Bongrain, Nozal to Rouch, Dufrèche to the naturalists.
Thomas is at the disposal of Senouque whenever he has need
of him, and Aveline at Godfroy's. The meteorological work,
after which Rouch looks during the day, is done at night by

Nozal, Boland and Jabet. In this way, all is going on, and should go on, as well as we can hope. The engineers' and carpenters' workshop is kept busy, the sailors are working well, and good health is general.

March 1.—In the evening the barometer, which had gone down to 720 mm., goes up a little, while the blasts are weaker and at greater intervals. In expectation of the wind jumping to the south-west, I have had put out on the port side astern a big tow-rope, fastened to an ice anchor wedged in some rocks. The task of stacking the cases of provisions is going on and we have begun to set up on Megalestris Hill the house from Wandel Island.

March 3.—The weather is better, but the thermometer is still below zero. The house is now in its place, and it only remains to construct a roof to replace that which was carried away. This sort of building is very practical, and no one could have told that it had stood four years in this rigorous climate. Right on the top of the rock, standing out against the blue sky, it looks very well, adding to the picturesque effect of our improvised village ; and further, it would be difficult to have, in these regions, a better meteorological observatory. The view from the interior, through the little windows, is magnificent. On the one side, the grand Lemaire Channel, with the fine mountains which make its two banks ; on the other, the high ground behind Cape Tuxen, which rises pale against the blue sky ; and lastly below, the whole of our picturesque encampment, with the *Pourquoi-Pas ?* in its haven, surrounded by our little buildings of weird and varied shapes, teeming with active life.

Four Megalestrides have been killed for the kitchen, and, unhappily for themselves, their flesh has been found excellent. We must be economical with them, however, for, like the big petrels, they help the naturalists by skinning the skeletons of the seals for them.

In the south fjord, exactly below the house, a fair number

An Arch of Ice.

of whales have been plunging, and from this height it is easy to observe their evolutions in the deep, transparent waters.

March 5.—At last the weather has turned magnificent, calm and with beautiful sunshine. This afternoon, a few banks of mist have passed, hiding the base of the mountains but leaving their summits uncovered but they rapidly dispersed and this evening all is clear, while each summit is adorned with a little white fleecy cloud, which looks like a plume on its top. Yesterday I went round the island in the pick-etboat. We came across a magnificent arch in a much-broken iceberg, through which I amused myself by passing. It is difficult to imagine anything more agreeably impressive ; one can never grow tired of this Antarctic architecture, it is so varied and unexpected, now graceful and now grand.

The meteorological hut is quite finished. Its roof has been cleverly and ingeniously made by Libois with scraps of old tin boxes, and the whole structure is kept up by a network of iron-wire and shrouds.

Rouch has installed there a registering wind-vane and his hackwatch, a Fortin barometer and a registering one as well. Just outside is the meteorological shelter which we put up when we arrived.

The naturalists have found and brought back two seals. These animals are now fairly numerous, and we do not require any more.

March 7.—We have been away and come back. The projected excursion to Beascocheia Bay was completely successful, and carried out more rapidly than I could have hoped. By way of precaution, and also to enable us to separate, if it should prove necessary to do so, I decided to tow the big canoe with us. We took tents, bed-sacks and provisions. Gourdon, Godfroy, Gain, Besnard and Denais were in the big canoe ; Bongrain, Nozal, Frachat and myself in the picket-boat.

At 10.15 a.m. we reached Cape Tuxen, and while Bongrain was surveying, we raised a cairn to serve as a hydrographic signal. An hour later, we started off for Cape Trois-Perez. The sea was completely free of ice-floes, and had only scattered over it a few icebergs and their remains, which we easily avoided. Between Tuxen and Cape Trois-Perez there juts out an enormous glacier, the biggest I have seen in the Antarctic. It receives numerous tributaries, and at its end is dominated by a sheer granite wall, topped by a layer of snow, which must be nearly 60 metres thick. We are destined to find this imposing and unsurmountable wall everywhere, seeming to forbid any attempt to penetrate into the interior of the mainland. The glacier's face, especially in the centre, is very high and disgorges enormous ice-blocks, which dot the sea.

We coast along Darboux Island, whose vertical cliffs are unfavourable to landing, and after threading masses of icebergs, and cutting through a stretch of new ice, which our picket-boat easily breaks, though its planks are scratched as though by glass, we double Cape Trois-Perez, when a magnificent spectacle is presented to our eyes.

Seen from the north, the Cape is already strange, with its enormous slanting menhir rising up from the principal mass, in front of two other peaks. On the southern side, as is the case with Cape Tuxen, cliffs of more than 500 metres in height rise up precipitously, majestic and sinister; but instead of being, as Tuxen is, tinted green with diorite, they are composed of veins of pink granite, wonderful in colour and arrangement. The picture is at once strange and beautiful. At its very extremity, the Cape forms a little bay open to the south-west, at the end of which is a wall with a jagged top. To the right, a grotto opens out, and a little beach of fine gravel runs down to the sea from a promontory full of little coves. Certainly when we, in the past, gave the name of three brothers whose memory is dear to us, it was to a place worthy of them and of our friendship.

We continue on our way towards the south-east, thus

getting into a large and deep fjord, bounded on one side by the precipitous and rugged mountain which joins on to Cape Trois-Perez, and on the other by the comparatively low range which continues Cape Lahille and beyond which rises a lofty range, evidently separated from the first by another fjord parallel to that in which we are. Cape Lahille itself is on a fairly long island, cut off by a narrow channel which runs into the fjord whose existence we presume.

We are progressing at a speed of about 5 knots ~~an hour~~, and for a long time we have reason to hope that we shall reach a strait or at least that we shall find an opening ; but to my great vexation there is nothing of the kind. Beascocheia Bay ends in a precipice and a big glacier full of ice crystals and crevasses, over which towers that vertical granite wall which turns up everywhere, unsurmountable and covered with a thin crust of ice. This is perhaps the upper plateau of Graham Land, but in any case it is impossible to reach it from this side. The end of the fjord is choked with big icebergs, their remains, new ice, and floes extending 2 or 3 metres beneath the water, which have evidently been detached from the glacier-faces or from the coast. It is very probable that, for some years, this bay has not been unfrozen, and that it is only thanks to the exceptional autumn that we have been able to get into it.

New ice, in this calm spot, forms about us with great rapidity, and by staying here any time with our little boats we should run a serious risk of finding ourselves blocked in. The weather, which was superb up to 1 o'clock, is clouding over, threatening from the direction of the offing snow and fog ; but we keep on all the same, and I make up my mind not to go about until 4 o'clock to return to Cape Trois-Perez. A fine sea-leopard, swimming majestically along, has been following us for a long time at some metres' distance, raising itself out of the water to look into the boat with its big, round, imposing eyes.

On reaching the cape our two boats separate, and while Bongrain, aided by Boland, Nozal, does some surveying, the others assist Gourdon in his geological searches. In the little bay in the cape three Crabbing Seals are moving about in the transparent water around the boat, playing about and snorting, and not even taking fright when we touch them with the oars. In this shut-in place we might believe ourselves in the Zoological Gardens, or in at Hagenbeck's famous Hamburg collection.

It is 8 p.m. when we think of returning. Night has come on quickly and threatens to be black, so that I hesitate for a moment whether to give the order to camp where we are ; but I fear bad weather. Besides, our programme is complete, and I take a little pride in accomplishing this long round in one day, and in overcoming difficulties of navigation by night.

Snow sets in, increasing the darkness, and we can see neither icebergs nor rocks until we are quite close on them. We progress by guesswork, and, although our look-out is very sharp, we get some heavy blows. In spite of the tension of our minds, or because of it, this is an impressive journey amongst the great icebergs which suddenly rise up before us, ice-blocks which we scarcely see in time to escape by a sudden turn of the tiller, and the reef black as night, whose presence we only discover by the noise of the surf. At last, after several detours, we recognize Deliverance Point, where we made so disagreeable a stay some months ago, and following the coast, which we know from this point, we double Cape Tuxen. By way of precaution, I had given orders for the searchlight on board to be started at 10 o'clock, and we now discern its light faintly through the mist. Half an hour before we get back the motor stops in the middle of an accumulation of ice-blocks, an accident having happened to the pump. We do not wait to try and repair this ; the big canoe goes to the front, to the great joy of its frozen crew, and, becoming the tower instead of the towed, brings us back triumphantly to our harbour amidst the jeers of the crew, addressed to Frachat, who is in despair over the breakdown of his beloved boat. He can console himself, however, for we have done 50 miles this day, often breaking through obstacles, and once again motor and hull alike have given the utmost satisfaction. The misfortune, as usual, comes about through the carelessness of the firm to which was entrusted the work of putting the boat together.

During our absence an iceberg, breaking up or turning over, had roused a great wave which lifted the ship up, gave a violent tug to the port chain, and precipitated into the cove the apparently solid rock to which it was laced. The chain, however, remains fastened round the rock, and I secure it there still more strongly by gripes. We are still firmly moored, but we shall perhaps have some difficulty in getting back our chain when we want to leave, even if we do not find it necessary to sacrifice one end of it.

March 9.—Gourdon, Gain, Godfroy and Senouque started out yesterday for the glacier in front of our anchorage. In spite of the great desire I had to accompany them and my love of climbing, I thought it better to leave them to go this excursion without me. I wish to encourage the utmost initiative in every one, to direct operations, as it were, from the rear, and above all, to show that I do not try to monopolize things. I believe, in this way, that the ultimate results will be the greater. I am convinced that all are animated by the best of spirits ; but the French character is such that the interest in the common cause gives place very quickly to the desire to act more on one's own behalf, and the leader who has in view only the object for which he sets out must, I believe, rule in accordance with the natures of those who are under him.

My colleagues came back the same night very delighted, having made a quick and easy ascent, but a very interesting one, which holds out some hope of a path leading inland. They had no difficulty in climbing the glacier, which comes down to the water-level in a small point. They were also able to hoist the Norwegian boat on to the ice, thus leaving it in safety until their return.

This night, at 4 a.m., we felt on board a violent shock, and the ship pitched and tossed for some minutes in an alarming way. This phenomenon, which repeats itself fairly frequently more or less strongly, is evidently due to the breaking up or capsizing of icebergs. To-day particularly, a very big one, stationed at the entry of the cove, has suddenly changed its shape. It is probable that icebergs, driven by the strong current from south to north, get stranded in the shallows which obstruct the entry to the little bay, and that the accident happens when, as the sea goes down, they touch bottom or lose their equilibrium. Whatever it may be, this is a source of real danger to the ship, for it is with difficulty that we keep her away from the rock to port, and the hull, in spite of its strength, runs the risk of serious harm from these shocks if they are frequently repeated ; also our cables might all break at once with a sudden strain, and the ship would then ground violently ahead. Two hawsers have broken to-night, and I am beginning to be really anxious. If this frightful weather continues long and we are not soon firmly frozen in, we shall never have enough hawsers to last out to the end. The number of ice-blocks and icebergs which are moving about in the channel is really extraordinary, and is certainly largely due to the exceptional weather this autumn. The loss caused to the glaciers by the heat is very great, and the production of ice-blocks is constant. Also (as we can readily show by comparison with the same season of 1904 in these regions) some usually frozen-up bays are now unlocked, setting at liberty not only the big ice-floes which cover them, but also the shore ice and the enormous masses from the glaciers which up to now they have held prisoners. Every moment huge fragments charge our boom, which I am in constant fear of seeing give way. Certainly even in this nook, where it seems as if

Our Quarters, Spring, 1909.

we must be so well sheltered, our safety is only comparative.

March 10.—The same party as the other day has set out for the glacier, approaching it from the other side. The face of this glacier, which is close to Petermann Island, almost opposite our anchorage, extends from Duseberg Rock to Cape Rasmussen, but it is cut in two by Mount Rude, of which Middle Mountain is a prolongation. The whole of the central portion of these two glaciers is composed of a magnificent, crevassed chaos, absolutely unapproachable, and it is only on the sides of the rocky masses which bound them that the ice is passable, being comparatively smooth and seamed by few crevasses, easy to get round or cross. The last time my colleagues landed near Duseberg Rock, which enabled them to explore east and north-east. This time they land at Cape Rasmussen to turn their attention to the south-east. I accompanied them off at 4 a.m., accompanied by Liouville in the big canoe, manned by Denais, Boland, Nozal and Hervé. An hour and a half after, making our way through a great quantity of broken-up ice, we reach Rasmussen and land without difficulty on a rocky point, on which the glacier rests. The place is very picturesque, for the cape is formed of a great cliff of black rock, split in two by a large rift, which makes a cove. Although the party is to return the same evening, in consequence of the distance we are from the boat, I have insisted on their leaving a camp and provisions on the cape, and while our men are putting the material on shore, I go a short way with the others on to the glacier. The ground is excellent, being formed of hard ice, on which one can walk without fatigue, covered by a layer of snow just sufficient to prevent slipping. The weather is superb and very mild ; indeed, mildness is the characteristic of this morning. The sun, scarcely up yet, tints with a pale pink, alternating with the bright or faint blue of the portions which are in the shade, the tremendous and indescribable chaos of the glacier which we are crossing, thus for an instant softening away the habitually sinister appearance of this piece of savage nature. After having agreed on a signal for the recall of the boat, Liouville and I return on board with regrets.

I get back just in time to inflict a vigorous whipping on Polaire. We are trying, with great difficulty, to teach this dog not to pursue and frighten the penguins. The latter defend themselves very well when she attacks them in front ; but whenever she can, and we are not there, she attacks them in the rear. To-day she set upon some megalestrides, and one of them is dragging itself along miserably over the island wounded. Evil befel Polaire, however, for another of these courageous birds, coming to the help of its comrade, gave her a sharp blow with its beak, and I for my part gave her a lesson which she will remember. We are obliged to kill for our collection, as also for our food ; but I do not allow useless cruelty, either on the part of the men or of the animals.

At 7.30 I go back to look for my colleagues at Rasmussen. They have walked for 13 hours, climbing to a height of 1,000 metres, and thus penetrating behind the big glacier situated between Tuxen and Cape Trois-Perez. The weather remaining very fine until this evening, when snow is beginning to fall again, has given them a chance of enjoying a magnificent view and of bringing back some interesting details about the neighbourhood. But there is scarcely any chance, they say, of penetrating into the interior on this side. I regret it, for Cape Rasmussen, although very far from our ship, offers a good basis for operations. The lie of the rocks not only gives an opportunity for the establishment of a camp (for one must always look out for sudden and prolonged interruptions of communications), but also provides a permanent place of disembarkation, whereas the other glacier, having no foundation supporting its end, might at any moment present an insurmountable wall to us.

Navigation amongst the ice has very much cut up the planks of the picket-boat and the big canoe. To avoid this dangerous wear and tear in future, I have nailed to the waterline of these two boats a sheathing made of the metal of old flour-tins.

March 15.—For the last few days the weather has been bad, sometimes horrible, the wind blowing from the east and east-north-east, accompanied by snowfalls and drifts of great persistence ; still there have been a few jumps to the west and the south-west, setting up in our cove an even stronger swell, and giving us fresh trouble with our cables. An anemometer placed on the summit of the island has been broken by the wind, and the cook, whose duty it is every day to go and verify the number of turns, has come back with the instrument in a sad state. Fortunately our engineers are clever, and under the guidance of Rosselin they have quickly repaired it and even made a spare one. The gangway, also, has almost been smashed against the rocks which support it, during the movements of the ship, which from time to time have gone near to causing serious damage on board. Chollet, with great ingenuity, has installed a stronger tackle purchase, which allows the gangway to be raised and lowered like a drawbridge. At the end we have put a rope ladder, and when the swell is on going ashore and coming on board necessitate an amusing little gymnastic feat.

A fairly large ice-block has succeeded in passing the boom, and has just come astern of us ; but I have had it pushed off at once to one side by aid of the picket-boat, and moored in such a way that it cannot do us any damage.

March 19.—Gourdon, Godfroy, Gain and Senouque have visited and returned from the glacier, where they have planted a line of stakes, which serve to measure the distance covered. With an additional crew of four men I accompanied them on the morning of the 17th to land their stores and run up the tent. At 9 o'clock we had soon hoisted the heavy sledge, and the camp was installed in a hollow formed by the eddying wind at the foot of a rocky crest which we call the Edge. It is from the summit of this crest that Godfroy will verify the alignment of the stakes and take their bearings.

From this altitude the view is magnificent over the Biscoe Islands, and stretches well beyond Victor Hugo Island. The sea is absolutely free; perhaps I should say desperately free, for we are all urgently praying for cold and good solid ice. About the same time four years ago we were frozen in at Wandel.

At the side of the glacier there are some large tracts, almost level, sprinkled with very few crevasses, and some seductive valleys seem to invite us to push forward into the interior of the land. Two of them have been explored, but offer no way through ; I hope that the third will not similarly disappoint us.

We lunched gaily altogether ; then I and my crew descended, leaving the others to their work. I was able to follow their movements from on board with the refracting telescope, and in the absence of marine ice to block them in there is no reason to fear about their return.

The next day was also fine and favourable to their work, but yesterday the north-easterly started to blow again with snow and sleet, and I saw the party from the glacier come down, leaving the camp, as we agreed should be done in case of bad weather. I went to meet them in a boat, and I had the satisfaction of learning that all appreciated the stores for the trip which I had so carefully prepared before they started. They even told me that they had no criticisms to offer. The contents of the excursion boxes in particular were a great success, the soup which formed part of them being really excellent ; and yet the weight was no greater than that of the rations carried by other expeditions. But as Gourdon had completely forgotten to take the petroleum they had to be content with an improvised alcohol lamp, and they cannot tell me if the little modifications which I made in the Nansen kitchens were successful.

Crossing a Bridge of Ice.

This afternoon a seal played a joke upon us. One of my colleagues came to tell me that a Crabbing Seal, stranded on the beach, was in death agonies. It might have been of the greatest interest to the naturalists to examine one of these animals dying a natural death ; and in order that the sea might not carry it away, we hosted it carefully on to the snow. The seal calmly allowed us to do this, and then, when we thought it safely fixed up, it slipped rapidly and with the greatest assurance between our legs and returned to the water, where it indulged in joyful frolics, which proved at once its good health and good temper.

Mid-Lent, postponed for a day to allow the trippers to take part in it, has been spent joyfully with the help of a wonderful preserved goose, which my devoted friend, Ch. Rabot, had given me for Christmas. In the jumble of our store-room, it was in vain that we looked for it at Christmas ; but the faithful Jabet during the last re-arrangement brought it to us triumphantly a few days ago, and we are glad now that we were obliged to keep it until this date.

A big hole has been dug in the ice, some sets of shelves have been erected in it, two of the dories have been placed over them as a roof, and in this way, in scarcely 2 hours' time, we have an excellent pantry, in which we put our stock of penguin and seal meat.

March 24.—We are again in the midst of a tempest. The temperature, which during the few fine days (if one can call by this name such grey and gloomy weather) had gone down to — 1° or —2°, rises to + 5°, and the horrible thaw commences again. Alternating with snow and sleet, rain falls abundantly, just as it does at Brest and Cherbourg, which seems ridiculous in these regions. I always find that one of the greatest comforts of this part of the world is precisely the absence of rain and the confidence with which one can go out without one's umbrella ! Now it is absolutely necessary for those of us who possess such things to show our respect for local colour and refrain from opening them, a proceeding which would entail the risk of seeing them carried away by the wind.

The swell is making itself more and more strongly felt. We are having perpetual trouble with our cables, especially through the fragments of ice. The east-north-east wind sends the latter towards the southern point of the entrance to our cove, and as soon as there is a calm the heavy swell drives them inward. A very large piece has balanced itself on the boom and finishes by breaking it, thus giving free entry to the others. We cannot dream of repairing the boom in this weather and shutting in the enemy with us, so we have to be content with clapping hawsers on the ice-blocks, either by taking advantage of their irregularities or by means of ice-anchors, and with removing them from the ship. But we are at the mercy of a break in one of the hawsers, and I pass anxious nights listening to the dull crashes to be heard alongside the ship. For a whole morning, amid snow and wind, we had to wrestle with an ice-block as big as the ship itself, which threatened to strike our stern, and would have smashed it up completely in a few seconds. We divided into two groups, one lot pushing the ice-block away, the other swinging on with the tackle, while the picket-boat strove to turn it aside. We only succeeded in removing it a bare metre away, and since then it has been hanging over our stern like the sword of Damocles.

The poor old cat which we took on board at Buenos Aires, and which presented us with six kittens, is dead. She was an affectionate creature, very touching in her maternal love.

March 25.—Yesterday evening, about 7 o'clock, the wind fell and immediately the barometer started to rise, tracing an almost perpendicular line. After a heavy snow-drift, mixed with rain, the wind started again from the west, blowing in great gusts.

The ship and the ice-block have exchanged some heavy blows, then suddenly the latter has capsized, by a miracle causing us no injury. The weather is grey this morning, but calm, and I have decided to clear our harbour of our terrible neighbours. We vainly try to blow up the biggest with a charge of gun-cotton. It capsizes again, all but sending into the water Bongrain and Lerebourg ; and at this moment our attention is called elsewhere. The news is brought to me, indeed, that the absolutely indispensable starboard chain threatens to come off the huge rock around which it is laced. The smooth walls of this somewhat conical rock offer no projections to stop slipping, and the very weight of the chain, on which I counted, is insufficient to withstand the abrupt pulls upon it.

With sledgehammers, chisels and pickaxes, and all the tools we can find, the men take it in turns for hours making notches in the hard granite. They succeed after a fashion, and finally fix some iron stakes in the clefts ; and the chain is now kept firmly in its place with strong tackle added as an additional security. We shall examine it every day.

March 27.—We have visited the glacier again. What I expected has unfortunately happened. At the spot where we usually landed a fall has left a vertical wall, impossible to climb, and we must look for another point more to the south. But this new way is difficult ; we have to cut steps and walk roped together along narrow tracks between deep crevasses, where a slip would be fatal. Nevertheless, it is by this route that we bring down the sledge and the greater part of the stores, leaving for future trips the tent, some bed-sacks, and provisions on the top of the glacier. This task recalls to me the time when in the Alps I enthusiastically aided the artillery-men to bring down their mountain guns, which went a long way to give me a taste for such adventures.

The difficulty in reaching the glacier leaves me somewhat anxious. The least landslip at any moment may cut off the road ; and, apart from the danger there would be for a party isolated from the ship, without the slightest chance of getting provisions except those they had taken with them, we might be totally prevented from continuing our excursions into the interior.

March 30.—The ice-blocks which were unwilling to leave our harbour have finished by wearing through two of our hawsers, which we had to fasten together as well as possible this morning. We absolutely must get rid of them at all costs. It is calm, and the usual current running north is very strong ; but at the point of our cove there is a back-wash to be dealt with. Also, the icebergs' draught of water obliges us to steer them round the shallows at the entrance. Hawsers are clapped round the masses of ice, and part of the crew hauls on to these on shore. Others in the big canoe try to tow them, while the picket-boat tows and pushes alternately. A Crabbing Seal in the water looks on at our work with a mocking air. I throw a snowball full in its face, and with an air of offended dignity it snorts its thorough disapproval of the liberty that I have dared to take. Finally, after more than 7 hours' work, we have succeeded in clearing our harbour. With six bights of iron-wire hawser we re-establish a boom, which we have every reason to believe firm.

Liouville has been out in the Norwegian boat, but the bad weather has forced him to abandon it on an islet, and we seek in vain to find it.

April 1.—

> " Avril vient de naitre
> Et par la fenêtre,
> Le soleil joyeux
> Nous fait les doux yeux."

This refrain, gaily chanted by a man on deck woke me up this morning ; and, as a matter of fact, yesterday's bad weather has given place to calm, and a ray of sunlight brightens up my scuttle. But in the afternoon the sky clouds over and it snows abundantly, with a feeble breeze from the south-east. However, the thermometer is below zero and the island is at

A Difficult Descent

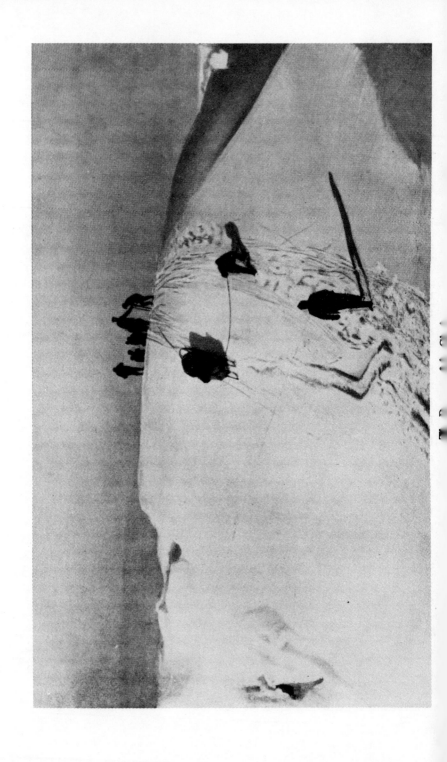

last covered with a fine, clean, white sheet, which pleases me very much.

April 9.—The commencement of the month is calm, with occasional clear-ups. Bongrain has been able to spend a day on the Argentine Islands surveying, and he has come back with 150 penguins, whose flesh garnishes the shelves of our meat department. In the course of this trip, Frachat and Boland were poisoned under the tent covering the picket-boat by carbonic oxide, the blast pipe having been badly fitted. Fortunately it is easy to put this to rights, while suitable treatment soon set the two victims on their feet again.

Thanks to a temperature of − 6°, some new ice is forming round the ship, and the slopes of the island are becoming very favourable for tobogganing. We give ourselves up to this sport furiously, and the toboggans which I had brought from Norway go up and down incessantly. The inequalities of the ground and the rapid slope cause a few accidents, but none are serious. Gain has a contusion of the leg, Gourdon skins his nose, and I myself · sprain my two heels fairly badly, which keeps me on my back for several days. This stupid accident prevents me from re-visiting the glacier. As for Godfroy, he gets a blister which stops him from wearing heavy boots. So our colleagues, to make up the party, take with them the cook, Modaine, who has been suffering from nerves for some time and will be benefited by this climb. In his absence Chollet, Jabet and J. Guéguen take charge of the cook's galley, putting on the symbolical apron, and like all good sailors they acquit themselves admirably. They start their important duties with a master-stroke, serving up a formidable pie of seal and penguin, seasoned with blubber, the composition of which, it seems, they have been thinking of for several weeks.

The excursionists come back the next day but one. They were stopped on their way by thick snow, into which they sank half way up the thigh, and they have not been able to discover whether the neck on which we build our hopes terminates in a practicable glacier or not. The bringing down of the stores was very difficult. While Godfroy, with a reinforcement of four men to aid them, climbed on to the glacier, I, incapacitated by my sprains, steer the picket-boat away from the glacier-face, which is perpetually crumbling, and a short time before, during a land slide, very nearly crushed our boats or at least swamped them in the huge waves which were stirred up. After having crossed crevasses and bridges of ice, our men succeed in letting down the sledge gradually on the end of a grapnel rope, and fortunately all goes off without an accident.

The navigation of the channel is now rather difficult, for it is choked with ice soldered together, with icebergs and their débris. Nevertheless, by making from pool to pool through winding ways, I succeed in getting on board, but it is clear that we must not count too much on navigating this autumn. Our island is gradually being deserted by its birds. All have already left their nests and many have gone away. The penguins come and go in groups, almost all the young ones being able now to go into the sea, and rest on the island after their fishing. The Giant Petrels and the Megalestrides are still here in fairly big numbers, attracted by the bodies of the seals, and so are some Sheath-bills. The pretty little Snowy Petrels (*Pagodroma Nivea*), arrived in bands at the same time as the ice coming from the south.

The men are building some snow-houses very skilfully. The veterans of the *Français* are teaching the new-comers to cut out with narrow spades big rectangular blocks of ice and to pile them up in domes. One of these houses has to serve as a supplementary larder, and when it is finished, its summit is adorned with a flag. On the other the flag is replaced by a small broom sufficiently indicating its purpose.

April 11, *Easter Sunday.*—I bring out of the reserve store of parcels which are only to be opened on fête-days a magnificent cardboard egg, which bears the label of a Guernsey firm, and makes me think of the frightful tempest which, just after we had left Cherbourg, forced us after two days of struggle to put into the pretty and hospitable little harbour of St. Pierre. In France the *Pourquoi-Pas?* had been given up as lost, as so many other ships were during this gale, but almost at the very start-off our stout ship showed herself capable of facing the worst of seas.

The barometer has started to go down again, the thermometer has risen to $+6°$, and the north-easter is blowing.

April 13.—The wind veers abruptly to the south-west, bringing down the temperature to $-7°$. Up to the present we have agreed, in order to save our coal for the summer campaign, to have no fires. So we have never had in the wardroom more than $6°$, and sometimes only $2°$ or even $1°$. In my cabin, I have even had a few degrees below zero. But it is rather the dreadful dampness of which we complain. We are almost all of us suffering abominably from chilblains, which poison our existence. I have never before been attacked by this malady, but I now understand the tears which they used to cause my little comrades at school. I had decided to light the stove to-day, and as I was slow in fulfilling my promise, Gain, in imitation of the old farce, surreptitiously put a candle inside, which gave a bright light through the sheet of mica covering the opening. Several of us on coming into the ward-room rubbed our hands, rejoicing over the pleasant warmth, and one even went so far as to complain that it was excessive!

At last we actually light the stove, and this important step makes me uneasy, for I am as much afraid of excessive consumption of fuel as of insufficient warmth. Happily my fears are not justified. The kind of stove we have does its work admirably, and with less than 20 kilogrammes of coal in the 24 hours it burns night and day while the arrangement of the rooms allows for an even temperature of $12°$ and $13°$ being kept up in all of them. Only in my cabin, further removed from the ward-room I have in great frosts a rather low temperature. What a difference now and on board the *Français*, where a wretched kind of stove, bought like all else at the lowest price, gave us so much trouble, sometimes getting red-hot with an unbearable temperature of $+25°$, sometimes smoking so badly that the sky-light had to be opened, which brought the thermometer down to $-10°$, if its absolute refusal to burn did not produce the same horrible result.

On the mess deck, a stove of the same kind as our own burns just as well as ours, and I feel reassured for the winter.

In the interests of health, it is decided that henceforward for a quarter of an hour every morning, a strong current of fresh air shall be let into the ward-room.

April 21.—The temperature remains low. The thermometer has even gone down to $-17°$, and the crew are already talking of the $50°$ below zero which they hope to have in order to be able to tell their friends in France about it later. However this may be, the dry cold weather is more agreeable and bearable than what we have been suffering from previously. Since we have had fires, whether it is from the absence of humidity, the warmth, or some other reason, we are suffering no more from chilblains, except one of us whose complaint is stubborn. This is a real consolation.

On the 14th, ' pancake ' ice formed round the ship. This name is applied to round slabs of ice with their edges slightly turned up by the action of the gentle swell. But soon the slabs are soldered together, and a few falls of snow gives them an uniform aspect. Godfroy has been able with care to reach over this ice his tide-gauge, which is set up against the rock at some distance from the ship.

A sea-leopard succeeds easily in breaking through the ice with its head, and looks at us curiously through the hole which it has made. This is the usual practice with seals for breathing when the sea is covered with pack-ice.

The channel is completely filled with stationary ice, which seems soldered together and stretches out of sight to the south. In the offing the sea is frozen over a fairly large expanse, and I seem to see on the horizon also some pack-ice. Nevertheless, in the passage which we took this summer on our way out between Petermann and the Argentine Islands there is still a large oblique rift, which stretches from the open sea to Tuxen.

The fairly abundant snow-falls make necessary a good deal of sweeping. The disembarkation of our stores was carried out in a full thaw, and to find again now what we want, which is being buried deeper and deeper under a thick, unmelting covering, we have to institute regular searches. The boats which are pulled up on shore need special care ; we have to prevent them from being covered up by snow, which, as it hardens, would encase them in regular blocks of ice, where they would stand the risk of being crushed, and from which we could not take them out without serious injury. To keep them safe, we dig round them deep trenches, which will at least stop the snow-drift. The picket-boat, which has become useless, is resting for the winter. Its motor has been taken out, and it is hoisted up under the bowsprit.

Toboggans and skis are our great distraction. Everybody is now more or less able to keep up on these latter, and some have even become very skilful. We have made a track to practise ourselves in jumping.

I heard that the 15th was Libois's birthday. Like Chollet, Jabet and J. Guéguen, he has been in my service for long years, all four having accompanied me to the Jan Mayen Land on my last expedition. He is a good fireman, carpenter and handy man, and a hard worker, eager to please one, never finding anything impossible, and gifted with an excellent disposition, which gives him a very good influence over his comrades. So I take the opportunity of celebrating the half century which he has attained.

The barometer went down on the 18th, to 718, and the thermometer rose to —1° 3 ; but the north-easter only blew for a very little, and the wind has come round to the south-west, blowing fairly strongly, with a temperature of — 13°.

April 26.—I have been to the summit of the island to observe the state of the ice. This climb, which is always monotonous, was made irksome and tiring by the crumbling snow, into which I sank half-way up my legs. From my observatory I see the pack-ice stretching very far over the high sea, almost up to the horizon, except to the north, where it is still free. On the channel side there is an accumulation of pack-ice, composed of new ice, bergs and big, thick floes, probably coming from the end of the bay ; but, on the other hand, big stretches of water separate the masses, and half Girard Bay, as well as the part of Lemaire Channel between Wandel and the coast, are completely free.

It will be some time before all is sufficiently firm to allow us to venture on this ice, but I do not wish to be found unprovided and I have made ready for trial a dory mounted on one of our sledges. These flat-bottomed boats, which are used by the Newfoundlanders, seem to me very practical for Polar expeditions. They can hold a lot of stores, carry a large number of men, and are yet so light that two of us were easily able to push one on the sledge over the ice. We also possess, besides two Berthons, a little Williamson boat of canvas with a flat bottom ; this excellent vessel, placed on a small sledge, might also be very useful for short excursions.

The ship's rat, the only one since his companion committed suicide by falling through one of the scuppers, after having given no signs of life for two months has again given proof of his existence by eating two birds prepared by Gain. It is sad that he is spoiling our collections thus, for the cats seem to trouble very little about him, and we too could easily have put up with him. I had even a scheme for taming him. How

Hauling the Norwegian Boat over the Glacier.

The Argentine Islands.

this poor solitary rat must be bored, and how much he must regret his choice of a ship!

On the 25th, about 1 a.m., we saw a Southern Aurora, so faint that several denied its existence. That it was there, however, was proved by Senouque's magnetometers, which registered a strong disturbance.

April 30.—On the 27th, the barometer dropped almost vertically to 720, but in spite of my fears of a gale this fall was only followed by overcast and foggy weather, a calm, a little snow, and a brief rise in the temperature. But there must have been bad weather some way off, for we hear the noise of the sea and the swell makes itself felt fairly strongly, in spite of the fortunate resistance of the ice.

We can venture out a little on the ice of our harbour, and Gourdon has begun to cut pieces out of it to measure its thickness and study it. Gain has been fishing for *plankton* at the entrance of the channel.

The ward-room skylight is covered with flowers, frost-flowers on the outside, and inside some superb hyacinths, which Gain and Gourdon are growing with the greatest care. There is even a regular horticultural battle on between them, and if Gourdon, who has some very fine blooms, is amused at seeing Gain's onions running to leaf, Gain on his side, proud of his cress, which takes very kindly to Antarctic soil, never ceases to sneer at his colleague's useless crops.

May 1.—Since yesterday the wind has been blowing again in a tempest from the east-north-east. The ice in the channel is entirely broken up and afloat with the wind. In our cove, great cracks have opened and the separate slabs thus produced, wearing themselves away against each other, crash against our hull more and more heavily as they get freer play.

There have been several hours of calm, during which the continual whistling of the wind among the masts and the sound of the rattling ropes and the flapping canvas of the awnings are followed by a great dull rumbling, which can be heard in the far distance, grand and awe-inspiring. The causes are the breaking of the sea against the shores and the icebergs and the movements of the ice. After this temporary pause the wind has sprung up more strongly than ever.

May 20.—For twenty-one days the tempest has continued without respite. We live amid snow, mist, and blinding drift. It is almost a torture to go out during the few hours of daylight, if one must give this name to the gloomy and foggy atmosphere which envelopes us.

The registering anemometer in the meteorological hut has been broken, but fortunately the engine-room men have succeeded in constructing another with a stronger axis.

Some of the men on May 4 remembered that it was St. Monica's Day, my little daughter's birthday, and J. Guéguen brings me what he calls ' a little boat in a little bottle for little Monica.' The men take great pleasure in constructing model boats of various sizes, but the present fashion is for boats inside bottles. Chollet is the great artist, and he gave us the other day a demonstration of the clever manner in which, in a very short time, he gets through the narrow neck of the bottle the compressed hull and rigging of the ship, and then with the aid of a little hook spreads it all out. To puzzle him, we gave him a small flask, but on the next day he gave it back to us with a full-rigged ship inside it. Liouville then gave him a tiny medicine-bottle, and Collet gravely, but triumphantly, brought it back containing a whaler manned by four oars.

On St. Monica's Day we dined with flowers on the table, real flowers coming from Gourdon's nursery, while a magnificent cake, a present from the cook, was put on at dessert.

The ice in our cove, broken up into small fragments, has been for a long time only kept in place by the hawsers, and at last all has got free and once more the ship is surrounded by open water. It requires both our absorption in work and our firmness of will not to let ourselves be downcast and thoroughly demoralized by these untoward changes of climate.

Day by day our observations continue their normal course. The whole staff works with its usual enthusiasm, without relaxing for a moment, happy at being able to collect interesting specimens or facts or to suggest alterations likely to be of service on board. Being convinced that with serious workers, who have made up their minds from the start to do their duty thoroughly, the maximum of results will be attained by such a method and such a display of confidence, I leave to each one the direction of, and absolute responsibility for, his work, restricting myself to asking for a monthly report ; and I do my very best to make easy every one's labour, and to assure to all the utmost possible comfort.

I must say (and I do so with a certain pride, since it is mainly due to the organization of the Expedition) that this comfort is real, and that it is already giving the results which I had a right to expect. Few expeditions, I think, have been so well apportioned from the point of view of scientific work. Every member of the staff has his own private cabin, where he can shut himself up and work. The biological and physical science laboratories, although small, are separate and comfortable ; the photographic laboratory is huge and well fitted. A nice warmth prevails all over the ship, and we are lighted everywhere by electricity, a luxury beyond value. Food is abundant, and one can have as much water as one wants to wash in, which is rare on Polar expeditions. We really lack for nothing, in some cases we have more than we want. The crew is sufficiently large to relieve us for most of the time of all fatiguing labour, and every worker has all the assistance he requires. Under the able direction of Rosselin, the engine-room men labour incessantly, not only at the ship's duties but also to repair, improve and construct scientific instruments and to increase the well-being of all. Poste, Monzimat, and Frachat are in particular very clever workmen. Libois is the excellent carpenter of whom I have already spoken, and the whole crew, with Chollet, Jabet and Besnard at their head, show the skill and ingenuity of sailors, animated by the best intentions, and do the greatest services to the common weal, making our task very much easier. Nozal and Boland, our young cadets from the Merchant Marine, are clever, hard-working and amiable, and assist in the labours of Bongrain and Rouch, to whom they are specially attached. Already the advantages of our comfort and organization make themselves felt, for, as the observations are taken, many of their results are immediately made clear and tabulated. In this way Bongrain has already been able to present us with a very satisfactory map of the discoveries of our summer campaign. I have every right to expect that, as soon as we get back to civilization, we shall be able to send to the Académie des Sciences a graphic sketch of our achievements. In our winter quarters we are like a set of working monks, who enjoy all the comparative well-being that can be expected in such isolation. I must, however, add that if this comfort is much to be appreciated with a view to the principal end of our mission, it has also its drawbacks. Naturally, those who have not taken part in any expedition, or who have not sailed except in the luxury of big ships, become exacting. For instance, if the electric light is temporarily stopped by a small mishap, even though it be replaced by a petroleum-lamp in each cabin, one sees long faces. If a dish be too salt or not salt enough, it is rejected with disgust; and so on through a whole series of things. Of course, this is very excusable. It is the case with all people, whose necessities increase with their good fortune. But I am convinced that those who complain the most would be the first to give a good example in case of accident. On board the little *Français*, where we had to set our hands to everything, to help the crew and protect the lives of the community, where we worked all crowded into a common saloon, where we had to economize food, clothing and light, while suffering from the cold, every small luxury and every slight improvement, for the most part introduced by our own ingenuity, was welcomed with the greatest joy. We should have considered then as an impossible dream the solid comfort which we have enjoyed during the second Expedition, which we owe to the experience we acquired and to the funds which I had at my disposal.

Since May 1, the winter programme has been organized. The rules of health, the same which were in force on board the *Français*, where they gave such good results, have been applied on the mess deck, and everything goes as well as possible. Open air exercise is one of the necessities to which I attach the most importance, and the men do not need much driving to this. In the morning, there is the task of getting the ice for the manufacture of fresh water, which necessitates a fairly long trip, followed by some active toil in cutting, gathering, and bringing back on the sledges, the blocks of fine clear ice. The diatoms which stain the snow, and still more the contamination of the latter by the detritus from the penguin rookeries, do not allow us to get our water in the neighbourhood of the ship. Sometimes the work is much simplified by the presence of a fine ice-block in the entry to our harbour, and we are pleased to be able then to take advantage of the delicious water which we get from it. Once the ice is on board, it is heaped up on deck, and thrown as we require it into a big butt holding 250 litres, which I have had placed for this purpose on the roof over the furnace of the cook's galley. Thus we have, with no additional combustion of fuel, abundant water, and there is no need to melt in small quantities, in buckets over stoves, the ice necessary for our drinking water, which was one of the long and tedious duties of our preceding expedition.

After this the crew devote themselves to various routine works, either on board or in our erections on shore. The snow has to be swept away from over our observatory, stores and boats. Meat has to be fetched from the larder, and sometimes the bodies of seals have to be brought from a considerable distance and cut up. The pumps have to be attended to, for we are still letting in water. The sledges have to be put together, which we brought with us in pieces to prevent their taking too much room. And there are a thousand other little jobs arising out of the needs of the moment, etc. After lunch the great joy is to have an hour or two ski-ing, and the whole station rings with merry cries and laughter over the falls and failures. Seeing these good spirits, I certainly do not regret having brought a plentiful stock of skis, which allows me to give each man a pair for himself and to replace from time to time those which have been broken. Work begins again immediately, and the days are thus well spent. An important part of our daily duty is concerned with keeping everything clean, and I spend much time in grumbling about this. I should like to see the boat as neat as a yacht. I recognize that this is rather difficult with the numerous different works in which all are engaged and amid the conditions in which we live. But recently I was reading in one of the books of Admiral Jurien de la Gravière, the following passage, which I marked for use :—' For my part I have always had a horror of a badly washed deck. In the midst of litter lying about, sang-froid is apt to evaporate. Before Sebastopol, General Pelissier was able to make cleanliness into a force and a virtue.'

Since the commencement of the month, we have organized optional classes for the crew after dinner, and the tasks set to the men attending them occupy the hours when they cannot work out of doors. Gourdon, Gain, Godfroy and myself are the teachers of arithmetic, grammar, geography, navigation and English, and once a week Liouville gives a lecture, which is closely followed and much appreciated, on the dressing of wounds and first-aid.

Saturday is given up to the washing of our linen. A great quantity of ice is brought on board the evening before, and during the night is melted in the washing-machines, the water being heated by burning seal's fat. The difficulty is to dry the linen, which when hung in the open has a disastrous habit of freezing and becoming as hard as a board. We succeed, however, by exposing it in small lots to the heat of the stove. In the ward-room, each one of us has a man who washes his linen once a week.

Sunday is a day of rest. The flag is hoisted at the end of the gaff, and if weather permits the day is spent in ski-ing, or in excursions over the island. If it is too unpleasant to go out we stay on board reading or having 'music,' when frightful things happen! My cabin is so placed that I am between the mess deck, the junior ward-room and our own ward-room. So it frequently happens that one gramaphone is going on the mess deck and another in the ward-room, and the Chief Engineer is playing his mandoline desperately and dispiritingly, accompanying himself, it may be, to the song, ' O Paquita, how I love thee ! ' Speaking for myself, I should say : ' How I have learnt to detest thee ! '

Whenever the opportunity offers in the course of a week, the flag is hoisted and the day is declared a fête-day. The work goes on as usual, but the menu is augmented. Thus, on the 10th, we celebrated Gourdon's birthday, which allowed me, in drinking his health, to assure him once more of my affection and tell how much I thought of this faithful comrade, so even in temper, so amiable, and so ready for everything, a perfect type of explorer, with his quiet and gentle manner hiding a rare energy and a strong will.

Finally I founded the Antarctic Sporting Club, and the first meeting, for which the crew prepared a long time in advance, took place with great success on the 9th. After the pistol-shooting, which members of the staff practise every Sunday, the crew assembled on the snow to the sound of the fog-horn. The course was marked out with ski-staffs decorated with gaily coloured flags, the gramaphone was playing its best pieces, and when the thirty members of the Expedition were assembled, it had all the air of a merry village fête. The programme included for the ski-ers a flat race, a race down the big slope, a test of graceful carriage ; and finally a fairly long race in which one might go as one pleased. This last race was much the most popular and the most interesting, for the course went up a pretty stiff ascent, over a fairly long flat surface, and finally down a rapid descent. Some were warm partisans of the ski, others of snow-shoes, while some claimed that good boots were the best of all. The skis had a big triumph, and the winners, who all used them, came in in the following order :—J. Guéguen, 1 ; Thomas, 2 ; and Frachat, 3. In the evening I distributed the gold and silver medals, cut out of preserved food boxes, and the cardboard medal. Lastly, on the unanimous recommendation of the jury, the consolation prize, consisting of two brooms crossed, was awarded to Modaine, who took part in all the races and was always amongst the three last. Every fortnight the Antarctic Sporting Club is to have a similar meeting.

In the ward-room, apart from the work which takes up the greater part of our time, every one finds some occupation to his taste. Cards happily are never seen, the games in favour being dominoes or chess, and we are perhaps the only civilized community which does not play bridge. Rouch striving hard to win a bet, provides us with an unexpected and much appreciated distraction by reading to us every evening a few chapters of a great serial novel which he finds the means of writing daily, entitled, ' *The Typist's Lover* ' !

On the 16th, the barometer goes down to 713 mm. The thermometer, for its part, has constantly wavered between $+ 2°$ and $- 14°$; for the last few days, however, it has stopped at about $- 10°$, and the ice is forming again around

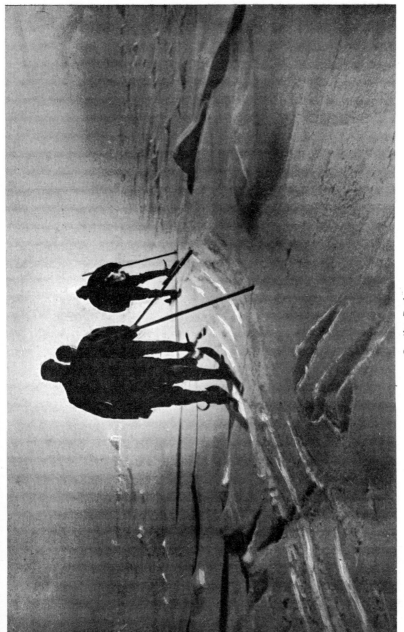

On the Pack.

us. The channel is blocked, but the sea, on the other hand, is still free to the west and the north and in consequence we are at the mercy of the swell. I am always looking at the map of our discoveries this summer, and I never cease deploring that we could not winter further south. Queen Mary of England, when she lost Calais, said that after her death the name of that town would be found written on her heart. I believe that there will be found written on mine the name of Marguerite Bay, which cannot but be flattering to my wife. Still what is the good of regretting the impossible? This frightful weather must be raging there as well, and if we had stayed on, exposed with no anchorage to the moving ice, our boat would long ago have ceased to exist.

May 23.—This is our first fine day since April 27. The thermometer, 5° below zero in the morning, goes down to 12° below at night. The weather is very clear, and the sun, during the very brief time that we can see him between Hovgard and the summit of our island, appears low on the horizon with a very sharply defined disc. We had come to believe that he had vanished for ever. For a few moments he gilds the mountain tops, which soon turn to a fine bright red. Joy beyond measure, it is absolutely calm!

The Antarctic Sporting Club has had its second meeting, with the same success as before.

May 24.—It is still fine! To-night at 12.30, the ship gave a great leap. She had been lifted up by a great rolling wave, which was heralded by a dull and awe-inspiring sound, caused by the breaking up of masses of ice. The same dangerous experience befel us on the night of the 17th about the same hour, breaking two of our hawsers and causing the ship to ground heavily. What is so curious is that the event happens always and only at the same hour, having been experienced by us four years ago at Wandel, at identical hours and dates. If the tide-register had marked a rather sharp curve, I should have thought that there had been a tidal wave, held in check by the accumulated ice, and suddenly bursting out ; but all that was registered was a movement of the swell. On the other hand, the seismograph has recorded nothing. It is, therefore, very probable that it is by mere chance that the hours and dates are the same and that this wave is caused by either the ' calving ' or the capsizing of an iceberg. One of these, a particularly huge one, has stranded at the entrance to our cove, and it is quite possible that fragments of it broke away this night.

The tide-gauge, which Godfroy had fixed to a rock, is no longer of any use owing to the ice and snow which cover it, so he sets up one to-day on a new model, copied from that used by the *Discovery*. It consists simply of a large trivet, 4·50 metres in height, supporting the tide-gauge. Along the latter there slides a weight, with an index-finger on it. The weight is supported by an iron wire, passing through a pulley fixed to the end of the trivet, and attached at the other end to a kentledge anchored to the bottom. The ice going up and down with the tide carries the trivet and gauge with it, and the index-finger on the latter, being motionless at the end of its wire, indicates the height of the tide. In order that the wire may not adhere to the ice and be frozen hard, it plays within a long tube filled with petroleum, which only freezes at 70° below zero.

J. Guéguen, while skylarking to-day on the mess deck with his friend Hervé, has fractured his fibula. This is an annoying accident when one thinks of all the chances there are here of breaking one's limbs off the ship. Liouville puts the leg in plaster. Guéguen had a hard time on the last Expedition and I hesitated to take him with me this time, but he begged me so hard and he is so fine and interesting a character, that I had not the courage to refuse him. He has never been better in his life than since his return to the Antarctic, provided that the forced confinement to his bunk now does not damage his general health.

May 25.—We seem to be always having fête-days. Yesterday it was Rouch's birthday, the 18th was the anniversary
of the launching of the *Pourquoi-Pas ?*, to-day it is the Argentine Republic's national festival. On the 18th we drank
to the health of the god-mother and god-father of the *Pourquoi-
Pas ?*, my wife and M. Doumer. Both of them are now thinking of their god-child and watching from afar over those on
board. The Expedition owes its very existence to both of
them. I need not insist on the part played by my dear wife.
Not only did she allow me to go away again, but subduing her
sorrow at the coming separation, she assisted, advised, and
sustained me in the arduous work of preparation, and was
successful in raising my spirits during my very excusable
moments of discouragement. I overheard lately a remark
of one of my companions, who probably did not know how
truly he was speaking : ' For the Commandant, his wife is
his conscience.'

As for M. Doumer, I hardly knew him when chance gave
me the opportunity of telling him of my schemes. He understood that my only object was to labour on behalf of my
country, he considered the work useful, and (as always when
it is a question of adding to the glory of France, the sole passion
of his life) he made a point of rendering my schemes possible ;
and he succeeded beyond my hopes. The organization of the
Expedition became possible through him. Out of what was
at first ordinary interest there sprang into being a personal
liking, which is to me a source of pride. But also there has
arisen a debt which I wish to repay, and which is always in my
mind ; for men who, like M. Doumer, devote themselves
entirely to a noble task have the right to be exacting toward
others.

The *Pourquoi-Pas ?* could not have two better god-parents.
Both of them in their own way set examples to the men and
women of France and are incarnations of the motto which
we have up on our poop-deck, ' Honour and Country.'

Nor have I forgotten, on this birthday of our ship, its over-modest builder, Père Gautier, the veteran of his profession, who threw all his heart and brains into the work, and who succeeded in proving, first with the *Français* and then with the *Pourquoi-Pas ?*, that our building-yards can strive successfully with those of other nations that are more accustomed to this kind of construction. With no help from luck, his one idea was to do his work well, and he succeeded to the full. Festivals like that of to-day are festivals of gratitude. This is a sentiment which I find no burden, and to which I attach the greatest importance.

This morning Gain came up to my cabin, bringing the gramaphone, which played the Argentine Anthem. The mere sound of the instrument made me catch up an avenging slipper, but on hearing the air which it played, I gave my approval to the feelings of gratitude by which Gain was actuated. We dressed ship with the flag of Argentina (the same which we had on board the *Français*) at the main, and it was with real emotion that at the little banquet in the evening I raised my glass to the prosperity and the increasing and well-merited greatness of this fine country. Its very real generosity with regard to my expeditions is all I need recall.

There was a superb sunset to-day. Some low, light streaks of mist threw veils of pearl-grey across the red, pink and mauve which tinted the mountain-tops.

May 30.—A somewhat low temperature has prevailed during the last days of the month, favouring the formation of the pack-ice, and yesterday we were able, for the first time, to venture some distance over the ice of the channel. Taking the precaution of putting on skis, I set out with Besnard and Lerebourg. The ice was firm, but unfortunately its surface was formed by the soldering together of all the débris of icebergs and floes which have choked the channel for the last few months. All the rough edges were joined by hard and slippery ice, and the resulting surface was so lumpy that a

Clouds round the Glacier Peak and an Ice-blocked Channel.

sledge would have been knocked to pieces on it very rapidly. At the foot of the great iceberg, whose smooth and shining wall towered above us, thirteen Crabbing Seals were sleeping. One of them was scored with innumerable bleeding gashes, from which few of these animals are free. At the entry to the cove there were two or three great frozen waves, evidently formed by the pressure when the ice was still very plastic.

Quite close to our haven a large strip of smooth black ice delights Gain and Godfroy, who have seized the opportunity of bringing out their skates and have been able to use them over a track as good as they could possibly imagine. This is a curiosity, for marine ice is generally rough, soft, and holding. No doubt what has occurred is this : the channel was choked with icebergs and their débris, all formed from land ice, of course. During the thaw the water produced by the melting of these, reinforced by that from the glaciers and the coastal snow, covered the sheltered parts of the channel with a sheet of fresh water of less density than the sea-water. Then, thanks to the fall in the temperature it froze, and thus its surface has all the characteristics of that of a lake of fresh water.

From the top of the island I have been able to discover that from west to north the sea is still open, so that our ice is at the mercy of the least spell of bad weather. I have never seen the sea so free, even during the summer of 1904–5. In the south-west and south the pack-ice stretches out of sight, uneven and divided up by big dark expanses, which are probably formed from ice like that on which our skaters are busy.

June 2.—With a nice little breeze from the south-east, and a temperature of —15°, I set off early this morning with Gourdon, Gain and Godfroy on skis to cross the channel. My object was to discover if the glacier fronting us is again approachable, for my secret hope is still to be able to climb the inland ice and make a long circuit into the interor of Graham

Land. The pack-ice is rough, but the heavy fall of snow yester-day and the day before has levelled it a little. But, like all snow falling freshly upon marine ice in a thin covering, it turns under pressure into a sort of pickle, which sticks to the skis, stopping all glissading and making them so heavy that one can no longer move one's legs. Nevertheless, in spite of this, we certainly progressed faster with their aid and they also permit us to pass safely over brittle ice.

The glacier-face, at the place where we climbed it the first time, has altered, changing into a fairly high and very much crevassed cliff ; but further to the north the glacier is lower. It will be easy to climb, the only difficulty to be overcome being that of crossing a little expanse of water formed by the move-ments of the tide between the glacier and the pack-ice. On our way back the still hidden sun gilds the mountain tops, then the dazzling light touches the big icebergs, and finally comes down on to the pack-ice, where all shadows lengthen out indefinitely and increase the fantastic appearance of the whole scene. But this is of short duration, for before our arrival on board the orb is again below the horizon. Thanks to the pack-ice, Rouch and Nozal, carrying the little sounding machine on a sledge, have been able to take a whole series of soundings and to get samples of water at different depths ; while Gain, with a trunnion also mounted on a sledge, has been able to fish for *plankton* at different depths.

June 10.—We are again in the midst of wind, snow, mist and damp. On the 3rd a total eclipse of the moon was pre-dicted, and as on the evening before the sky was absolutely clear, we were rejoicing, some over the observations which would be possible, others over a new distraction. But, just as if we had been in a fine observatory in the neighbourhood of Paris, the sky clouded over completely, and it was only on the strength of the calendars that we could guess anything about the moon.

We meet with the usual mishaps in the Antarctic as much

as in France. Monmizet made Liouville as fine a pair of skates
as any turned out by a big manufacturer, Godfroy completely
spoilt some quite new town boots by fixing his on to them,
and a great skating carnival was announced. Immediately
after this, as after the notices of the Skating Club in the Bois
de Boulogne, the ice cracked and became covered with water,
and all skating was impossible. I very much fear that the
smooth ice will not return and that the fine new skates will
have no other use but to augment the collection of objects
manufactured on board.

The day before yesterday was particularly disagreeable.
In a few minutes the thermometer went up from $-13°$ to
$-7°$ and then to $+0°3$, to go down with the same rapidity
to $-5°$ and up again to $+2°$. The north-easter blows in a
regular tempest.

Four years ago to-day our first expedition returned to
Paris; and Gourdon, without saying anything about it,
had organized in concert with the men a little display in my
honour on the mess deck. Gourdon and Rosselin gave the
toasts. My brave and faithful follower, Chollet, companion
on my journeys for twenty-five years, pushed forward by
Gourdon, tried to speak in his turn, but he was very agitated
and after a few stammering words, he thought of something
better, for he shook my hand in such a way that I understood
the affectionate devotion with which he was overflowing.
I was extremely touched by this manifestation, the responsibility for which Gourdon and the crew laid on one another.
The veterans had already shown me their affection and confidence by asking to join the new expedition, and I have every
reason to believe that their sentiments towards me are shared
by the new-comers. We drank champagne, ate plum pudding,
and chattered gaily.

June 12.—Overcast, but south-south-west wind fairly strong.
Still, there is a little change. About 2 o'clock, there were
some very fine light effects caused by the twilight. Although

in the latitude where we are wintering the sun never remains
constantly below the horizon, yet, even if the nearly always
overcast sky allowed us, we should not see it more than a short
time, for it is so low that it remains hidden by Hovgard and
the high parts of our island.

Many of us are suffering from rheumatic pains, evidently
caused by the continuance of this frightful weather. Chollet
has a stiff neck, and with a sealer's cap on his head, a huge
pair of brown goggles on his nose, his neck rigid and wrapped
in a dirty stocking—for it seems that, to do any good, the
stocking must be dirty—he looks like a Dutch doll.

Most of the birds have left Petermann. From time to
time we are visited by a few penguins, which come to fish in
the neighbourhood and rest on the island. A large number
of Snowy Petrels, charming and elegant little birds, white as
the snow from which they take their name, live around the
boat still, feeding on the scraps thrown away from the kitchen.
Only the beak and eyes of these birds are black, and when they
fly over the snow their bodies are lost against it, and three
tiny black points seem to be crossing through space. These
birds have taken the place of the Sheathbills which lived in the
same away around the *Français*, and which are rather scarce
this year. We have had to kill a few of the petrels for our
collection, but we leave the others in peace, and they let us
come near them without fear.

Gain has found some interesting parasites on their heads.
And one of them which was killed had a congenital anomaly
in the shape of only one claw ; we have seen several others in
a like case. One of these birds made his way into the cook's
galley, and the cook soon tamed him. He was feeding him
on rice ! This is certainly an unexpected diet for an Antarctic petrel. Unfortunately, at the end of a few days, the poor
little bird burnt his wings cruelly, and we had to kill him to
put him out of his suffering.

June 16.—The vile weather from the north-east has come

back worse than ever, and yesterday the barometer went down to 712 mm., while a blinding and stifling snowdrift covered our island. All the ice in the cove has gone, and the ship rolls from side to side. The ice which supported the trivet for the tide-gauge has gone like the rest, but fortunately the apparatus has been fished up without great damage. One of our Norwegian boats, which we had intentionally stranded close to a little cove where the seals sometimes come, was in danger through the abrupt departure of the ice. We were able to save it, but it took a regular little expedition to do so. It would have been a pity to lose one of these boats, which are of the greatest service to us. They are so very light that two men can draw them up on shore or launch them. Thanks to their raised bows, one can readily land on the ice from them ; and lastly the two skates fixed to each side of the keel allow them to be dragged without much difficulty.

June 17.—This day has been terrible. The north-easter raged through the whole night. Owing to the strength of the wind, the starboard chains and hawsers have slackened, and the ship has been dashed against the rock to port with great shocks, followed by ominous sounds. Further, a counter-current set up at the entrance of the harbour and two big ice-blocks came through, breaking down the boom, which was already much damaged. Before we could even try to interfere one of the ice-blocks struck our stern violently, and a great piece of wood, which was rapidly borne away by the wind, proved to us only too clearly that an important part of our rudder had been torn away. For the moment it is impossible to discover whether the injury is serious or slight ; but there is cause for anxiety, since our scheme of summer navigation may perhaps be ruined by what has happened, and the ice-block threatens us with fresh injuries. After four hours' continuous effort, we succeed in mooring one block in such a way that it wards off the others a little, but we are dependent on the strength of a rope. Without loss of time, taking all advantage we can of the few hours of twilight, we fix up on the other side three fish-tackles, which keep us off the rock.

June 18.—A slight calm and the transparency of the water enable us to see that almost two-thirds of our rudder has been carried away, and that at least two of the braces are broken. In order to be able to steer, it will be absolutely necessary to take off the rudder and repair it as best we can, but the fid is lying at a depth of 2 or 3 feet below the surface, and I fear that we shall have great difficulty in getting it up.

I am anxious, indeed very anxious, for the future. Now that the channel is again free, and our boom, which it is impossible to think of repairing for the moment, is broken, fresh ice may come in and cause irreparable damage, and even bring about an inglorious end to the expedition through the loss of the ship before we have accomplished more than an insignificant portion of our task. Responsibility weighs more heavily on me than ever, and to distract and encourage myself, I re-read my diary on the *Français*, written during a period quite as agonizing as this. I light on a passage where I assert that, if ever I return to France, I will embark no more on such adventures. A few weeks after my return, I was thinking of nothing but the organization of a new Expedition, and three years later, I started off again! Is this my reward for my persistent efforts? Obstacles seem to arise everywhere in my path. After the summer campaign (which, it is true, was very fruitful) we found ourselves prevented from wintering where we wished, and we have to put up with a most detestable and troublesome of winters. Certainly our work is progressing well, but the trips on which I counted so much seem spoilt by the perpetual changes in the state of the ice. The passage of time does not bring us deliverance, as to so many expeditions, but merely the necessity of commencing the struggle afresh for the honour of our enterprise and our country ; and with this object in view, irreparable injuries are the last thing we want. Perhaps others could content themselves with the work already done ; I cannot do so. I have to combat the possible demoralization of my companions and to watch over their state of mind. So my discouragement lasts but little. Besides, Shakespeare, my faithful friend, fore-seeing everything, comes to my aid :—

> ' When good will is showed, though it comes too short,
> The actor may plead pardon.'

June 21.—This is the official start of winter. It is also the date when the sun begins to climb up the heavens again and the days to get longer. The south-easter has been blowing for some hours. Does it herald at last the true winter, which we desire so much ? I should have liked to have entered upon this new period cheerfully, but alas ! it is with anxiety and apprehension only too well founded that I see it opening. The torments of these last days have been nothing (for material damage can be repaired) compared with what occurs to-day. The so-called ' Polar anaemia '—or perhaps it is scurvy, which is just as much to be feared—has made its appearance on board.

For a fortnight past, I noticed that Godfroy was growing pale, and that he, so enthusiastic, so vigorous, so ready always to diffuse his cheerful personality, so eager for the success of the Expedition, which he had made his own, was entirely losing his good spirits. Now his legs are very much swollen and he complains of violent pains. For my own part, I notice in myself a shortness of breath without any cause, and a per-manent pain in front of the heart. To-night my legs also are swollen. Need I say through what alarms I go, what re-proaches I heap on myself, how hard I strive to find the reason of this misfortune ? I never believed in ' Polar anaemia,' which is a meaningless expression, but I had been obliged to acknowledge the Polar myocarditis of which Matha had so bad an attack on board the *Français* and from which he recovered by a miracle. I myself felt a few trivial symptoms, which I overcame, as I believed, by physical exercise, almost by over-fatiguing myself. On other expeditions there had been deaths, and now two of us are attacked in the same way as Matha. Liouville also has a little œdema. I anxiously await the examination of the whole personnel of the ship to-night. If others are attacked, it is probably scurvy to which we have fallen victims.

The examination has taken place, and certainly we are the only two attacked, which is a good thing. I have no intention of allowing myself to be downcast, and if I take certain precautions in case of anything happening to me, it is because my rôle of leader of the Expedition impels me to do so.

June 27.—After getting worse, the condition of myself and Godfroy remains stationary. His legs are more swollen and more painful than mine, but on the other hand, his heart is sound, while I am suffering from pronounced myocarditis. We are still the only two invalids on board, and in these circumstances I abandon the idea of scurvy to fall back upon Polar myocarditis, the origin of which is as yet unexplained. We have nothing wrong with our gums, none of the classical symptoms of scurvy. However, the treatment which we are following is that which would be applied to this malady. With great kindness, the crew has spontaneously gone in all directions to look for seals and for penguins and other birds. Dufrèche has even nearly drowned himself while setting hoop-nets for fish on the edge of the pack-ice, which has formed again in the cove. We are taking considerable quantities of citric acid, and I get as much exercise as my miserable condition allows me.

To-day, as we could not walk, to take advantage of the fine weather, Godfroy and myself established ourselves on deck in our bed-sacks. What weighs most heavily upon me is this physical weakness. I have always been so strong and able to endure everything, and have never allowed anything to stop me.

Gourdon.

Rouch.

Liouville.

Charcot.

Bongrain.

Gain.

Godfroy.

Senouque.

THE STAFF IN JULY, 1909.

June 29.—This night, about 2 a.m., there were two or three great heavy rollers, followed by violent shocks, and this afternoon, also about 2 o'clock, the same phenomenon occurred. The tide-register indicated a wave of 1·16 metres. These tide-waves are difficult to explain, for we have neither heard nor seen any iceberg breaking up. Perhaps there has been a big slide of ice-cliff, but if so it was at a considerable distance from us. All the ice in the cove has been smashed up, and those of us who were on shore had the water up to our knees. The hawsers held good, but they have been subjected to a great strain, and this must not happen too often.

July 7.—A few days of fine calm and cold weather have allowed the ice to re-form around us. The thermometer marks —18°; at Wandel, on the same date in 1904 we had —34°! Our state of health is a little better, and I take advantage of this to get as much exercise as possible; but the irregularity of my heart is marked and on the same day my pulse has given 22 beats and 124! The œdema of the legs comes on and goes off without reason, and I often have more in the morning in spite of a night of complete repose. The same is the case with Godfroy.

I have recently turned out from a locker complete files of the *Matin* and the *Figaro* for two years before our departure, kindly presented to us by their Editors. Every day I put on the ward-room table the numbers corresponding to the present date, and personally I have never read the papers so attentively or thoroughly. If I must confess it, the news, now so ancient, the scandals, the *affaires,* interest me just as much as if I had never heard of them. I had forgotten them nearly all and I await the next day's issue with impatience. I am now much better acquainted with my country's politics and the world's happenings in 1907 than I have ever been, and probably than I shall ever be again.

With the help of some shanks of iron skilfully turned out by Rosselin the key of the rudder has been fixed up, and we are only waiting now for a fine day and a favourable state of the ice to unship the rudder itself.

July 14.—Overcast weather, fine snow up to 3 p.m. Wind from south-west and south-east, temperature — 16°. From 8 o'clock the ward-room gramaphone has been playing the ' Marseillaise.' Three shots from our little cannon, brought up on deck for this occasion, are fired, at 9, 12, and 6. This same cannon, which was constructed for the first trials with melinite, has saluted July 14 at Jan Mayen in the North and on two different occasions in the Antarctic.

Gourdon, who is housekeeper on board, has decorated the wardroom with a profusion of little paper flags and the National colours. The *Pourquoi-Pas ?* has hoisted her ensign, and the island is covered with all that we possess in the way of foreign nations' flags and with rows of signals on ski-staffs. When the snow is good enough to stop, the effect produced by all these brilliant colours against the white background is really charming.

In the afternoon, the Antarctic Sporting Club had a shooting competition. The prizes were solemnly distributed in the evening as follows :—Poste, 1 ; Nozal, 2 ; Jabet, 3 ; Lhostis, 4 ; Rosselin, 5 ; Modaine, 6 ; Frachat, 7. As for all the rest, to console them, they were given a bottle of grog, which was very well received. At dinner in the evening, most of us appear in full dress or in any old clothes of the civilized world that we can find in our cabins. The menus, written by Paumelle, the mess steward, on red-white-and-blue paper, were as follows :—

DEJEUNER.
Hors-d'œuvre, saucisson, divers.
Potage aux tomates.
Vol au vent a l'Australe.
Tête de veau en tortue.
Petits pois à la Française.
Chaussons de Pommes à la Normande.
VINS FINS.
Chateau-Cambusard à discretion.

DINER.

Potage jardinière.
Homard vinaigrette.
Poulet à la gelée.
Filet de bœuf champignons.
Fonds d'Artichauts.
Plum-Pudding.
Compôte de fruits.
VINS FINS—Champagne.

At 6 o'clock, there is a torchlight-tattoo, with all the crew carrying preserved-food boxes filled with tow soaked in petroleum. Then we had a display of fireworks got up by Gain, consisting of crackers of his own composition, which went off well, of Bengal lights made by the same manufacturer, which did not burn or which, as Chollet put it, ' gave a black light,' of set-pieces of iron-wire wrapped in tow, soaked in spirit and powdered with magnesium, which we happily knew were supposed to represent trees, suns, and an interrogation-mark, and lastly, a huge feu-de-joie, composed of penguin-fat and the body of a seal, all abundantly soaked in spirit, which continued to blaze, illuminating the island in fantastic fashion, until 5 a.m.

About 11 o'clock, Liouville, Gain, Godfroy, Gourdon and myself went on to the mess deck, where the greatest gaiety was in full swing. Dufrèche was playing the accordion for the others to dance to, and my colleagues joined in the dances with the crew. On the smoky mess deck, divided up by the solid wooden ribs of the ship, the crew, with their energetic faces and their picturesque clothing, patched up according to taste, with knives at their waists, and their hair and beards flowing loose, leapt about and shouted loud challenges to one another. One might have thought oneself carried back a century to the 'tween-decks of a piratical ship rejoicing over a fine prize and careless of to-morrow's combats. And are not our men, in reality, the sons of those corsairs, from whom they have inherited the taste for adventure, the character like a big child's, the courage and the feeling of honour? These few minutes spent among them with their free but always respectful gaiety, drinking their half-pints with them and smoking the tobacco which they cordially offered us, have done more to raise my spirits than any amount of reasoning could have done.

July 15.—The weather is very fine. A little breeze from the south-east first scatters and then brings back a slight mist. A white frost covers the ship with its elegant flowers, which attach themselves to the smallest cord. Once more our flags decorate the island as they flutter in the breeze; but this time it is not by my orders. It is known that I am forty-two to-day, and with one accord it has been decided that this shall be a fête-day.

Chollet is the first to come and shake hands, then Libois as the eldest on board brings me an address signed by the whole crew. It is one of the documents which I prize most dearly.

' DEAR COMMANDANT,' it runs,—

'ON the occasion of your birthday, I, as the eldest of the crew, am given the task of offering you the best wishes and compliments of the crew of the *Pourquoi-Pas?*, begging you to believe in our entire devotion and our confidence in the success of the Expedition which you are leading with such confidence and singleness of purpose, and above all, we are happy to notice the apparent restoration of your health and hope that it is permanent.'

Poste brings me a panel of copper on wood, very artistically designed and executed by himself, representing an escutcheon with the arms of the ship, supported by two heraldic lions, and another very charming panel, which he has executed after Liouville's design, to serve as a background for the little old figure of the Virgin which adorns the ward-room.

The menus have again been remarkable, the cook having

surpassed himself by putting before us a set-piece of nougat and spun sugar. Owing to these successive fête-days the good fellow has only slept four hours in two days. For my part, the dinner was washed down with some of the fine wine coming from the special cellar which my mother-in-law fitted up for me before we left, but which, following my invariable principle, I have never touched without the others joining me. After dinner the hour of the great surprise arrived. As a matter of fact, it was not altogether a surprise, since for over a month (though I concealed my knowledge in order not to spoil their pleasure) I have been aware to some extent that rehearsals were going on, directed by Gain in secret in the engine-room, in spite of the great cold.

The table was quickly removed and also some of the doors, and when the crew had entered the ward-room, singing a special chorus, the affair began   This was the official programme —

PART I.

' L'Epave,' by François Coppée	.	recited by PAUMELLE.
' Le Parjure,' ballad	. . .	sung by AVELINE.
' Maman La Bataille '	. . .	,, PAUMELLE.
' Il fait soleil,' ballad	. . .	,, LIBOIS.
' L'Automobile du Colon,' comic song	.	,, PAUMELLE.
' J'viens d'être enlevé '	. . .	,, PAUMELLE.
' Lettre à Columbine,' song	. .	,, MODAINE.
' Réponse de Colombine '	. .	,, AVELINE.
' La tringle ' comic monologue .	.	recited by MODAINE.
' L'O dans le Q '	. . . .	,, MODAINE.

' La Leçon d'anglais,' Burlesque and Critical Fantasia, by M. J. LIOUVILLE.
Played by F. LIFOIS and J. JABET, *alias* ' Le Bosco.'

PART II.
VIVE L'ARMÉE.
(Comedy in one Act, by PIERRE WOLFF.)

Mlle. Bouboule (aged 26)	. . .	PAUMELLE.
Caboche (dealer in sugar)	. . .	ROSSELIN.
Pied (1st-class trooper in the 1st Cuirassiers)		LEREBOURG.

The scene is laid in Paris.
Scenery and costumes by MM. Gain, Liouville and Gourdon.
Stage Manager, M. Gain.

PART III.

Artistic Living Pictures of the Journey of the *Pourquoi-Pas ?* by M. A.
SENOUQUE.

The success was complete, the actors playing their parts to
perfection, in most unexpected costumes. Lerebourg's helmet
and cuirass, in particular, were absolute marvels, and made
one forget that the cuirassier's sword was only a naval officer's
sabre wrapped in silver paper.

We came out of the theatre at 1.30 a.m., without any disorder in the cloak-room, and only then did we notice that
the — 23° and the calm of the afternoon had been followed
by the usual gale from the north-east, which whistled through
the masts of the *Pourquoi-Pas ?*.

July 24.—Still, still bad weather. The ice has been
broken up and dispersed by the wind, and we have been able
to go out in the dinghy and land on the glacier facing us. In
the channel, icebergs and ice-blocks innumerable go slowly
south before the wind and come back again during the too
infrequent calms, driven by the current. We know nearly all
the large bergs, which pass and repass us in the same order like
the supers in a ballet.

Our hawsers are always breaking and we repair them rapidly,
as best we can. The picket-boat, being in a dangerous position as she hangs under the bow of the ship, has been put
ashore. We spend our time in taking counsel, watching, and
strengthening our position, but we cannot foresee the chances,
and the boom, which we restored yesterday with the greatest
care, has been broken during the night.

The evening of July 15 has whetted the men's appetites,
and they have come to ask my permission to found a Musical
Society to meet on the mess deck every Sunday. Then from
bags and lockers are brought forth all the song-books, a haphazard medley of old ballads, sailors' choruses, sentimental songs
and music-hall trivialities. Every Sunday the programme is
brought to me, whereon every one is down for his little con-

tribution,which he sings lustily or chaffingly, as the case may be. We pass an hour together, and we are amused, which is the principal thing.

July 31.—The bad weather continues, more intense than ever, and we have a perpetual tempest about us. One of the anemometers has been broken again ; happily we have a spare one, and we have replaced it at once. On the 25th, during a fine spell, we succeeded in unshipping the rudder. For a long time all had been prepared for this operation, which is difficult to carry out afloat, and in an hour and a half it is on the deck. The injury is even more serious than we feared, and if we had had to navigate under such conditions, we should have exposed the ship to grave danger, even apart from the fact that in the Polar regions the steering must be quick and sure. Two of the pintles have been broken off in the gudgeons. We succeed in getting them out with a curved iron shank, but we shall have to make fresh rudder-irons, and this is a hard piece of blacksmith's work. We have no wood strong enough for the repair of the check-piece, so we shall have to give Libois one of our two spare spars, which can be cut in pieces to make just what is required. The same is the case with the irons. I had an idea of cutting a piece off the beam of the waist anchor in order to forge them from it, but in the end we find a spare bolt for the thrust-block of the engine, which may serve our turn. To protect the gudgeons and the stern-post against shocks from the ice now that the rudder is un-shipped, I join together three thick stakes and pass them through the rudder-hole, keeping them in place by tightly drawn braces. I regret that I did not, at the beginning, think of unshipping the rudder and taking this precaution.

Polaire has again given birth to two puppies, of which we decide to keep one. This four-footed son of the Antarctic, who is to be called by the strange name of Gugumus, is going to live with his brother Bibi, his mother Polaire, and his father Kiki, on the most intimate and friendly terms with the three kittens born at Buenos Aires and the cat taken on board at Cherbourg.

The thermometer has risen to $+3° 5$ this evening. Fortunately I have had the starboard stern hawsers tripled, and all the hawsers we have are now in use. A large quantity of ice, composed principally of the débris of bergs, has invaded our cove, and chokes the entrance for a considerable distance. A string of colossal icebergs, the biggest which we have yet seen in this region, have stranded to the north, close up to the island, and another of these ice monsters has stranded to the south. Unhappily this dyke does not prevent the swell from being felt very violently between 10 and 5 o'clock, and it is a wonder that no cable has broken. The struggle with the ice-blocks begins again. We cannot shut our eyes to the fact that the ship is in danger. Should a hawser break and an ice-block charge us violently, we might go to the bottom very quickly. Also the neighbourhood of these enormous icebergs is a perpetual menace, for if one of them breaks up or capsizes, the wave may drive us I know not where. To prepare for such an emergency, therefore, I have had taken ashore and put in our provision-store all our bed-sacks, the matches which we brought in soldered boxes, and a certain stock of clothing.

As soon as these precautions have been taken, however, the ship grows more at her ease again, still rolling a little and reeling under the violence of the gusts, but not putting too great a strain upon her cables.

A new boom, which I have had constructed with the greatest care, has resisted the ice well. Abandoning the actual entrance to our harbour, where all the others were so soon broken, I have had this one stretched obliquely across the centre of the cove, in the direction of the prevailing wind, so as to allow the ice-blocks to slide along it. Lastly, I have had the six lengths of steel wire protected with old preserved-food tins, to prevent wear and tear, while half a dozen empty hogsheads support the whole affair.

August 2.—The swell has completely ceased, despite the continuance of the wind, and I discover the explanation of this unaccustomed calm by climbing to the top of the island. The whole offing, as far as can be seen, has been suddenly invaded by dense pack-ice coming from I know not where, but never at any time, even on board the *Français,* have we seen as much.

There is only a little circle of free water, starting from near Darboux Island, passing by the Myre de Vilers Islets, to touch Wandel in the north. Lemaire Channel, apart from the icebergs, is free, and thus makes a large lake.

Our life on board goes on, at once busy and monotonous ; and if the months pass quickly, the hours are long. So true is the saying that ' the hour which one watches stands still.' Of course, in spite of all our efforts to make distractions, these are few. We know every inch of the island where we are so closely confined, and the bad weather does not usually make walks agreeable.

We have fortunately an extremely well-furnished library with about 1,500 volumes of scientific works, travel-books, novels, plays, and artistic and classical literature, to distract, instruct, or help us in our work. The crew has the right of dipping into these to a great extent, but I have thought it best to strike off the catalogue for their use a whole series of volumes that seemed to me harmful, or at least useless, to most of these good fellows, who are happily still very much children of nature. The volumes which circulate most in the ward-room are undoubtedly those of the Dictionaire Larousse, which, apart from the instruction which it gives us in our isolation from the rest of the world, cuts short if it does not completely check, discussions which would otherwise threaten to be interminable. Whether or not Larousse provides the solution, in a life like ours discussions are inevitable. They are one of the occupations, often one of the plagues, of Polar expeditions, and I well understand why, during a celebrated English Antarctic expedition, they should have been punished by fines when they overran the comparatively short hours when they were permitted. I must hasten to add that on our ship they seldom turned bitter, and the clouds which they may have raised quickly dispersed.

Further, most of us are watching one another, trying (to use the expression of one of my colleagues) to ' study the psychology of the restricted community.' Much has been said about *cafard polaire* (though it is too frequently invoked as an excuse), and it is certain that this life in common, with no possibility of finding distraction from temporary failure of nerves, with no hop e of being able to take a meal alone or in other company, has its painful moments. Our arrangements on board at least allowed every one to find solitude in his own cabin, contrary to the rule of most expeditions, where two and sometimes three lived in the same room. This is one of the reasons why I advocate that even the crew should have a place to shut themselves in.

As a moralist has said, in a maxim of which I can only recollect the sense, ' It is often more difficult to bear the daily pin-pricks than the great griefs.' An innocent crotchet, a mere mannerism in sitting down, blowing one's nose, or helping oneself to food, which in ordinary life would not even be remarked, becomes the cause of annoyance and may even assume the proportions of a grievance ; but all that is wanted is a little education and self-control to counteract this evil tendency. My small experience of two winter seasons with different companions allows me to assert that *cafard polaire* does not create new defects. A good fellow remains a good fellow, and a man distinguished for his manners remains distinguished. What happens is that characters are made to show themselves as they really are, with their weaknesses or defects no longer under the mask by which, either designedly or of necessity, one hides them in ordinary social life. But here, as elsewhere, education plays the chief rôle, and a man who has been well brought-up will always avoid being a nuisance in the wardroom, even in the Antarctic, or rendering his presence insupportable to his comrades. My companions, in the course of these long months, were able to avoid the annoying tendency to form antagonistic cliques.

Meals play a great part in these expeditions. This is the crucial moment when all are collected together, when discussions arise, and tempers have free play. On the other hand also, it is the moment when feelings are appeased and reconciliations are made. The food itself has an unsuspected importance. It is very difficult to satisfy eight persons of different tastes, often inclined, in an access of bad temper, to find everything bad in advance—especially as, whatever the care that has been devoted to the choice of provisions, culinary resources are necessarily limited. We must all, and I more than the others, be grateful to Gourdon, who accepted the thankless and difficult job of commissariat officer, for his unwearying patience and the tact and devotion with which he carried out his additional duties to the very end. I am sure that Gourdon, for his part, will be glad for me to record with what devotion Quartermaster Jabet, who was in charge of the provision room, seconded his labours, invariably goodhumoured, content, and prepared for all.

August 23.—I read in to-day's (?) *Matin* that Casablanca had just been taken by our Marines. Now one of our men, Thomas, was in the company that landed. I take the opportunity of going on to the mess deck, and after a few explanatory words to his comrades, giving him a special packet of tobacco.

We have had for a few days a breakdown of the electric light. The bearings of the motor had worn out, and we had no spare ones. Bongrain searches in vain for a piece of bronze which he can turn to replace what is wanting. At last it occurs to me to give him the old screw of the picket-boat. After considerable difficulty he succeeds in casting it in a satisfactory fashion, and once again our fine electric light replaces the petroleum-lamp. From every point of view I am not sorry for this. Good temper returns, and above all, we are not wasting more of a combustible of which our stock is, through an error in my calculations, rather limited.

Whether it is through the seal's meat—seals of the Weddell species having appeared in great numbers last month—or for some other reason, the improvement in the health of Godfroy and myself increases daily. I enthusiastically prepare for the trips which I wish to undertake in September.

On the glacier which we shall have to cross, the motor sledges will probably be useless, and our first attempt will have to be purely a trial trip. I decide that six of us shall go —Gourdon, Godfroy, Gain, Senouque, a sailor and myself, divided into two parties, each with their own sledge, tent, and separate stores. I have loaded the sledges with the weights which we shall have to carry, and for some hours every day we practise ourselves in dragging them over the most difficult parts of the island. I am studying also the question of foot-wear, which is one of my great preoccupations, and I make some slight alterations in the frost-nails, which we have had made like those of the *Discovery*, which Captain Scott, with good cause, praised to me very highly. I wish to leave nothing to chance, while the particular conditions of climate under which we live oblige us to take additional precautions. We have not only to struggle against cold, but also against abrupt and considerable changes of temperature, against incessant snow and persistent wind.

Our excursion-provisions are unanimously admitted to be excellent and their stowage in little boxes for three men each day is practical. In this way meals can be prepared in the minimum of time and food-depôts easily fixed up. Before our departure, I arranged everything with the utmost care ; but the final dispositions can only be made on the spot. We have now but to wait for circumstances favourable to our setting out.

August 29.—Alas ! I cried ' Victory ! ' too soon. Godfroy has fallen ill again, and I very soon did the same in my turn. Our condition is worse than ever, but I will not give way, and so, panting and my heart beating like a clock, I force myself every day, whatever the weather, to climb to the summit of the island and to take long walks. Oh, these 200-metre climbs, most of the time in solitude, so that there may be no witnesses to my weakness ! I have to take 350 steps to reach the summit, and out of breath and choking I count them, obliged to stop every ten steps, my heart leaping as though it would break and my swollen legs giving way under me. I am joyful when I succeed in taking 50 steps without stopping. With frost-nails on my boots, I drag myself along miserably every day, sometimes in soft snow up to the knees, sometimes over the frozen surface laid bare by the wind or through snowdrift. How well I know all the corners of the island, all the rocks where I can take shelter and behind which I fall beaten ! There is in particular, on the north-east side of the island, a fine, picturesque ravine, both narrow and deep, where in my solitary walks I gladly sit down when tired out. Sometimes I push on as far as a huge stray rock, oval in shape, split in two by frost, and looking like a monstrous Easter egg. I halt in this rift, pressing my hand to my breast, until the cold forces me to move on again ; and my moral suffering is still worse than the physical. To despair at my own weakness is added anxiety over Godfroy's condition. If his heart is not affected like mine, his legs are more swollen, he is pale and thin, and his hands are covered with horrible ulcerations. He treats himself by rest, puts up with all the regimens and all the drugs, very rational in their way, which Liouville recommends to him ; and I confess I cannot urge him to follow my example.

To-day's splendid weather is a relief after the long and constantly bad days through which we have passed. To the south there is a very remarkable mirage effect, which lasts quite late in the day. In a region where I know very well that nothing of the kind exists, there rises a high and magnificent wall of ice, which starts from the coast and loses itself in the horizon out to sea. We make out all the details of its perpendicular face, and it is quite certain that a passing explorer would affirm, with the best faith in the world, that there is at this spot a barrier similar to Ross's.

September 5.—It is no good. My condition gets worse, and Godfroy, who is following a regimen the reverse of mine, is no better. I do not wish to confess it yet, but evidently I cannot lead the excursion. I cannot walk, I crawl, and at the end of a few hours I should be obliged to have myself carried by the others.

To give the crew some useful exercise and to lighten the upper part of the ship in view of the coming summer campaign, I have the spare screw, which weighs 1,500 kilos, lowered to the bottom of the hold.

Libois has done his work admirably, and the new rudder is almost finished. Protected by sheets of iron, it will be stronger than the other. Rosselin, for his part, has forged some rudder-irons, which will last better than our former ones.

September 13.—Alas! I am forced to abandon all idea of a trip. In spite of all my efforts and all the will-power which I use to drag myself along, I am beaten. My legs can no longer carry me and my heart is very low. I suffer from palpitations, or, on the other hand, from a slowing down of the action, and from choking fits ; and at night there is a painful praecordial affliction, which makes me think that I have a touch of pericarditis. I can barely drag myself about on board.

Godfroy's heart is all right at present, but his legs are even more weak than mine, and the ulceration of his hands increases. Both of us have a few spots of *purpura*. I have now to lie on my back nearly the whole time. After thinking it out, I have arrived at the conclusion that we are suffering from scurvy, or more precisely, from preserved-food sickness. I have decided to remove from our diet all preserved meat and to eat only seal, penguin, garlic, sauerkraut, jams, etc.

I am going therefore to entrust to Gourdon the command of the excursion. It is heart-breaking for me, but I could not put it in better hands. This excursion is, properly speaking, a trial trip. If the regimen I have adopted succeeds, perhaps I shall be able to join him later or start out with him again on his return.

I attend with the greatest care to the preparations. These excursions are a hobby of mine. I devote a lot of thought beforehand to their organization, and I am anxious my comrades should lack nothing and find themselves in the best possible position. With Gourdon will go Gain and Senouque, accompanied by Besnard (who took part in our excursion in 1904), Hervé and Aveline.

To-day Gourdon, Gain and a large party succeeded in crossing the ice and hoisting on to the glacier a considerable portion of their stores.

On board our regular life continues, and the ordinary work is increased by extras. Bongrain seizes every opportunity to go off with Boland surveying. Rouch succeeds one calm day in inflating a balloon with one of our tubes of hydrogen and sending it up to register atmospheric currents. We attach a message to this balloon, without the slightest hope, of course, that it will ever reach any destination.

One of our dogs, Bibi, has been away for 36 hours and we feared that he had met with an accident, but this morning he turned up again quietly, rather abashed and very hungry. The crew say that he has passed all this time in a crevasse at some distance from the ship, into which he must have fallen, and they have indeed found a tuft of his hair. The poor beast does not seem to have suffered very much from the 20° below zero.

September 17.—Godfroy and I feel perhaps a little better, but we are still very weak.

Yesterday was Chollet's fifty-second birthday. I got up a little banquet on the mess deck and sent for our good skipper to come to the ward-room and have a drink with me. He has made himself loved and esteemed by the whole of the staff, to whom his ingenuity and skill have been of the utmost service.

There have been a few changes between fine and stormy, but the weather is a little calmer than last month. The sky, however, is always grey and overcast, and the falls of snow are frequent and abundant.

September 18.—My companions have started on their trip. While shaking their hands and wishing them good luck I felt very sad. Except for Rouch, Godfroy, the cook, Robert, Chollet and myself, every one else on board accompanied them to drag their sledges as far and as quickly as possible.

Our regimen has certainly had a good effect, and this morning I felt considerably better. The same is the case with Godfroy, and we were able to set off over the ice, like two cripples, to meet the party which is coming back this evening. All went off well. The stores are on the top of the glacier and our six comrades well on their way, though unfortunately much troubled by the thick snow. The weather is calm and overcast. May they succeed in finding the much desired way into the interior !

September 23.—We are getting better and better. It was certainly the preserved-food sickness from which we were suffering for more than three months, and it is evidently the same thing which afflicted Matha in 1904. All the so-called Polar anaemias turn out to be nothing but maladies allied to scurvy. In the past, when crews lived almost entirely on salt meat they were attacked by the well-known variety of scurvy, with large black spots, ulceration of the gums, etc. But everything changes, even diseases, and with the modern preserved-food the classical scurvy has been replaced by the curious kind from which we suffered, characterized especially by oedema of the lower limbs and myocarditis, without anything wrong with the gums. Something of the kind, moreover, showed itself in our Army during the Crimean War.

Seals, fortunately, are again abundant and we can kill more than we require for our food supply. On board the *Discovery* there was also a serious outbreak of scurvy, much more classical in its nature than ours, which was rapidly and completely got rid of by using the flesh of these animals. This meat, which it is difficult to compare with anything else, and which is pleasant to my taste, is a precious resource for Antarctic expeditions and furnishes us with a diet of which we do not get tired. When cooked in steaks with a little butter I have consumed great quantities of it with sauerkraut, of which I laid in an ample stock.

The men, in their anxiety to see us cured, hunt for seals on every side and even risk their lives to bring them in. So I have to watch them and prevent them from being too rash. To-day I am told that a fine seal is asleep on one of the little islets to the south. I go to the place from which it can be seen and make out not one but two, the second appearing quite small. With some difficulty we get near them and find a female Weddell's Seal, which has just given birth. With the greatest precaution, in order not to frighten them, we approached the interesting couple. The mother seemed in a condition of considerable prostration. Nothing could have been more touching in the midst of this gloomy scenery, so little suggestive of life, than the little seal, disconcertingly human, charming alike in physiognomy and size, beside its mother with her massive and clumsy form. Covered with a thick, soft fur, yellow spotted with black, it spent most of its time on its back, amusing itself like a child, stretching out its flippers, playing about and rubbing itself against its mother, with its quaint little round face and fine large eyes full of astonishment and roguery.

While we were watching it, a male of the same species, no doubt the father, appeared through a hole in the ice and started to intone for the benefit of the others a curious, if not particularly melodious, little song.

We photographed this Antarctic family group from all sides, and then I drew close and took the little one in my arms. It was delighted, showing no fear, but acting just like a baby, and when I put the soft little body back on the ice again it came crawling up to me, rubbing up against my legs and asking for fresh caresses. Must I confess that the memory of a little being which I left at home in France came to me so sharply that there was a catch in my throat ? I felt ashamed before the rest of the party, and I did not take into my arms again the little seal which caused me so much emotion, though I would have liked to fondle and embrace it. The mother seal was a little anxious and snorted and protested loudly, trying to frighten me, but she was immediately reassured when her infant came back to her. He began to suck at once, so greedily that the milk ran out of his nostrils.

There was no need for me to order that these animals' lives be spared, for I very much suspect (and some words I overheard confirmed my suspicions) that the men who accompanied me, nearly all of them fathers of a family, had felt the same emotions as myself.

To-day is the first day of spring. It is grey, gloomy and windy. At midday on the 18th, the official hour of the new season's commencement, we sounded the bell on board full peal and the crew sang a few topical verses, scarcely in harmony with the climate in which we still have long months to live.

The weather has been particularly atrocious these last few days, the barometer having even gone down to 703 ! We took advantage of the bad weather, which offers few inducements to go out, and of the temporary thinning out of the ward-room, to go through our cellar and make an inventory. Not only in France, but at our different stopping-places, too, presents of wine were made with the greatest generosity, and we are more plentifully provided than we could have ventured to hope when the Expedition was being organized. Of course this is a luxury, but there is nothing disagreeable about luxury, and it has not cost us a farthing. We have the finest varieties of Madeira, and Argentine and Chilian wines, side by side with the best known brands of Bordeaux, Burgundy, and Champagne. One of my old school comrades, who became a wine merchant—the medical career leads to all sorts of things, as I am myself a proof— kindly sent me on our departure a few hundreds of wonderful bottles of Nuits, which we drink on fête-days with the respect that is due to it. We do not make undue use of our cellar, for good sense and economy alike forbid this. A second winter may become necessary, and it is then that we shall be glad of our superabundance.

I may say that the Vin Ordinaire on board, otherwise called Chateau Cambusard, is excellent, and that our pur- veyor showed himself a man of conscience. The French sailor is one of the best of fellows, but, unhappily, he must have his regular ' rations,' without which he considers himself lost. This was one of the troubles of storage on board, for the number of hogsheads it was necessary to take occupied a huge space, which I should consider better occupied by other provisions. I got over the difficulty partly by bringing wine very strong in alcohol, which we dilute with more than the same quantity of just warm water before giving it out. Thus a considerable space is saved. During the excursions the men put up with the total absence of wine, though they often speak of their half-pint waiting them on their return. It is a sad thing that for the great majority of our country's sailors all the comfort and joy of life seem to be concentrated in a plentiful supply of wine or alcohol. Can we blame them for this widespread notion, when we of the richer classes are the first to manifest our joy and honour an occasion by open- ing a bottle ? Still, we live soberly in the ward-room and

I have succeeded, without any difficulty, moreover, in abolishing the word 'apéritif' altogether. Would that all our fellow-citizens at home would follow our example !

For four days I have not been able to pay another visit to the little seal, the ice being broken up and the gale allowing no launching of boats. This evening, during a calm, I went there again and found mother and child doing well. My little friend was sleeping beside his mamma. At the noise which I made he woke up and began once more to frisk about quaintly. He had grown a little and had become a little more active in his movements. I made a fuss of him again, and I was allowed to do so ; but now, whether it was in play or whether it was to show that he was a big child, he opened his mouth threateningly and snorted like his father and mother. Mrs. Seal, who was a little anxious about me at the start, soon discovered that she has nothing to fear from me. To give her confidence, I caressed her also, and after this she allowed me to do as I liked with the little one. In my presence she taught him to walk, getting him to pursue her, showing him how he must sweep away the snow with his head as all seals do when they advance ; although the light covering of snow to-day made such a precaution unnecessary. It is very probable that the father comes to visit his wife and child fairly frequently, for close at hand there is a seal-hole with marks of recent use.

A flight of about 200 cormorants has passed over the island, stopping at various spots as if looking for a favourable place to establish themselves in. But apparently they did not find what they wanted, for they have gone away. The manœuvres of these birds are the more curious because quite unusual. We always see them fly straight ahead without a stop, like busy birds with a definite object in view. Almost every day, about the same time, we have remarked a single cormorant coming from the direction of Wandell or Berthelot Island. As there is a rookery, even in the winter, on both of these islands, we look on this cormorant as the courier of the two colonies.

Since we have been on an exclusive diet of seal's meat, the ulcerations on Godfroy's hands, which looked so serious, have totally disappeared with surprising rapidity, and he seems completely restored to health. As for me, I have no more oedema of the lower limbs, only my heart refusing to grow regular again. Still, I find myself so well after these months of sickness that I have made up my mind, if our comrades do not return in five or six days, to go to meet them on the glacier. I shall take with me Jabet and Thomas, who are very excited at the prospect, and I have prepared to this end a lightly loaded sledge, so as to be able to advance rapidly. Our re-victualling will be done from the food-depôts on the way.

October 2.—I have had to renounce my project again, for at 11 o'clock I espied our six excursionists making the pre-arranged signals on the glacier. The whole ice surface of the channel has been broken up by the constant gales, but fortunately there are a few passage-ways of open water which we can use in going to meet them. But we must be quick about it, for these passages may close up as rapidly as they opened, and we should then risk being isolated from one another for a very long time. In a few minutes, but not without difficulty, in consequence of the lowness of the tide and the amount of ice débris, the big canoe is launched, and I start off with Godfroy and four men. To get out of our cove we have to carry the boat over the ice, whereby I get a bath almost from head to foot, and after a bit of a struggle, we reach the glacier-foot. Recent falls oblige us to cut steps before we can get on shore. The ice is closing up so quickly behind us that we have only just time to shake our comrades' hands and find out that in spite of their fatigue they look well, and then, putting in a safe place the stores, which we shall come to fetch later, we re-embark and get through the ice just in time before our retreat is cut off.

As is shown by Gourdon's report, which sums up the work of the party better than I could do it, if the object, which was to discover a route to the supposed inland ice of Graham Land, was not attained, the trip was in any case interesting from many points of view and does great honour to those who carried it out. They all come back delighted, in a good humour, and satisfied with one another, which is the best point in favour of them all. But I knew that this would be so at the start. Gain's carefully taken meteorological observations will be most useful for comparison with those taken at our station.

REPORT BY E. GOURDON ON AN EXCURSION INTO GRAHAM LAND

From September 18 *to October* 2, 1909.
On board the *Pourquoi-Pas* ?
Sunday, October 3, 1909.

COMMANDANT,—

In reporting to you on the mission with which you entrusted me I must first of all call attention to the devotion, endurance and good temper which my colleagues, MM. Gain and Senouque, and the sailors, Besnard, Hervé and Aveline, displayed in pursuance of their duty. I am happy to bear witness to this and to thank them before you. Our mission was to ascend on to Middle Glacier to eastward, where an elbow of the mountain noticed in the course of the spring trips allowed us to suppose a passage into the interior of the land. We were to verify the existence of this and then to push a reconnaissance a few days beyond.

We managed to reach the point indicated and we have ascertained that unfortunately there is not in this direction any means of crossing the line of heights by way of a pass or of reaching the upper part of the plateau by a glacier with a gentle slope.

In spite of the negative result as far as the main object is concerned, the trip has not proved useless, for profitable glaciological, topographical and meteorological observations have been brought back, and also the party has gained experience in sledging.

There were put at our disposition a month's food for six persons, two tents with room for three each, and two sledges. Moreover, a depôt of fifteen days' provisions and a tent were placed in reserve on the coast at Mount Diamond. A cache containing three days' provisions for six persons could, in case of need, be found at Edge Hill, situated to the south of Middle Glacier. The two sledges with their full loads had been brought on September 15 to Middle Glacier, at a height of 350 metres, thus giving us a good start-off.

On September 18, at 8 a.m., we finally left the ship in clear but somewhat overcast weather. Bongrain and Liouville, with six sailors, accompanied us on the first day. We put on our skis and had only to carry as far as the sledges a cold lunch, our Thermos flasks, and our cameras.

From Petermann Island to the glacier the crossing of the ice covering the channel was made rapidly, although the melted snow stuck to our skis. At 11 o'clock we reached the sledges and at once harnessed ourselves to them. We pushed on till 3 p.m., with a half hour's stop for our cold meal of sausage, tunny-fish, corned beef and jam. The soft snow and rather steep slope only allowed us to make about three metres, which brought us to 12 kilometres from the coast and to a height of 500 metres.

At 3 o'clock our companions say good-bye to us, and after many handshakes start back for the ship. We establish our camp on the glacier, not far from the western spur of Middle Mountain. The two tents are put up side by side. According to your instructions, the party divides itself thus :—

Tent No. 1, Gourdon, Senouque and Besnard ; Tent No. 2, Gain, Hervé and Aveline. Senouque examines the horizon with the theodolite. The apparatus is placed on a little mound of beaten snow and firmly fixed. At the back of sledge No. 1, with Besnard's aid, I fix a bicycle wheel fitted with a register to measure the ground we cover. At 7 o'clock, the food is cooked in the Nansen kitchens, and soon we have some hot soup, washed down with half a pint of coffee. Then everything is put in its place in front of the tents and the bed-sacks laid out on the canvas matting which is to keep them from contact with the snow. The thermometer registers — 2 °7, the sky is overcast, and a little wind is rising in the north-east. We make haste to slip into our reindeer skins and at 8.45 I blow out the lantern.

It is not a particularly grand night for most of us. It takes some time to get used to one's bed-sack. One finds oneself squeezed up and stifled if one closes oneself up too much, while there are draughts of air if one opens the bag unduly. Violent gusts shook our tents, and the snowdrift rattled down upon them.

In the morning this snowdrift and the exceedingly heavy weather prevent us from starting. It is not until 11 o'clock that we can get off. We have put on one sledge about 200 kilos of provisions and instruments. We shall take this as far as possible and come back to sleep at the camp, which we leave standing. So we push forward north-eastward, all six harnessed to the sledge and shod with snow-shoes. The surface of the glacier is smooth enough and without crevasses, but the extreme sharpness of the slope in places and still more the thick covering of soft snow make our advance extremely slow and difficult. It is snowing and the wind is keen. We have to send one of the party on ahead in turns. He takes a hundred steps, stamping down the snow, and then comes back to harness himself to the sledge, which advances along the path thus made. In this fashion our

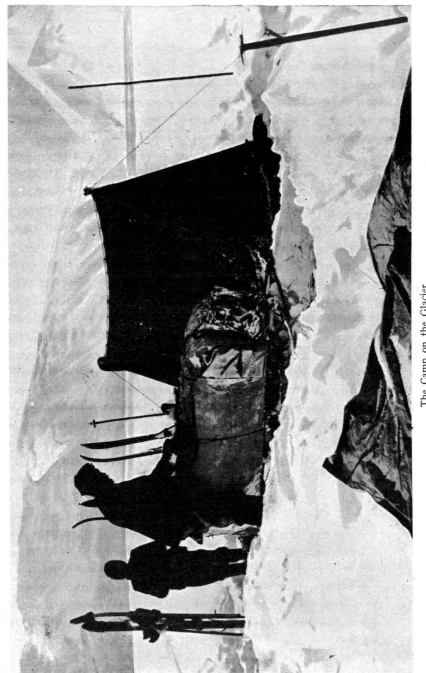

The Camp on the Glacier.

journey is long. At 4 o'clock, we are about 750 metres up,
at the foot of Middle Mountain. A tablet of chocolate and
a half-pint of lemonade restore us a little, and then, leaving
our sledge behind and putting on our skis, we glide down the
slope on our way back to the camp. At this moment a break
in the weather restores calm to the elements and brings back
our good spirits. The soup is put on the fire and soon swal-
lowed, and then we sleep, while a little sleet, mingled with
rain, rattles on the tents.

Next day, September 20, we rise at 6 a.m. The weather
is calm and clear, despite some mist. At 8 o'clock, the sun
appears. The thermometer marks — 4°. Owing to the difficulties of sledging, caused by the state of the snow and the
slope of the ground, I decide to leave here a portion of our
provisions, the place being well marked out by Senouque's
bearings. We leave, therefore, a depôt of eleven days' provisions (for six persons), the two canteens of rum, and two
cans containing five litres of petroleum. We have with
us seventeen days' provisions, which gives us a freedom of
action quite sufficient for our reconnaissance. We set out
on our way in fine, even rather warm, sunshine, and about
1 o'clock we reach the sledge brought on in advance yesterday.
We employ the halt to dry the tents, eat a tablet of chocolate,
and load the sledges afresh. Meanwhile, Senouque examines
the horizon with the theodolite. The number of bearings
that can be taken is indeed considerable. Behind us, that
is to say, westward, the glacier descends in long undulations
towards the sea, whose horizon, in the far distance, is marked
out by pack-ice. On our left Mount Diamond, with its summit
on a level with the horizon, terminates the range which we
have skirted. White Hill, a huge snowy ridge, partly hides
from us the lofty mass of Glacier Mountain. Then comes
the jagged outline of Wandel Island, which loses itself behind
Cape Cloos, itself dominated by the high summit between
Girard and Deloncle Bays. A long crease of snow, in which

several crevasses appear, allows one to guess the presence of these two bays, basins with a regular girdle of glaciers about them. Between the high points can be seen to the north Mount Français. Finally in front of us are twin masses, round and perfectly white; to the right of these opens the valley which should lead us into the interior, and above us rises Middle Mountain, whose high rocky wall is clear grey in colour, streaked with thin lines of darker hue. Unfortunately no rocky point is accessible, and it is impossible for me to collect a specimen.

Our observations being at an end, we start our journey again, only towing a single sledge between six of us. About 3.30, just as we are reaching a region of crevasses, the fog envelops us and forces us to stop. It is snowing, and we go back to fetch the other sledge and put it with the first. The camp is established and the lamps are lighted for the evening meal. The fog is thick, it drizzles, and the thermometer is 3° below zero. We get to bed very quickly, and after examining my companions' legs and assuring myself that they are in good condition, I blow out the light. It is 7.30.

Next day, when we awake, the fog still envelops us. It has snowed abundantly in the night, and sleet is falling continuously. We can do nothing but shelter ourselves. Still in the afternoon, with Gain and Senouque, I reconnoitre the region in front of us, and, coming back to fetch the rest, we go off on skis in the direction of the bearings we took last evening, and advance cautiously with the help of a compass for about a kilometre and a half. Then, planting our skis in the snow, we return to the camp, stamping down the ground to prepare the path which our sledges must take to-morrow. We have an early meal and at 7 o'clock we are in bed.

September 22, one of our best days. The weather is clear and the sun even makes a momentary appearance, lighting up in the west a magnificent sea of clouds, over which we seem to float. The thermometer has gone down a little to — 6°, driving away the damp which was so disagreeable yesterday. To-day is Gain's birthday, so I run up the National flag, and we congratulate him warmly. A box of sweets kept in reserve will lend special éclat to our meal on the journey. We set off gaily with the first sledge over the track prepared yesterday and then come back for No. 2. Our second trip is finishing when suddenly a thick fog envelops us. We have fortunately had time to take our bearings and we can continue on our way with the compass. But travelling becomes very slow and the freshly fallen snow makes it very difficult. Starting off on skis, one of us a hundred paces in advance, and guided by the compass, we journey on some time ; then replacing the skis by snow-shoes, we come back, stamping down the snow, an irksome, discouraging and fatiguing task. We have turned into regular fullers and weariness falls upon us amid the fog. We make our way down with short steps, silent or cursing. Now, harnessed to the sledge, we climb up again, encouraging ourselves with loud cries. Then comes the descent once more, with the breast-strap about us, the traces hanging, and our feet enlarged by our snow-shoes until we look like the heavy spare horses of the Paris omnibuses, coming slowly back to find at the bottom of the hill another 'bus. This comparison amuses us. Finally, the two sledges are together again, and before us stretches the white and powdery surface through which we shall have to dig our way, making the same journey five times for every stage forward.

In the afternoon we were favoured by clear weather, though the sky remained grey. The snow got better, or, I should say, less bad. We resolved to make an extra effort and take the two sledges at once. Besnard and Hervé, the two best in the collar, harnessed themselves with me to the front sledge, which was the more tiring job. Gain, Senouque and Aveline followed immediately after us. This was a success, with a record for pace, in spite of the often pretty stiff slope. It was not until 6 p.m. that we camped, but we were merry and good-tempered, being delighted with our progress of 7 kilometres, which brought us to a height of 900 metres. The highest point reached in the spring has been surpassed. In the evening, Gain provides us with some excellent hot chocolate, which brings us all six rather close together into his little tent. I produce some packets of cigarettes, and this happy day ends most cheerfully. Outside the cold is keen enough at —7° 1. The moon, with a halo about her, lights up the immense glacier, whose sparkling whiteness gives the dead landscape the dazzling beauty of marble.

The night was so cold that in the morning we found all our footwear frozen, even those of us who took the precaution of putting them beside us in the bed-sacks. Up to the present we had journeyed in ski-shoes made of sealskin, covered with the Alpine hunters' cloth socks. We had to replace them by reindeer hide mocassins, and we found these so good that henceforward they were the only footwear used. Their sole drawback is that they wear out rapidly.

The sun is shining, but the cold is keen at — 7°. We start our march again under the same conditions as yesterday. Behind us Middle Mountain, an imposing triangular pyramid, cuts the surface of the glacier into two branches. To the north lies that over which we have journeyed, to the south an immense channel, split up by crevasses, which descends to Cape Rasmussen. To our right the horizontal crest of the Mounts of Ice stands out boldly, while to the left the white dome of the Breasts stands out in a semi-circle, and to the east a series of heights bar the road before us, and at their meeting-point with the Mounts of Ice, make that corner whose mystery we have to clear up.

About 3 o'clock the opening commences to widen, and

unfortunately the eastern flank runs more and more behind the Mounts of Ice. If there is a way through, it must be terribly narrow, and in the direction of the south. It is with gradually tottering hopes that we push on, when suddenly the fog descends and completely cuts off our view. We go back to the sledges and put up our tents, for we must renounce all hopes of reaching to-day the solution of our problem.

At 6 o'clock the snow began to fall. Without rest or respite, the white flakes must have been falling down upon us for 96 hours. Next day the wind rose and soon changed into a furious hurricane. From the bottom of our half-opened bed-sacks, we watched with fright the leaps of our tent, desperately swollen out by the wind, which passed through with a terrific roar, while the uprights quivered as if they would break in the infernal dance of the gusts. We remained 48 hours without communication with our neigh-bours, though they were only a few feet away from us. The snow piled up rapidly about the tents and worked its way in at the sides, over the canvas, to such an extent that the two outside bed-sacks were soon buried under a thick blanket of snow, which at every movement of the sleeper pressed more closely upon him. We had the horrible sensation of being held in a vice which only just left us room to move and forced us to sleep in the least comfortable position. One night in Gain's tent, they could only sleep two at a time ; in ours Senouque was obliged to get up at 3 in the morning to sweep his place clear !

Otherwise we tried to kill time as best we could and endured our ills patiently. We spent the morning in the warmth of our bed-sacks. A cake of chocolate sufficed for breakfast, and all the scraps of newspaper found in the parcels were read and re-read. With the aid of my sketch-book, I manu-factured a draught-board. In the afternoon the bed-sacks were folded up at the back of the tent, the carpet was placed over them, and installed on this improvised divan and some-

229

what wet with the water that leaked through the tent, we devised no end of things while the food was cooking. Sometimes we added a cup of chocolate, and then invitations passed from one tent to the other. Next we swept around the tent as well as possible and proceeded to get to bed, a most complicated operation in so narrow a space.

At last on the evening of the 27th, there was a lull, which permitted us to catch sight of a corner of the mountain. With what joy we greeted it! The snow stopped, and the valley was bathed in wonderful moonlight. Mars and Venus appeared in the sky. What a pleasure it was to go to sleep peacefully without the rattling of the snow on the tent and the howling of the wind.

On the 28th, we awoke in fog, and I thought for a moment that our prison walls had closed upon us again. But at 5.30 a pink haze appears in the east, and so we are up and away. The weather is calm and the thermometer registers − 19°. The fog takes long to clear off, but we advance carefully. The snow is good for our skis, our beards are loaded with icicles, and the dry cold braces us up. From time to time there is a crash of avalanches close at hand. A half-break in the darkness allows us to double the spur of the Mountains of Ice, and we make our way into the pass at the end of which we hope to find a way through. Alas! when the sun smiles upon us at last and lights up the mountains which surround us, it is to reveal to us on every side an insurmountable rampart. We are in a vast amphitheatre, but in a cul-de-sac. In an apparently horizontal line, which is perhaps the edge of a plateau—and this makes our disappointment more galling than ever—there is a weltering chaos of glaciers coming down in an irregular stairway. The valley through which we are passing is choked with snow, and at its end fearful avalanches have broken off from the flank of the mountain enormous masses of ice, which lie at its base, all broken up, in long slopes of blocks and dust.

We call this place therefore the Amphitheatre of the Avalanches. The mountain flank where it is laid bare reveals rock ; unfortunately it is too abrupt for us to reach it and amid the ice-débris I cannot find the smallest fragment of rock to show me its character.

We take our time now contemplating the beauty of the scene, and truly this ' end of the world ' is splendidly striking. This chaos of ice, grooved in places by the raging torrent of avalanches crashing down the slopes and spreading themselves out in a fan at the foot ; the sun multiplied six times in a parhelion with its many-coloured circles, like some fairy halo ; the air all sparkling with diamond dust, and the wisps of white mist streaming from summit to summit, give us an unforgettable moment which rewards us for our pains and lessens our disappointment.

On our return to camp we prepare to depart. Our tents have disappeared at the bottom of a ditch, surrounded by a wall in which we have to cut a stairway. To unbury our sledge we have to sweep away a depth of 2 metres of snow. It does us good to handle the spade in this dry cold, which at 6 o'clock reaches — 23° 5, and we have all the enthusiasm of captives set at liberty. A fine sunset favours us with its golden rays.

On September 29, we strike our camp under a fine sun and with the thermometer at — 12°. In the distance on each side of Middle Mountain, the sea, covered with pack-ice as far as the horizon, shows itself over the slope of the glaciers. The ground, whose softness we have been fearing on account of the great quantity of freshly fallen snow just now, has hardened again in the very keen frost, and having the slope now in our favour we make an attempt to drag the sledges on our skis. The result is excellent, the only difficulty being to keep the sledge upright. Remembering the good effect of the arrangement which we tried before when dragging a whale-boat over the pack-ice in our 1904 campaign, I lash firmly across the front part of the sledge, above the load, two tent-uprights. Thus we get a firm rail by which to keep the balance on either side, and Senouque and I, being well matched in height and strength, push against these two horizontal arms, while Besnard pulls. This arrangement succeeds very well with sledge No. 1, but unfortunately our comrades with No. 2 cannot adopt it because of their greater height.

The caravan was getting along well and we were about to reach the position of our camp of September 20, when about 3 o'clock snow began to fall, accompanied by wind. Up to 4, we were able to get along with the aid of the compass, but the wind got steadily stronger, so we had hastily to encamp and take refuge under our tents. In the evening we went to sleep with the rattling of sleet on the canvas and the groaning of the wind.

On the 30th we were back again in the worst phase of our captivity. Rising at dawn to take advantage of the first break of the weather, we were obliged to stay in our tents by the violence of the gusts, the thickness of the fog, and the abundance of the snow. Our draught-board and a little English vocabulary, which Gain discovered, were our only distractions.

Next day opened as unpleasantly, till at 11 a.m. the fog broke up. We hasten to strike camp in spite of the still very keen wind and the freshly fallen snow, into which our sledges sink. Long waves of spoon-drift give the ground the appearance of a frozen sea, and make our progress very uneven. On the slopes, where we occasionally are carried off our feet by the speed, the sledges rock like a launch, and we have numerous falls, which are fortunately comical rather than dangerous. The afternoon is clear. We make good progress and at 4.30, we stop where we placed our depôt on September 19. Everything has disappeared and there is not a trace in the thick mantle of snow. While Senouque tries to find the place, first with the compass and then with

The Return of Aveline, Besnard, and Hervé.

the theodolite, we put up our tents and prepare the meal. The sky is clear and the thermometer registers — 16°. We go to sleep under a fine starry night, in the hope that to-morrow it will be in our berths on the *Pourquoi-Pas?* that we shall rest.

The 2nd of October starts with a rather thick mist, it is true, but accompanied by wind. At 8 o'clock we have not yet had the slightest break, and it is impossible to go on with our search for the depôt. As I shall have to come back here sometime to complete my measurements of the pace of [the glacier, we can collect our stores on the same occasion. It is useless to waste time, so we pack up traps and start. The snow is in good condition, in spite of the high waves caused by the drift, and as the slope increases our speed becomes fast. At 11 the fog clears off, and the pack-ice comes in sight, looking very bad, full of crevasses and broken up. Shall we be able to cross it, or shall we be condemned to stop in quarantine in sight of port? But there is Petermann again, with the masts of the *Pourquoi-Pas?* We hoist our flags and almost immediately we are answered on board. As was agreed, we keep only one flag flying, signifying ' Send to fetch us.' It is with some anxiety that we await the answer. A signal runs up at the mizzen-gaff, another at the main. This means that the operation will be difficult. A third would show that it is impossible, but happily it does not appear, and hope returns. An hour later we have reached the first depôt. With the aid of field-glasses we see a boat leaving the harbour in the middle of the ice. Beneath our feet, to reassure us, the glacier was bathed by an ice-free sea, and indeed before we could get down, your greetings reached us ; a few minutes later we had the pleasure of shaking hands with you, Commandant, coming off personally to meet us, with Godfroy, our old comrade on the spring excursions, and also with the sailors who accompanied you.

In the course of this fifteen days' trip, which took us to a height of nearly 1,000 metres and to a distance of some 25 kilometres from the ship, the state of health of our little party always remained perfect, in spite of the very unfavourable atmospheric conditions with which we had to put up. Good spirits and cheerfulness prevailed throughout, to which contributed very much the excellent choice of provisions due to your care. Our equipment would certainly have given equal satisfaction had we not met with humidity very contrary to what one expects in these regions.

The meteorological observations, summed up herewith, were taken regularly by Gain. The route, recorded by Senouque, was traced out by means of three stations of the theodolite and seven of the compass, in the course of which 64 points were taken. Middle Glacier, which we climbed to its source, is remarkable for an almost complete absence of crevasses, those which we noticed in the spring being at this season hidden by snow-bridges. Only the lower part of the glacier, for about a kilometre before one reaches the sea, is seamed by large cracks, due to a rapid clearing away of the snow. Before it reaches Middle Mountain, the glacial stream forks and sends out to the south-west an arm, unlike the other, very full of crevasses, which embraces Middle Mountain, Mount Rude, and the Edge, whose mass is thus nothing more than an immense *nunatak*. This arm rejoins Middle Glacier again, so as to present a single front to the sea. At the level of Girard Bay another part of the ice leaves the principal current to fall in cascades into that kind of funnel which breaches its right flank. This glacier is fed comparatively poorly and from one source only. It does not appear that any considerable masses fall from the crests of the Mountains of Ice, as would be the case if they were the waste-pipe for the regions inland. The quantity of snow which falls locally is sufficient to explain how it is that glaciers of such importance can be without a feeding-basin of any size ; for in four days

—it is true we were specially favoured—we saw the level of the ground rise more than 2 metres.

As for the nature of the regions inland, this important problem remains unsolved. Undoubtedly the long horizontal ridge of the Mountains of Ice suggests the edge of a plateau, particularly when one remembers the frequency of this horizontal contour at other places on the coast, in De Gerlache Strait, at the end of Beascocheia Bay, and at the end of Matha Bay; but this is only an hypothesis. Likewise we have discovered no indication of the presence of an inland ice-plain. Perhaps we shall have the opportunity later of making a new reconnaissance at another point.

I came across no rock which I could reach, but from the similarity of aspect presented by those I could see at a distance to the specimens picked up at the Edge and at Cape Rasmussen, I may conclude in favour of a stereoscopic formation. I took myself about sixty snapshots.

I finish, Commandant, by thanking you for the honour you have done me in entrusting me with this mission and by assuring you once more of my entire devotion.

E. GOURDON.

October 8.—Gourdon and Godfroy came to tell me in turn on the 4th that they had oedema of the legs. This did not alarm me beyond measure, for I knew the treatment now and I was convinced that, by taking the malady at the start, all would be right in a few days. I put them, therefore, on an exclusive diet of seal's meat. Surely enough, at the end of three days, every symptom has disappeared. I have not ceased to reflect upon the cause of this scorbutic disorder. What proves completely that it is provoked by the preserved-foods and not by the absence of fresh meat is that the symptoms disappear, not by adding fresh meat to the diet, but by the total suppression of preserved-food.

On the other hand, not all preserves can be to blame,

since, fore and aft alike, we are eating identically the same products, coming not only from the same purveyor but even from the same boxes, and the crew have been totally immune, only the ward-room suffering. Now in the ward-room, at the beginning of the Expedition, there were certain protests to the effect that the menus ought to be a little different, and although I should have preferred to continue with one menu for all, as on board the *Français*, I had to allow there were certain advantages and very few drawbacks in making some differences. These consisted almost exclusively of hors-d'œuvres, coming not from the stores chosen by myself with great care for the trip, but from various presents, over which, of course, we had exercised no supervision. The facts force me to conclude that the cause of ill must lie in these boxes of hors-d'œuvres. But the treatment is so simple and easy, especially since with the spring the seals have become abundant, that I am no longer anxious about the matter.

The ice still stretches out of sight to seaward, and it seems that we are completely encircled. De Gerlache Strait, however, and Lemaire Channel, between Wandel and the coast, having always been free during our first winter, I hope that the same will be the case this year and that we shall be able to get out easily when the plug which is at the mouth of this channel shall be removed. I should like to be ready to start on November 15; for, since we can no longer hope for an important excursion into the interior, I think it would be more interesting to commence our sea-work very early and to put in some productive labour in the South Shetlands before turning south again. Therefore I have commenced preparations; for the persistent bad weather, which stops all work for days at a time, my keen desire to leave under the most favourable conditions, and the trouble we have over the indispensable sweeping away of the snow, which takes us several hours a day, make this necessary now.

The *Pourquoi-Pas?* and her surroundings in October, 1909.

The ice accumulated around the boat bothers us a lot. For one thing, it prevents us from putting the rudder back in its place, and for another, it surrounds the cables, threatening to break them and subjecting them to heavy strains. I no longer dare slacken them, since the gusts of wind and the movements of the swell are so sudden here that the ice might be broken up in a few seconds and a mishap overtake the ship before we had time to haul them taut again.

The crew cheerfully work at breaking up the ice and we lend a hand, looking for weak points, increasing the cracks and splitting up the large blocks with improvised levers. As soon as enough has been cleared away, we attempt to put the rudder in its place, taking advantage of the transparency of the water, but we have to hoist it on land again to make a small alteration in one of the irons.

A couple of cormorants have returned and taken their place again on a point of rock. In the autumn, Gain had fastened about their legs a band of coloured celluloid, as he had done with a large number of penguins. In this way he was able to ascertain that they are the same ones which have returned.

I have just learnt that the stock of nails on board is exhausted, which is not very astonishing, seeing how large a quantity has been used in the construction of the observatories and for the numerous cases enclosing the naturalists' collections. We want nails, but I am not very worried about this, for I have promised a glass of anisette to every man who brings me a hundred. Immediately all the pincers on board are requisitioned to pull them out of old boxes, and if this goes on, we shall have more than we had at the start.

October 15.—The outfitting and repair of the ship is being pushed ahead very actively. The roofs of the cook's galley and the laboratories having been much affected by the temperatures to which they have been exposed, I have them re-covered with painted sail-cloth. In various places the deck has been

re-caulked as best we can. The spirit store-room has been
looked to and the lead which lines it has been re-soldered
wherever there is a crack. We have still almost 6 tons of
spirit to carry with us. Herein there is considerable danger.
Thanks to the precautions which we took, all accidents were
avoided during our first campaign, and I have every reason
to believe that these precautions will continue sufficient, provided we look after the lining of the room and the ventilator.

The rudder was shipped without difficulty, in such a
way that if there is a fresh mishap its unshipping will be
comparatively easy.

All the sails, after the sail-makers had examined and
repaired them, have been bent. I have had a supplementary
crow's-nest of canvas set upon the top-mast cross-trees. More
accessible than that at the top of the mainmast, its height
is quite sufficient for the ordinary conditions of navigation
amongst ice. The Lucas sounding apparatus, whose electric
motor is not strong enough, has been brought from the stern
to the port-side forward. After a series of attempts, Rosselin
succeeded in connecting it with the little engine of the picket-
boat brought back from Wandel, and its working seems as
if it ought to be quite satisfactory henceforward. At Rouch's
orders, Nozal has installed astern a hand-trunnion, which
allows the rapid taking of water at various depths during
deep soundings.

All these operations on board have no effect on our scientific work, which continues with the greatest regularity
throughout the winter.

One solitary penguin has come back, apparently to examine
the rookery; perhaps sent by the rest to report on the
situation. From my notes I see that the same time four
years ago there were twelve penguins back at Wandel, but
there was then much more free water about the island.

The general health is satisfactory, and there are no new
cases of scurvy. But Poste and Modaine have been prostrated

with violent neuralgia for several days. Liouville too, who, entrusted by me at the start with the medical superintendence of the ship, has devoted the utmost care and attention to his duties, has himself been in bed for some days suffering from stomach or liver, but he now seems quite recovered.

On the 12th a black ice-block ran aground close to the island. Gourdon and I have examined it and, as we expected, find its colour due to the abundant sediment imprisoned in the ice before it got afloat. It is very common to find bergs or blocks thus freighted with various geological specimens, but we have rarely seen one so big or so full of mud and gravel. Meeting one like it at sea, even at close quarters, one would be excused for marking down a rock on the chart.

October 19.—If the ice is constantly broken up by the wind in the direction of the channel, to seaward the pack extends out of sight. Beyond the Le-Myre-de-Vilers Islands it is fragmentary, and so also to the south; but along Petermann, Hovgard and Wandel Islands it forms, under a very thick covering of snow, a fine, smooth surface, over which we venture frequently, both for work and for exercise.

Yesterday, while Bongrain took Boland surveying to the Le-Myre-de-Vilers Islands and Gourdon was geologizing on Hovgard, I decided to go with Gain as far as Wandel to discover the condition of the ice in Bismarck Strait. We set off on skis at 10 a.m. The pack-ice was excellent; a little soft and uneven in places, very dense to all appearance, but almost entirely composed of a thick layer of snow through which our staffs pierced easily. Although the thermometer stood at −16° and we were very lightly clad we really felt the heat of the glorious sunshine to which we had become unaccustomed. The reflection was very strong, and we dared not leave off our glasses for fear of the very painful snow-ophthalmia. Thanks to our yellow glasses, recommended by a surgeon-major of the Alpine Rifles, none of us has been troubled with his eyes in the present expedition, whereas in 1904 ophthalmia

239

was the curse of our existence. Apart from their excellent qualities, yellow glasses have this great advantage over smoked ones, that they impart a more agreeable and cheerful hue to the scene, which means a good deal to those who cannot do without glasses. People vary a lot in this respect, for I have seen some attacked by ophthalmia after taking off their glasses for a ridiculously short time, while others have never felt the need of them.

This was the first time since my four months' illness that I had taken part in a trip of any duration, and I started off as gaily as a schoolboy on his holiday, rejoicing in the apparent total recovery of health. Alas! I presumed too much on my strength, and I had a day of physical and moral suffering such as I had never experienced before. After two hours' journey my heart began to trouble me. Palpitations and irregularity were followed by violent agony, accompanied by shootings in the shoulders and arms. But I resolved to go on and tell nothing to my companion, who must have found my conversation singularly spasmodic.

We reached the headland of Hovgard without difficulty, and came across a female Weddell's seal with her young one, her head all powdered with fine snow. In spite of our reassuring words, the poor mother displayed a fear which is unusual in these animals. We crossed the headland and found more good pack-ice leading to another cape, where we rested and ate a tablet of chocolate. Next we went on to a small cap-shaped island north-west of Hovgard, whence we saw Salpetrière Bay covered by the same thick pack, sprinkled with numerous big icebergs. The seals were very plentiful, including six Weddells with their young and a whole family of Crabbers. My heart grew worse and worse, causing me horrible pain. For all my energy and pride, I was forced to stop every hundred steps and lean on my staffs. I was eager to keep up to the end, but the thought of return caused me great anxiety.

About 3 p.m. we reached Wandel. The magnetic hut was half buried in the snow and it would have been impossible to open the door without protracted labour. So I was obliged to rest in a hollow of snow formed by the wind. Stretching myself on my back with my arms above my head, I succeeded in easing my pain a little, but the cold, which made itself felt as soon as I stopped walking, prevented me from keeping still long. While Gain went on a visit to the cormorant-rookery, which was inhabited all the year round, I managed with the greatest difficulty to get to the cairn, awful cramps suddenly attacking my legs and being only got rid of by rubbing and violent slaps.

The whole of Wandel was buried under a thick layer of snow such as I had never seen before, and the pack-ice stretched out of sight everywhere. Even in the haven of Port Charcot there were imposing ice-blocks, and it is certain that a ship wishing to winter here in this exceptional year, with its ice-free sea right into August, would have been in a very awkward position and would probably have been shattered against the rocks or crushed by the ice-blocks.

The discovery of this condition of the ice made me very anxious, for how and when could the *Pourquoi-Pas?* make her way out? My patience has been sorely tried. For the greater part of the winter we were much troubled by the bad weather and open state of the sea, but we hoped at least to get away early and to find but little ice on our route. Unfortunately the contrary is the case, for we have never seen so much ice at any time! But we are only in the middle of October, after all, and happily a great deal may happen in a month.

On our way back to Petermann the sun was hidden and a fresh south-west breeze made travelling a little less painful. It was necessary to get back before nightfall, and in spite of the condition of my heart and my fear of more cramp I made every endeavour to push on as fast as possible. At last we reached the foot of the island and had to climb up about 150 metres before descending to our quarters. I was at the end of my strength. A false step caused me to pitch into the soft snow and I should not have been able to pick myself up without help. Gain, however, proved the best possible of companions. He was both patient and energetic and uttered no word of complaint at having to drag me behind him all the way. He showed clearly his greatness of heart, not only cheerfully lending me his aid but also successfully soothing the shame which I felt at showing my weakness before him.

Gourdon, being somewhat anxious, had come to meet us on the summit of the island, and at 11 p.m. we were back on board. I had walked for thirteen hours, covering more than 35 kilometres, in spite of my myocarditis. For the first effort of one recovering from four months' illness this was not bad!

October 31.—The fitting up of the ship goes on apace, and the stores are piling up in the holds. The picket-boat has been carefully repaired and fitted with a well-made and apparently very useful hood, and to-day she has been launched. The task is a delicate one, owing to the extent of the sheet of ice projecting over the sea, and the whole of the crew has to take part in the operation of getting her afloat.

The birds are coming back to Petermann Island. They herald the end of our troublesome winter and furnish us all with a distraction, while to Gain they mean a fresh start of his interesting studies.

November 1.—All Saints' Day, Todos los Santos! Therefore it is the birthday of Madame Santos Perez, the wife of my dearest friend at Buenos Aires, Dr. Perez, to whom the Expedition owes so much, for he it was who influenced public opinion and interested the Government of his country in my two enterprises. So we drink the health of this charming lady, who can have no idea that at the end of the world the thirty members of the Expedition are making the icebergs ring in her honour.

November 12.—The temperature is higher, varying generally between − 5° and + 4°, but the weather is still as desperately bad, and the gales of wind are followed by heavy falls of snow, which do not make our work easier. Often after these big falls there is, in a very short space of time, a series of thaws and frosts, which cover all the tackle with solid ice, outlining their shape and giving the ship a most picturesque appearance. But when the temperature goes up again there is much danger in stopping on deck, for the ice detaches itself and falls in heavy masses from the masts, or in long swords from the rigging. There are a few accidents, fortunately not serious; but Jabet has had a narrow escape from being killed by a block which fell beside him.

The tarpaulins have been taken off fore and aft, the deck has been cleared and cleaned, the funnel replaced, and the ship has resumed an appearance of active life which is pleasing to see.

On the 7th, after a strong gale of wind, the channel was completely unblocked for several hours and we were able to go hurriedly and recover the sledges which we had had to leave on the glacier the previous month. Since October 2 it has been totally impossible for us to go there, and if by a mischance we had not succeeded in fetching our comrades off that day, they would have stopped in their tents facing the ship for more than a month without being able to communicate with us. The sledges and all that belonged to them were buried under a thick covering of snow, the only indication of where they were being a few tent-poles. We were able to bring back all except one tent and a depôt of provisions, which we abandoned at the top of the glacier.

While the picket-boat was alongside the ship, Frachat, who was in charge of the motor, set fire to the spirit; immediately a long flame shot out and he had only just time to save himself. Happily a Minimax extinguisher was within reach, and in a few seconds the blaze was put out. This probably enabled us to save our precious picket-boat without serious damage, although its reservoir at the moment contained more than 30 litres of essence.

Two other cormorants have returned, also with their rings about their legs, so that all those of last spring have come back to their old home. The penguins for their part are extremely numerous and afford us, as was the case on the *Français*, one of our principal distractions.

The two couples of cormorants have established their nests on a little point dominating the noisy and ill-kept rookeries of the Adélie penguins. With their cleanliness, dignity, and calm elegance, they make a contrast to the dirty chattering crowd of penguins, who are quarrelling and rushing about just as if they were mere human beings. A great number of these penguins have the rings which Gain put on their legs in the spring. It is proved that we are only seeing the adults back again, not one of the nestlings hatched on the island the previous year having returned. It even seems that these penguins come back to the same places in their rookery. The little family which used to live in a cavity in the rock is back again, but the 'loony' is missing; perhaps they have had to shut him up in an asylum.

On the 9th the first egg was laid. Access to one portion of the rookery was henceforward totally cut off, so that Gain might continue his embryological researches under the best possible conditions. I lent him my bacteriological stove, which is transformed into an incubator for hatching out the eggs of various species of birds.

The seals on the ice are also in great number, and we have counted as many as fifty individuals in a group.

Lerebourg has replaced Dufrèche as assistant in the laboratory.

November 14.—One of our great anxieties for the moment is to find how we can fill our boiler and our casks with fresh

We begin to put the Stores on Board.

water. If necessary, we could use sea-water for the first, but it has been kept in such good order hitherto that I shall only risk this as the last extremity. To-day Guéguen, helped by some of his comrades, is busy digging trenches to try to catch the water which the thaw sets running under the glacier covering the island. In spite of all his efforts the quantity which he gets is still insufficient. Guéguen, however, does not despair, and night and day we see him wandering about with a bucket, a spade, and a length of hose. He is a sworn foe to the ice and makes violent attacks on it. When we have to get some off an ice-block or to break or moor one of the blocks, Guéguen is always to the fore, and the usually gentle fellow becomes violent, hitting out wrathfully and insulting his enemy under his breath. He was like this on the first Expedition and has become remarkably clever at his work. He knows the ice and all that can be done with it, and if he cannot find water no one can.

Jabet has come to tell me of some curious black marks on the high cliff of the glacier in front of us. With the telescope I discover, to my great astonishment, that these black marks are nothing else than thirty penguins. The glacier shows traces of the road which they traversed ; they climbed up at the spot where we landed ourselves, mounted right up on to the top of the glacier, and then, probably thinking that they were returning to the water, let themselves slide down a slope which they could not climb again, thus finding themselves about 40 metres above sea-level on the cornice of the steep cliff. The poor birds were in great danger of dying of starvation. We saw them for three days in their evil plight, but on the fourth they had disappeared. Perhaps they ended by jumping into the sea.

November 17.—Guégen's ingenuity has only succeeded in getting 6 tons of water for the boiler, and we want about 18. As I am determined at all costs to fill it with fresh water, I have had a small fire lighted up in the furnaces with a few briquettes and some old boxes, so as to melt gradually the snow which we shall throw in. To get this snow I lay out a line between the ship and the summit of the ice-cliff to starboard. On this line runs our biggest washing-bucket. A party on shore fills the bucket with snow and lets it run to the ship, where another party empties it into the boiler ; then it is again sent back to the cliff. I have calculated that it will take one hundred journeys to finish our task. We all work at it hard, and by dint of urging on the men with a stop-watch, the bucket's full journey is completed in 45 seconds. At 5 p.m. not only is the boiler full, but we have provision of water for two days more. We have been able to light the boiler and as soon as we have a little steam up, the auxiliary gear is successfully tested. Then Rosselin increases the pressure to 7 kilos and, to let me know that the engines are ready, sets the whistle to work. This unwonted sound, which we had forgotten for so long, is at once strange and pleasant. Three-quarters of an hour the engine has been working in a satisfactory manner, and I feel real emotion at hearing the heart of the *Pourquoi-Pas ?* beating once more.

With the engine working it becomes quite easy by means of the pipe for this purpose to melt the ice rapidly and to pump the water into the casks. In a few hours all is finished, Guéguen giving himself the pleasure of destroying a whole ice-block to supply the necessary ice.

We are ready to start, therefore. The only operation remaining to be carried out is to take up the chains and hawsers. These latter, in spite of all our precautions and the clearing work we have done at various times during the winter, are buried under a thick covering of ice and snow, and the men have already begun to dig trenches more than 2 metres deep. I fear that we shall also have some difficulty with the chains, especially with the port chain round the rock which fell at the beginning of our winter season. It is not until the very day of our departure, however, that I shall venture to cast them off entirely and take them on board, for even yesterday a large piece of the cornice came down, stirring up a wave which gave the ship a violent shock, scraping our starboard chain and breaking three hawsers, including the big tow-line.

The state of the ice is so far satisfactory. From time to time there is a certain loosening in front of our haven, which allows us to make some interesting dredges and to take bearings and soundings, but the pack-ice in the offing scarcely alters at all. South of the channel it is quite compact, and in the north, between Wandel and the land, the accumulated ice-blocks appear to present an absolute barrier. A large iceberg seems actually buttressed at its two extremities to the two shores and by its own mass to block the whole of the narrow passage.

I am very anxious about Chollet's health. He has fallen a victim in his turn, but to a much more ordinary form of scurvy. He has great black spots on his thighs and can no longer keep on his feet. He is the only man on board who feels towards seal's flesh a repugnance which no amount of effort can overcome. Fortunately the penguins are abundant, and also they are beginning to give us eggs in fairly large quantities. Yesterday we were able to eat our first omelette, which all declared excellent.

Every morning, under the leadership of Gain, some trust-worthy men go to gather the eggs, but I am obliged to watch carefully and to show my anger frequently. Some of the crew, at other times most docile, go completely mad where there is a question of eggs, which they try to crack and swallow raw, to the loss of their more obedient comrades.

On the 15th we celebrated the national fête-day of Brazil with the flag of that fine country at our masthead, and I may assert that the wishes we expressed for the prosperity of this generous nation were sincere and came from the bottom of our hearts.

November 23.—Some considerable loosenings of the ice

247

have occurred, and the iceberg in Lemaire Channel seems to have shifted a little.

I had insisted that the observation huts should remain to the last moment for the carrying out of our work, but now I give the order for their demolition and the putting on board of their contents. I have decided to leave nothing here. We have before us a long campaign in the unknown and these buildings may be of great service to us. The gangway is lifted up and the topgallant yards lashed together and stowed away. The explosives and the spirit are shipped in their turn, and lastly, on the site of the movable house on Megalestris Hill we build a cairn, surmounted by a signal and supporting a large leaden tablet on which are engraved the names of those taking part in the Expedition.

November 25.—The weather is grey but calm. It seems to me from the summit of the island that a very narrow passage will allow us to enter the portion of Lemaire Channel which is hidden by the mountains and which I suppose at least to be free. I have decided to leave to-day, before midnight. The work done during the day is formidable. We all take part in it, toiling like navvies.

The port-chain, caught under its rock, is fortunately freed by a sharp tug of the steam windlass, and then, with a party of ten men armed with pickaxes and levers, I go down into the trench dug down to the starboard-chain, which, not without considerable difficulty, we succeed in releasing from its covering of ice. We bring it neatly on board without mishap. Meanwhile, the picket-boat and other boats are hoisted and secured.

We free the last hawsers and we are even obliged to cut some of them. The ice-anchors are brought on board. Finally we destroy the boom which has resisted so well for three months, and nothing remains on shore except three men whose duty it is to loosen the hawsers which prevent us from swinging.

An Argument!

Out for a Walk.

At 9 o'clock we get under way, the manœuvre being diffi-cult owing to the accumulation of ice; but Godfroy, who made the plan of our harbour with great care, knows every detail thoroughly, and at 10.30 we are outside. The men left on shore return in the dinghy. The three cairns and a heap of empty preserve-boxes are the only indications at a distance that the island has been inhabited.

Farewell, Petermann! Here for more than nine months, amid snow and fog, we have lived through the tiresome mono-tony of an almost continual gale, and have been through hardships and sufferings, but we have accomplished our task without quailing. The wind will continue to sweep your hills, snow and fog will always envelop you, but man has been able to safeguard his life in your unfriendly neighbourhood and to struggle victoriously against the forces which protect you, and which, as in the stories, have in the end spared him and revealed to him their secrets.

Full of enthusiasm and hope, after this long stop, we set out again to continue our work.

PART III

THE SUMMER OF 1909–1910

BEFORE we are able to draw up a definite programme of our summer campaign we must go to Deception Island, where I have every reason to believe we shall find some coal. We have succeeded in saving about 80 tons of our stock, and if the whalers can let us have another hundred we shall have an unhoped-for opportunity of carrying on the Expedition.

Our short previous stay at this island showed us how much profitable work remained to be done, and at all events we must continue some of our studies there. Our observations, and our collections still more, would be the more valuable for a rather prolonged visit.

November 26.—Our voyage has begun again. We progress slowly, pushing with difficulty through the big floes which block the channel. The current, which is usually so strong in the direction we are going, is hardly to be felt amid the ice, which confirms what I notice from the crow's-nest as we gradually approach Wandel Island. It seems, in fact, that the channel at this spot is hermetically closed. Soon the marine ice is succeeded by a great stretch entirely covered by the hard ice of glacier-débris, and these fragments, small though they are in size, are so heaped together that we can scarcely cut a way for ourselves. Then we get into a perfect maze of icebergs, some of whose summits tower far above our masts. After advancing slowly and steering with the greatest difficulty to avoid dangerous collisions we find our-

250

selves irremediably checked. The big flat iceberg which I saw from the top of Petermann Island completely shuts up the narrow channel and others have come up too to assist in the work. There is in this place an unparalleled accumulation, extending over a wide space. We needs must put about and try to make De Gerlache Strait by way of Salpetrière Bay. This manœuvre is not easy in the narrow passages between the icebergs, full of huge blocks which restrict the effective action of the rudder. Shocks are frequent, and the silence of this calm night is broken by the noise of the ice, which we are displacing, the tinkling of the engine-room telegraph, and the repeated commands, ' Starboard,' ' Port ! ' ' Helm amidships ! ' But we make our way between Wandel and Hovgard.

I have often been over the course we are trying to take, but only in a small boat, and if I know its principal dangers many shallows and rocks may have escaped my notice. A great strip of pack-ice blocks our way. We hurl ourselves forward at full speed. The ship, being lighter than formerly, climbs up, but she is too broad, and in spite of our repeated efforts we cannot break through. There is a passage about 20 metres wide just open along the coast of Wandel. There is a chance of getting aground, but we have to make up our minds to run the risk if we do not want to go back to Petermann. Uneasily and slowly we make our way into it and get through, thus entering Salpetrière Bay. This is sprinkled with icebergs, but by unforeseen luck quite free from marine ice. Through the narrow Rallier-du-Baty Channel, where Matha fortunately took some soundings four years ago, we steam past our old anchorage. I should have liked to stop a few minutes at Port Charcot, but the whole bay is filled with solid pack-ice and the north-easter is beginning to blow. Farewell once more, Wandel, shall I ever set eyes on you again ? The big cairn seems to me to stand out sadly on the top of its hill, but I cannot get rid of the idea that some day this station will be again inhabited, an outpost of civilization established by us.[1]

Scarcely have we emerged from Rallier-du-Baty Channel when once more the pack-ice stretches before us, completely filling up Bismarck Strait as far as the eye can see. It is extremely dense, being composed of slabs of moderate size made very thick by the snow and cemented together by a freezing pulp. The ship progresses with great difficulty through this stuff, the floes will not budge, and our stem cuts into them without shattering them. We go forward therefore desperately slowly. At last in the evening Roosen and Peltier Channels come in sight, completely free of ice. We thread the latter channel and arrive before Port Lockroy. This harbour is entirely filled with very thick pack-ice, and consequently we must abandon the idea of entering.

While our naturalists go ashore in a boat to visit the rookeries, on board we have a good dredge and survey. When our colleagues come back we continue our voyage. Passing Casabianca Islet, Gourdon lands to deposit a new message in the cairn. This polar letter-box has been regularly cleared for some time past, but up to the present we have been the only postmen.

November 27.—In Roosen Channel we meet nothing but bergs, ice-blocks, and débris, and the case is the same in De Gerlache Strait. The ice-blocks most to be feared are those of rounded shape, of a size quite sufficient to make them dangerous, but with so small a portion rising out of the sea that they may be mistaken for an insignificant lump of ice. An error of this sort, abreast of Two Hummocks Islet, has let us in for a violent shock, happily without serious consequences.

About 10 a.m. we enter Bransfield Strait, where our ship

---

[1] Since the *Français* Expedition the Argentine Republic has cherished the scheme of setting up on Wandel Island a permanent observatory similar to that which it has maintained in the South Orkneys since 1904.

Hovgard and Wandel Islands, as seen from Petermann.

begins to dance, and at 12.30 the north-easter sets in strong. Deception Island grows up on the horizon and platonic wagers are being made as to whether the whale-men have arrived yet, when the discussion is abruptly cut short by the appearance of one of the little whale-boats coming full speed toward us. She passes close and salutes us with her flag, while the caps of her crew wave in the air; but the sea is already rough enough to cut off all communications, and after her courteous greeting she puts about to continue the chase. These brave fellows are the first we have seen for a very long time.

This whale-boat is the *Almirante Valenzuela*, of the Magellan Whaling Company. So we know that the factory-ship *Gobernador Bories* is at Deception; and she promised last year to bring us our mail. Our mail! The words are the cause at once of delight and of dread, since for nearly a year we have been cut off from all and whatever the news which awaits us, we must go back into the unknown again for many long months.

We advance through the narrow channel, with grave faces and with but few, forced jests on our lips. The *Gobernador Bories* is at her usual anchorage. Parallel with her lies another ship, the *Orn*, and in the middle of the roadstead is a steamer of strange appearance, which we learn later is the *Telefon*. Already plentiful carcasses of whales prove that the work has begun. When the high cliff no longer hides us, the Chilian and Norwegian flags run up at the mastheads and the decks are covered with people. We moor in a depth of 60 metres and at once I have a boat manned to take me on board the *Gobernador Bories*.

I find in the clean and well-kept ward-room, with its decoration of flowers, M. and Mme. Andresen, still accompanied by their parrot and their Angora cat. They give me a charming welcome, cordial and affectionate. My first question is about what is most important to the Expedition—coal—

and M. Andresen tells me that he can give us 100 tons. So my mind is at rest about our remaining work. During our short conversation on this subject, Mme. Andresen, guessing my thoughts before I speak, with the tact characteristic of sailors' wives, has been to fetch a big packet of letters and sets me in front of a table, bidding me attend to my mail. Alas ! as far as I am concerned, Deception Island this time has earned its name. Probably in consequence of a mistake, or rather through anxiety not to forget them and the consequently excessive care taken of them at Punta Arenas, there are no letters for me from my family, so I know and shall know nothing about what has happened at home ; and the same is the case with several of us. In the impossibility of receiving news it is easy to imagine that all is going well, which explains the saying, ' No news is good news ; ' but now, with letters in our hands dated a little more than a month ago on board a ship arriving from the civilized world, it is quite another matter. I am assailed by the blackest of thoughts, suggesting to me in spite of all my efforts the most foolish and gloomy ideas. Still, one must continue the struggle, voyage on for days and days, and perhaps even risk spending years of anxiety and uncertainty. It is the hardest trial I have ever been called upon to go through ; but as Dumont d'Urville wrote on the day of his departure, ' I have filled the cup and I must drink it.'

Through my hosts, whose good hearts are anguished at not having been able to bring me happiness, I learn the most interesting to us of the great events which have happened in our absence, the discovery of the North Pole by the American Peary and his controversy with Dr. Cook, the magnificent exploit of the Englishman Shackleton, at which I rejoice sincerely, and lastly the crossing of the Channel by our compatriot Blériot. Unfortunately there are no newspapers, and all these tidings are necessarily given to us briefly and without details.

I hear also the history of the *Telefon*, the vessel lying in the roadstead, which aroused our curiosity. On December 27, 1908, that is to say two days after we left, news reached Deception by one of the little whale-boats returning from the chase that a ship bringing a fresh stock of coal for the whalers was stranded on the rocks at the entrance to Admiralty Bay and had been abandoned by her crew, who were able to reach the station in boats.

Immediately all the little whale-boats at Deception Island, belonging to the various companies, set out for the scene of the wreck, and a desperate race began. The *Almirante Valenzuela* made a late start, but she was the fastest of the squadron. They were all on the winning-post when she shot ahead. Andresen leapt on board the *Telefon* and hoisted his flag, and since the ship had been totally abandoned by her crew she was considered his fair prize. With great difficulty, seeing the limited means at his disposal, he got her off the rocks on which she was stranded and brought her back to Deception. There could be no idea of repairing her at this moment, but Andresen had his scheme for the future and he stranded his prize at the end of Deception Bay, opposite Pendulum Cove, where he left her for the winter. At the beginning of November, i.e. earlier than usual, so that the rival companies might not on their return take possession of the wreck, the *Gobernador Bories* reached Deception with a captain and a crew of six for the *Telefon*, a little boiler and a pump, a diver, some materials of all sorts and above all numerous bags of cement. But the ice which we met in such abundance during our short passage was here also, and a thick covering of it filled the whole bay. Andresen had some sledges made of planks, and twelve men set off to look for the *Telefon*. She was entirely frozen in, bunkers, boiler, and engine being all in one compact block. Norwegians, who are the best sailors in the world, are not disheartened at so small a thing as this, and with desperate labour, using the little boiler to melt the ice, they lightened the ship sufficiently to get her afloat after several attempts. The diver began his work. Without any water-tight gloves—for the poor fellow did not expect to find the sea so cold—he plunged into the water at a temperature of − 8°, and after a few minutes of work under these conditions he had hours of suffering. He went on, nevertheless. The *Telefon* was afloat and, helped by a temporary loosening of the ice, she was brought into Whalers' Cove. The injuries to her hull are tremendous, but Andresen is convinced that he will be able to patch them up sufficiently with cement to take back his 4,000-ton prize to Punta Arenas and even to Europe, where thorough repairs are more easily carried out than in South America. ' She's a fine whale,' he says to me with a smile. He is even sure that he will be able to clear boiler and engine of all the ice which encases them, and as the windlasses and other gear are in good condition he cannot see why the engine should not be the same. So he wishes her to make the voyage by her own efforts and not under tow.[1]

Already the empty hogsheads and the coal which constitute the cargo have been unloaded ; and it is thanks to this additional stock of fuel that we are enabled to refill our bunkers.

Lastly Andresen gives me the excellent tidings that the workman on whom Liouville operated in the December of last year is completely restored to health.

All the evening on board comment never ceases on the news I bring back, and the fresh and unexpected tidings give such an impetus to conversation that both ward-room and mess-deck are unusually animated.

November 28.—The north-easter, which began to blow

---

[1] On our return to Punta Arenas we saw the *Telefon* arriving calmly from Deception at a speed of 10 knots, her colours flying in the wind, clean and repainted, carrying on board not only Andresen, but also Mme. Andresen, who insisted on making the passage with her husband. This was the finest piece of salvage-work imaginable.

An Iceberg off Petermann Island.

yesterday before our arrival at Deception, continues and even increases in strength. The thermometer is — 2°.

During the whole time we were in winter quarters, in fact ever since she grounded in January, the ship has always leaked a little; but now Rosselin comes to warn me that we are making as much as 2 tons an hour ! We seek in vain to find how this water gets in, carefully examining the whole of the interior of the hull. Is it a case, as some suppose, of a weakening of the planks of the ship or, as I continue to believe (although we see nothing coming from this quarter), is it merely the injury to our bows, the full extent of which indeed we do not know ? It must of course have got worse during the summer campaign, and our struggle with the ice in getting away from Petermann can but have increased it. Or is it perhaps, on the other hand, a fresh injury arising from the repeated and frequently violent shocks the ship sustained in winter quarters ?

M. Andresen, whom I go to see in the afternoon and whom I tell of our leak, very kindly offers to have his diver examine our hull and insists that I shall accept.

When it grows a little calmer the *Telefon* is to go alongside the *Gobernador Bories* to unload some cargo, and then we are to take her place to embark our coal. M. Andresen tells me that he insists on giving me this coal in exchange for a similar quantity which he will take from our reserve at Punta Arenas. To remove all my scruples about accepting, the best he can find to say is that our arrival has saved him a great deal of time and also of coal, since he had decided, had we been a month later, to come to look for us with his whalers at least as far as Wandel. I could not have expected such generosity, for it would have been quite natural for him to make me pay a big price for this coal, and in the condition in which we are I expect that I should have complied with all demands. He offers me also some petroleum, of which we are short, and sends me in the afternoon a fine present of two sacks of potatoes. Mme. Andresen has found out that Chollet is suffering from scurvy. The charming lady at once despatches to him the whole of her own little stock of apples and oranges. She sends to me, with these, some pots of flowers, which she cultivates with great care. How could I ever sufficiently thank these excellent people ?

In the evening the wind drops and Gain goes with some of the crew in the dinghy to look for eggs in a big Antarctic penguin-rookery near the entrance. Further south we have never come across this kind of penguin except one at a time. Here they live in thousands. The seals are equally numerous, and their steaks, with our new supply of potatoes, make a regular treat for us.

November 29.—The north-east gale has started again more strongly than ever, accompanied by snow. I have been fearing all the morning lest we should drag, for one cannot anchor here except in very deep water and the holding is bad. The whalers, too, have warned me that we must keep a look-out, for in spite of all the precautions with which they surround themselves (which we cannot take for so short a stay) they are frequently driven ashore, they say. Happily the anchor has a good grip, and we are holding so well that I am afraid it may be fouled by the chain of the *Gobernador Bories*. We cannot complain for the moment, but we may perhaps have great difficulties in consequence when we want to get under way.

The weather is still moderate this morning, and Bongrain has succeeded in taking ashore the seismographic hut and has begun to set up the instrument. Godfroy, for his part, has been able to instal his tide-gauge. But in the afternoon the weather becomes frightful. Although we are only two cables' lengths from the shore, from which the wind is blowing, the sea grows so heavy that we cannot put out a boat. The dinghy has broken its painter and has drifted away. Fortunately the wind must have carried it right into the basin, but in this raging tempest of snow it is impossible to see it.

At 6.30, in spite of the thick weather, the *Svenfoyn,* another factory-ship, comes into the roadstead, accompanied by its little whale-boats, and anchors near us. These Norwegians are certainly famous sailors, for all the whalers are out hunting. One of them has even come in with two whales in tow and gone out again without waiting.

November 30.—There has been a slight calm, and I went out with Godfroy in the picket-boat to look for the dinghy. We saw it at last in the midst of the ice in the big basin. With great difficulty we cut a way for ourselves up to it. It was full of water, but has lost nothing except its rudder, and as Libois made one for the *Pourquoi-Pas ?* he can make one for the dinghy. We had scarcely brought the truant back when the weather again became bad. Nevertheless, Bongrain succeeded in fixing up the seismograph and setting the apparatus to work. At 4 o'clock I went on board the *Orn,* where Captain Paulsen received me very affably. I had heard that he had the last edition of the English map of the South Shetlands, brought up to date by the aid of our labours on the *Français,* Nordenskjöld's, and the information given by the whalers. He very kindly agreed to lend it to me to have it copied. He gave me some interesting details about his work here and told me that when the *Telefon* was wrecked his young wife was on board, on her way to join him. She had to spend six hours in a small boat, and this year he did not allow her to accompany him.

December 1.—The gale still continues from the same quarter. This morning a new ship has arrived, the *Bombay,* which was expected by the others on this very date. She belongs to the same company as the *Orn.* New Sandefiord (it is thus that the whalers, in memory of the port at which they fitted out in Norway, call the cove to which we give the name of ' Whalers' Cove ') now shelters all the ships expected, and the poor whales are in for it. The young Danish doctor engaged for the season by the three companies should be on board the *Bombay*.

The wind is strengthening so much this evening that I have the fires made up to be ready for all emergencies.

December 2.—Wind fairly strong or moderate, varying from north-east and north-west to west, and going back to north in the evening. Temperature $+ 2°$.

The ice from the end of the bay is entering the channel in great masses and chokes the greater part of Whalers' Cove. The little boats, therefore, enter and return with the greatest difficulty. The captains tell me that they have never seen so much ice in the four years they have been here. This evidence agrees with what we ourselves found further south, and yet the winter for us was exceptionally mild and the ice very late.

I profit by the ice all around us to take in tow to the picket-boat a big floe, which I have moored alongside us. We cut it up in pieces, which are thrown into the boiler. The water thus obtained is a little briny, but good enough for the engines. Most of the members of our staff scatter over the island. There is work for all, and I have reason to believe that our stay here will be most profitable.

December 3.—Very fine weather, variable breezes, a clear sky, and temperature $+ 4°$. I have the fires made up early and we start to weigh anchor at 6 o'clock, to go alongside the *Gobernador Bories* and get our coal on board. Our anchor, as we supposed, was fouled by the chain of the other ship, but by heaving in to a short stay, going ahead gently, paying out cable a little, and shortening in again, we succeed in getting under her stem. The *Gobernador Bories* then hauls taut her chain, sends us a line, and we end by clearing our anchor and getting ourselves alongside abreast of the after hold, where is our coal. Unluckily, while getting under way, a regrettable accident happens. A length of the innumerable whale's intestines which are floating about the cove having wrapped itself round the chain, Hervé got down into the bowsprit shrouds to take it off. The chain was coming up at this moment and Hervé's foot was caught in one of the links and pulled into the hawse-hole. Fortunately, a very thick boot partly saved him, but he has a bad wound on the joint, which will probably necessitate surgical aid. I am all the more grieved because he is one of our best and bravest sailors ; but the victim himself takes it very cheerfully.

At the moment we come alongside, several cats look down on ours and one of them decides to pay a visit of courtesy. Trying to jump on board, it miscalculates its distances and falls between the two ships. Happily for it Denais saw it and, risking getting crushed himself, he went overboard with the agility of a monkey and saved the poor beast.

We are now in the midst of cut-up whale corpses and others being cut up. Everything is covered with oil, and the odour is very unpleasant ; but one gets used to anything.

The whalers' doctor, by name Malver, has come to pay us a visit. He is a very intelligent young man, but is making his first voyage and is much astonished at the life he is living and all he sees about him. He speaks French and English fluently, and is enchanted when I talk to him about his beautiful city of Copenhagen.

In the evening I am invited to dinner by M. and Mme. Andresen. For the occasion I get into civilized garb, with a linen shirt, a starched collar, cuffs, tie-pin, and all the rest. I must confess, moreover, that I found myself immediately at my ease and that I mechanically put into my pockets the useless objects I had given up for so many months ; but it was impossible to get into my town shoes and I had to be content with substituting for my boots an enormous pair of snow-shoes.

The dinner, at which Captain Stolhani was present, was delightful, and the dishes excellent. Amongst other things we had chicken and some oranges! Must I confess again, at the risk of disillusionizing my readers on my return, that I found chicken and oranges excellent, but they made no more impression on me than if I had eaten them the night before! The parrot dined with us and took a most amiable part in the conversation.

December 4.—The weather is overcast, with a calm or light breezes. At 6 o'clock we began to put the coal on board. The men work without stopping all day at the dirtiest job possible; for not only must they pass the coal into our own bunkers but they have also to get it out of those of the *Gobernador Bories*. Moreover, our bunker-holes are necessarily very small and the stowage is very difficult. After 12 hours of this work an easily intelligible lassitude prevails, but with kind words and encouragement I succeed in re-establishing peace, and the work goes on till 7 p.m. By shutting the ears to some grumbling on the part of our mercantile sailors, by showing confidence in them and by appearing at least to leave the initiative to them, one gets all one wants.

A serious question at Deception Island is that of fresh water. The whalers have need of very large quantities for their work, and to procure it they bring with them a whole outfit of canvas hose, metal pipes, planks for making gutters, and pierced hogsheads. With great ingenuity they catch the water coming from the little cascades formed by the melting of the snow on the top of the ice-cliffs, or else that coming from the snow covering the beach. Sometimes they go very far afield, as far as the fossil glacier extending between Whalers' and Pendulum Coves. To bring back this water they have astern boats towed by motor-canoes. Unfortunately the temperature up to now has been rather low, and the water only runs in small quantities and during a few hours of the day. The hot water springs are useless because sulphurous. In spite of the competition between the different companies, the directors, captains and crews make no attempt

262

to injure one another and give mutual help in all things, especially in the matter of water. One and all work for the common service.

We benefit by this also, and M. Andresen with his usual kindness saves us numerous journeys by sending us water direct from his engine-pump.

We have been fortunate enough in our turn to render him a little service. The lack of gloves prevented the diver from working more than a few minutes under water. The captain of the *Telefon* had very cleverly cut him out a leather pair, but the seams nevertheless let in the water. We have found on board some tubes of liquid rubber, which enables the gloves to be made perfectly watertight, and this apparently insignificant gift is of priceless value in our friend's work.

I have made the acquaintance of the captain of the *Telefon*, a superb type of Norwegian, of uncommon vigour and shrewdness. He has recently strained his foot seriously, which does not prevent him from jumping a distance of 3 metres, without turning a hair, to return my visit.

The harvests on shore continue to be rich. Gourdon has brought back some fine mineralogical specimens, Gain some Yellow-crested Penguins (*catarrhactes chrysolophus*), and both have succeeded in making interesting observations in their different departments. On the south-east coast, which is bathed by Bransfield Strait, there is a rookery of 50,000 Antarctic Penguins, and in the middle of this is a rookery of Crested Penguins numbering about 1,500. The two species apparently live on very good terms. The sea breaks with considerable force on the coast, and Gain brings back some amusing photographs of penguins in the midst of the breakers. On the west coast is another big rookery of Antarctic penguins, numbering more than 50,000. These birds generally lay two eggs in the nest.

December 5.—The north-easter begins to blow again. While all the rest are still asleep, the ward-room has been converted into an operating-theatre, and Liouville, Gourdon and I have examined Hervé's wound under chloroform. The articulation of the first joint is laid open, but we agree, from the healthy appearance of the wound, that the amputation which we dreaded is unnecessary, and we content ourselves with some stitches. I have put Hervé to bed in the cabin next mine, where he will be better off than in his own berth, and I shall be able to watch over him by night. It would be difficult to imagine a better patient, always cheerful, content, and good-humoured. This gentle Breton giant, since he has been on board, has never had a moment of bad temper nor aught but a smile on his good-natured, intelligent face.

M. Andresen has given me to understand that to-day being Sunday he would prefer that no work should be done on board his ship. For my part I am not vexed at giving this well-earned day's rest to my crew, but of their own accord this morning the men have gone down into the bunkers and finished the stacking of the coal put on board yesterday.

In the evening we had M. and Mme. Andresen to dinner. We did our best in their honour, our service with the arms of the *Pourquoi-Pas ?* on it being brought out, while we got together with great difficulty two unbroken tumblers and five champagne glasses. We had some dozens of them when we left Punta Arenas, but the mess-steward tells me that the causes of their disappearance are firstly the rolling of the ship and secondly the cold, and lastly, he adds, everybody knows that glass is fragile ! As I do not wish to appear more ignorant than ' everybody ' and as my scoldings would do no good, I can only be resigned. We produced the best from our stores and our cellar, and I must say that our guests were good enough to appear to appreciate French cookery and the generous wines of our country.

December 6.—In overcast and calm weather, with the thermometer hovering about zero, we continued our work on the coal, finishing at 2.30 and then giving up our place to the *Telefon*, which came alongside the *Gobernador Bories* again.

This morning our two naturalists, Liouville and Gain, accompanied by Senouque with the cinematograph, went out on the *Almirante Uribe* for a whale-hunt, M. and Mme. Andresen being of the party. It was an unique and unexpected opportunity for them to study close at hand the two species of balaenoptera (*B. musculus* and *borealis*) and the megaptera (*M. longimana*) which are to be found in these regions. I was convinced, before we came back here, that the whalers encouraged such observations, and I was not wrong, for not only was Liouville, who is particularly interested in these cetaceans, invited on board all the whale-boats, but every one was eager to give him all the information possible and to bring him any portions worth notice ; and so especially our own collection has been enriched by specimens of the parasites of whales.

The *Almirante Uribe* came back at 9 p.m., bringing a Blue Whale, and our colleagues are enchanted with their day and the manner in which they have been treated on board.

December 7.—To-day the weather happens to be superb, and M. and Mme. Andresen have the excellent idea of coming to take us all out whale-hunting on the *Almirante Valenzuela*. As on my first visit I am struck by the extreme cleanliness of these little vessels, the very practical system in vogue on them and the real comfort displayed in their fitting up. This is one of the most up-to-date and possesses all the latest improvements. For people really fond of the sea she would make a wonderful little yacht.

I need not, I think, give another description either of the boat or of a whale-hunt.[1] From noon until 2.30 a.m. we were afloat, searching first along the coast of Livingstone Island and then around Sail Rock. Several times we sighted and

[1] See p. 41.

went in pursuit of whales, but they always succeeded in escaping us or presented a poor target for the cannon. It seems that a rather heavy sea is better for the chase, since the body of the animal stands out better among the waves and allows an easier shot. In spite of my desire to see our hosts successful and to be present myself at the various phases of the catch, I confess that I was not sorry each time one of these magnificent, peaceful and amiable brutes managed to escape, and that it was with joy that I saw fading farther away the little black patch on the calm blue sea, with the jet of noisily spouting vapour above it.

Nevertheless, after we had pursued a couple of Blue Whales sailing along happily and unsuspiciously, a series of very adroit manœuvres brought one of them within the right distance of our cannon. The captain fired calmly, and the beast was hit, making the foam fly up around her and disappearing with a tremendous leap. The cable is paid out with wonderful rapidity and already the windlass is ready to haul it in again, when suddenly the tension stops. It seems that the harpoon has broken near its head and the prey is lost. We look round on every side to see the wounded beast reappear, but the captain says that she was killed on the spot. This being so, she has sunk and will not rise to the surface before three days are over. In the distance I see her poor companion, now left all alone. No longer will they swim together, in an intimacy which perhaps had its pleasures, through the great green expanses and among the valleys and the fairy grottoes beneath the icebergs which should have protected them from the cruelty of man.

A few hours later we chased four Fin Whales manœuvring in line abreast without gaining or losing an inch on one another, magnificently calm and ignorant of the danger threatening them. They presented a poor target, it seems, and I am not sorry. Certainly I could never be a sportsman.

The whalers, however, who are not working for the pleasure

of the thing, are upset, for hunting is bad this season. Perhaps, they tell me, this is due to the absence of icebergs, which are indeed very scarce about us ; for it seems that these animals like to haunt the neighbourhood of these masses of ice. A naturalist would find interesting microscopic study in the subject of whale-food—the infinitely small denizens of the water—which must count for much in explaining the routes the whales follow ; and science once again would hereby render eminent services to commerce. The bad weather which has lasted since the beginning of the summer campaign, unparalleled both for persistence and violence, troubles the fishermen a lot.[1]

There is perhaps also another reason, more important and serious for the whalers. Through dint of being over-hunted in the one region, these animals are perhaps becoming warier and instead of coming down south, as they used to do, by way of Bransfield Strait, they may take a devious route, away from Deception Island. Lastly, the reckless hecatombs of four years, numbering sometimes over 2,000 whales a season in this limited region (the whalers themselves are the first to deplore them, without being able to remedy the matter) must necessarily reduce their number and may even bring about their extermination ; for a whale's period of gestation is about a year, and as the pregnant mothers and young whales are hunted with the rest there can be no restoration of the balance.

At 3 a.m. we returned on board, while the *Almirante Valenzuela* took a little more coal and some provisions and started off again. These boats indeed only rest once a week, on Sundays, spending the remainder of their time out of harbour in pursuit of their work. The men take watches

---

[1] On our return to Punta Arenas we learnt that the fishery improved later, but that the whalers had to go as far as the entrance of De Gerlache Strait to find their prey. Nearly 1,500 whales were brought in during this season to the five factory-ships.

as on board all ships, but as soon as a whale is sighted every one must be on deck, even the men available for the engine, and under these conditions they can rarely get four consecutive hours of sleep. Far more frequently they pass 24 hours without going to bed. The only moment of real rest, for the captain as for the crew, is when several whales are being towed back and there is no possibility of pursuing others for a time. But all these men, though their fixed monthly wage is small, make money when the catch is good, and they forget the miseries of this arduous profession when they think that the wife and children at home in Norway lack nothing in the clean little cottage where they themselves may perhaps one day enjoy their hardly earned repose.

December 8.—Yesterday's fine weather has not lasted, and the east-north-east wind has begun again.

The diver, M. Michelson, an intelligent Norwegian, has been down to-day to examine the hull of the *Pourquoi-Pas?*. He has been at work nearly three hours beneath the ship, examining minutely all the submerged portions. The low temperature of the water compels him to come up to the surface practically every ten minutes, and even then he remains a few moments without power of speech. Before he began his inspection I asked him, if he found anything serious, to tell no one but me. His report on the hull, apart from the bows, is satisfactory, and is given out aloud. He has discovered a curious big hole on the port-side, extending a long way; a good deal of wood torn off where the hull struck the rock several times at Petermann Island; a few grazes almost all over, caused by the ice; and, finally, what we saw ourselves, a fragment of the false keel torn off astern. Our new irons on the rudder have held good. But when the diver comes up after examining the bows he contents himself with saying, in front of the crew, that there is evidently an injury, though of small importance; and he makes a sign to me that he wants to speak to me in private. A few minutes later I go to see him on board his own ship and, looking rather pale, he tells me that he has discovered a most serious injury. The whole stem below water-line is torn away as well as several metres of the keel, the wood being pulped right down to the rabbet, and splinters sticking out on all sides. ' You cannot, you must not navigate in such a state in the midst of ice,' he says to me. ' Mere ordinary navigation is already dangerous, and the slightest shock might send you to the bottom.' [1]

A few minutes later M. Andresen comes to look for me and tells me that Michelson has begged him to speak to me and explain to me the seriousness of the matter. I thank them both, but in my turn beg them to let out nothing of what they know. We must continue the task we have undertaken, our honour and, still more important, that of our country being at stake. Nothing will make me renounce this summer campaign, bad weather and the observations now in progress alone preventing me from starting at once. These strenuous men understand me and shake my hand. They would do the same in my place.

---

[1] When the *Pourquoi-Pas* ? went into dry dock at Montevideo in April we were able to verify Michelson's statements. The big hole on the port side extended for 15 metres, cutting clean through the outer planking in places. We could not make out either how or when it was made ; perhaps on January 8, 1909, when we felt no shock but that curious rolling motion. In any case, it is certain that it was caused by a rapid passage over the top of a rock. A few fractions of an inch more and the ship would infallibly have gone to the bottom fast. As for the damage to the bows, it was most serious and took a long time to repair. The water which effected a lodgement on board came in there in floods, and with my pocket-knife I was able to cut right through the wood and make new openings in it. The wood was so pulped that the whole of the bows looked like an enormous brush. Our hard struggle with the ice since we grounded, during both the first and the second summer campaigns, had considerably increased the damage and had it continued must in the end have worn out what still held firm.

Our making two tons of water an hour was caused solely by this injury to the bows. The rest of the hull was in admirable condition, proving its excellent construction and solidity, and showed not the slightest trace of weakening or wearing out. When once this injury had been repaired through the good offices of the French Montevideo Co., the ship no longer made a drop of water, and her hull might be considered as good as new.

I think it right to tell at least a portion of the truth to my colleagues on the staff, but it seems to me useless to alarm the crew ; and yet I feel sure that if both parties had known all, not one among them would have dreamt of an immediate return home.

I try in vain to induce Michelson to accept some remuneration for his examination of the ship. He answers with a laugh that he did not come to Deception Island to dive around the vessels of scientific expeditions, so that this has been a pleasant distraction for him. I feel that by insisting I shall in the end offend him, and I have to content myself with expressing as best I can my gratitude and my admiration for his disinterestedness.

December 9.—The north-easter is blowing very hard and soon turns into a gale. If we remain moored to the *Telefon* it will be dangerous for both of us, so we must anchor in the roadstead. I desire to take advantage of our move to sound and dredge in the basin of Deception Island. Just as we are starting we have a great shock, for news is brought us that the engine-room, which was made dry an hour before, has over 40 tons of water in it. After yesterday's report we have reason to believe that something serious has occurred suddenly and surreptitiously. Happily after examination we conclude that the valve of the pump must have accidentally jammed ; and when the water has been exhausted it does not come back more quickly than before—which was quite enough.

The thermometer registers − 2°, and with the wind that is blowing the weather is very cold. We go to the end of the basin, sounding and dredging as we go, with very good results. The ice, since our arrival, has gradually left Deception, and there is now but little, all of it to the south-west. At 5 o'clock we anchor in Pendulum Cove, where the gusts are as strong if not stronger than in Whalers' Cove, but the holding is good at a moderate depth. I should have liked to stop here during the continuance of this gale, for at the other anchorage I am always afraid of driving or of losing our anchors in the network of chains belonging to the whalers ; but Gourdon, who has gone on a trip in the picket-boat is to rejoin us there, and his observations with the pendulum and the seismograph are not yet finished. So we return and try to moor as close to land as possible, in the hope of finding bottom at less depth and with better holding. But all of a sudden we drive and our anchor-shackle breaks and is lost. Luckily I had taken the precaution of bringing five. The weather is so bad that it is extremely difficult to manœuvre in the midst of all these vessels and we run dangerously near the high cliff. Not till 9 o'clock are we able to moor again, but we are now holding so well that I believe this time we are caught in the chain of the *Bombay*.

December 18.—The weather has been so frightful these last days that despite our close proximity to the land, off which the wind is blowing, we have scarcely been able at short intervals to communicate with the other vessels or leave our ship. For three successive days it has been impossible to launch a boat. The whalers have been unable to go out and those outside have quickly returned. Even to leeward of the island the sea seems to have been tremendous.

We have nearly finished our labours, and I should like to be once more on our way, but we cannot hope to do anything at sea with these gales and the snow, which cuts off the view. Here at least we are not burning coal and we are not wasting our time, for there are always interesting pursuits for us all. The soundings at the entrance to Whalers' Cove are incomplete or erroneous ; and, since this place is now frequented, as from its situation it deserves to be, both by whalers and by scientific expeditions, it is right for us to try to rectify and complete its charting. There is work therefore for our officers, while the naturalists and geologist have plenty to do for their part.

As I still believe that we are moored to the chain of the *Bombay* and as it may in consequence take us a whole day to get under way, I have made up my mind on the first lull to attempt to get our anchor up and then to go and moor in Pendulum Cove, whence we can start out whenever we want and in a very short space of time.

I could have wished, before going south, to do a little more work in the neighbourhood. We are sure of making profitable researches here, and, in case our navigation into the unknown turns out fruitless, we shall thus have made certain of a good haul in the way of collections and observations. The programme which I have mapped out for myself is to try to reach Esperance Bay, where Duse and J. Gunnar Andersson, of the Nordenskjöld Expedition, wintered under such dramatic conditions. Professor Nordenskjöld gave me in writing information to enable me to recover some fossils which they were obliged to leave behind. Lastly the whale men are very anxious to know whether there cannot be found in the bays of Joinville Island some good anchorages, at which they could carry on their work. It comes within the scope of our duties to discover this for ourselves and to try to bring the information back to them.

We have offered our hospitality to Captain Stolhani of the *Gobernador Bories* and to Captain Rouvre of the *Bombay*. Both are very interested in our Expedition, and are pleased to see that we are paying attention to their labours. In conversation with them we, on our side, pick up useful information about these regions, and we tell them in return what we can about Port Lockroy and De Gerlache Strait, which it may be advantageous for them to know. But I am astonished at the difficulty which we have in learning anything precise about the weather conditions at Deception. We meet with contradictions every moment from one and the same person. So when the young Danish doctor on the station, Dr. Malver, comes to dine with us I ask him whether he would care during his stay to make some meteorological observations. He has very little to occupy him and is delighted to oblige us while doing something in the cause of science. I give him therefore a little programme drawn up by Rouch and a sling thermometer.[1]

Captain Rouvre has given us a huge piece of whale-meat. This meat, of which the whalers themselves are very fond, is simply exquisite. It may be compared with the best veal. Unfortunately it does not keep and must be cut from the animal as soon as it is killed.

The fresh water problem still worries us and, in spite of everybody's kindness, we can with difficulty keep our casks full. Still, this will not keep me from starting, for I am convinced that we can complete our watering at Pendulum Cove.

December 20.—All our erections on land have been taken to pieces, and as the weather was a little finer yesterday we attempted to get under way ; but our anchor is in fact caught in the *Bombay's* chain, and we must take the greatest care not to lose it and at the same time two links of chain. We worked up to noon, but the wind rose again, and as we had to abandon the operation all has to be done over again. This morning we recommenced our work in calm weather and at 7 p.m. we were able to ship both anchor and chain. A little whale-boat, the *Svip*, came back while we were at work, with the fine catch of seven whales all on her own.

At last at 8 o'clock we anchor in several metres of water in Pendulum Cove. Before leaving, in case we cannot return to Deception, I hand to M. Andresen our mail and some reports which he undertakes to transmit to the Académie des Sciences if he gets back to Punta Arenas before us.

Hervé is getting better and better, and has been able to

---

[1] I have since received from Dr. Malver a very interesting series of observations, which he made with the utmost care. It is most curious to compare them with those which we made further south. I hope he will allow me to offer him here my sincerest thanks.

return to his bunk on the mess-deck. Chollet, thanks above all to Mme. Andresen's fruit, is on the road to complete recovery.

December 21.—It is exactly a year since we arrived here the first time, in identically similar weather, fine and warm.

In the morning we all scattered, Gourdon, Gain and Senouque going out in the picket-boat on a trip to the other side of the basin. Bongrain and Godfroy have been surveying, and Rouch sounding. I myself go with the men to look for a watering-place, and in the end I find some cascades which we tap by means of our canvas hose. We have also to clean up the ship and her boats as much as possible. In consequence of our stop in Whalers' Cove, everything is simply covered with a thick and disgusting coating of oil which we cannot get rid of. In the evening, I go to look for Gourdon and his companions at the spot where the *Telefon* passed the winter stranded. In this part of the island there are a number of undoubted smoke-vents, and Gourdon says that he found at the height of about 100 metres, plain traces of volcanic activity.

December 22.—The weather remains good, and while Gourdon and Senouque make the ascent of Mount Pound I have everything got ready for our start and go to leave a new message in the *Uruguay's* cairn.

At 4.15 we got under way, and half an hour later stopped at Whalers' Cove, where I went on board the *Gobernador Bories* to say goodbye—or *au revoir !*—to M. and Mme. Andresen. Then we start off, saluted by the flags and whistles of all the steamers. The weather is magnificent and the little wind which is blowing is astern. At sea we meet the small whalers and exchange salutes with them. Unfortunately, at 6.30, Rosselin comes to tell me that the gear of the high-pressure cylinder is broken and that there is an injury to the air-pump. This repair will take four or six hours' work and we are too close to Deception Island to hesitate to go back. At 8 p.m. we are again in Pendulum Cove.

December 23.—Our repairs are finished about midnight and we are off again at 7 a.m. The weather is superb, the sky cloudless, the horizon clear, and the sea smooth. The thermometer, at + 5° in the afternoon, goes down at night to — 2°. Everything promises a fine voyage, and the coast stands out clearly, tinted with that old-gold which is peculiar to Polar lands under strong sunshine. We mark out on the map, as we recognize them one by one, the lands discovered by Dumont d'Urville and surveyed by Lieutenant Duse and Captain Larsen, who completed the study of this region, one of the smallest but not least interesting portions of the work of the Nordenskjöld Expedition. We are already anticipating all the pleasures of a landing in this neighbourhood, historical since their time through their dramatic wintering there, when once more ' we find ourselves in the hands of the gods like flies in those of naughty children.' Sixty miles from land, apparently starting from Astrolabe Island, the ice lies before us, composed of jagged but fairly big floes, which are more and more closely packed as we make our way in. In the distance, nearer to land, the ice even looks as if it formed a dense pack ; on its border are great indentations, but its general trend is towards the north-east. I search in vain for a passage, for I am not thinking of breaking through the ice to take the *Antarctic's* channel. To have any chances of success we should have to expend upon this attempt, which is only an extra in our programme, too much coal and perhaps too much time. We should also have to run the risk, not only of being reduced to inactivity for long weeks at the mercy of the ice and thus of compromising the rest of our campaign, but also of seeing the *Pourquoi-Pas ?* (in this case without absolute necessity) finish her career in the same way as the *Antarctic* did so gloriously. It will be remembered how this vessel was lost after having vainly attempted, while trying to pick up Nordenskjöld and his companions wintering at Snow Hill, to pass through the ice-choked strait which bears her name. Captain Larsen, who was in command of her, succeeded in turning Joinville Land, but after landing Duse, Gunnar Andersson and a sailor in Esperance Bay, the *Antarctic*, crushed by the ice in spite of all the skill of her commander, sank in sight of Paulet Island. The rescue of the whole expedition thereafter makes one of the finest and most extraordinary chapters of Polar history. Now that year the ice in Bransfield Strait was in a condition very similar to what we have come across ourselves. When the *Antarctic* was there, the basin of Deception Island was choked by ice, as it was for us during the greater part of November, and it was almost in the same latitude, to seaward of Joinville Land, that the *Antarctic* met it again.[1]

I have therefore resolved to follow the line of the pack-ice, pleased if I can find a way through, but with no intention by trying to force one.

December 24.—Magnificent weather, with a light breeze from the south-east, or calm. The pack-ice, in which the floes are getting more and more gigantic, runs on still north-eastward, leading us away from Louis Philippe and Joinville Lands. At 4 a.m. Bridgmann Island is in sight. No expedition as far as I know, at any rate no scientific expedition, has yet landed on these islands. Several reports from captains, notably one from one of the whalers that we have just left, are to the effect that Bridgmann Island is in full eruption, so that it is interesting to try and land there. At 7.30 Gourdon, Godfroy and two men start off in the dinghy and succeed in getting ashore on a little beach to the south-east, somewhat sheltered from the swell prevailing at the moment. During this time we take a sounding, which gives 328 fathoms. On the beach, the only spot on the island where the shore does not rise up in cliffs or in high steep rocks, Gourdon saw some thirty seals,

---

[1] We have learnt since that, while at Petermann we had a troublesome but comparatively warm winter, in the South Orkneys, on the contrary, the cold was very severe.

a few Adelie and *Papua* penguins, some terns and sheathbills.
He did not discover the slightest trace of present volcanic
activity, but numerous proofs of comparatively recent activity. We reached the same conclusion while making a circuit of the island as close as it is safe to go. It is clear,
as often happens, that the ' smoke ' and ' vapours ' mentioned as proof of volcanic activity, were nothing but piles of
dust raised by the wind, clouds clinging to the summit or even
snowdrifts. A few years ago, at Jan Mayen Island, we had to
penetrate right into a blown-out crater before we could persuade ourselves that it was really dust and not smoke that was
coming out of it. This rugged, barren and almost snowless
island is a curious sight as it rises in isolation from the midst
of the sea, tinted by the brick-red tufa and yellowish scoriae.
We take numerous photographs of it, of which one notably
proves not only the skill of the artist accompanying Dumont
d'Urville, whose picture is before our eyes, but also that there
has been no change of shape since the passage of the *Astrolabe*
and the *Zélée*.

Since Joinville Island is beyond our reach, I decide to turn
back to Admiralty Bay, the refuge of the old-time sealers,
which was of recent years, and may be again, a whaling station.
Apart from the physical and natural history observations we
shall be able to make there, it may be interesting to make a more
minute and exact survey than those engaged in these commercial undertakings have yet succeeded in getting. In still
magnificent weather, which allows Bongrain to take bearings
of the land and outlines of the coast, we skirt the south of St.
George Island, and at 4.30 p.m. we reach Admiralty Bay.

The end of this huge bay, which is a kind of arm of the sea
open to the south-east, splits into two profound culs-de-sac,
clear-cut and picturesque, and walled in by glaciers and steep
mountains. The north-western branch is itself divided into
two narrow channels by a high island. At present, we penetrate into the north-eastern branch. The ice-blocks which

have come from the cliffs are rather numerous but give way before us, driven by the north-east wind, which is beginning to blow pretty strong. We look for an anchorage, and first of all, at a distance of scarcely 50 metres from a big beach, the slope of which we hoped to see stretching down gently toward the sea, we sound and find 150 metres of water. At length at the end of the cul-de-sac, in a very sheltered spot, we find at the foot of the glacier a muddy bottom with good holding, varying in depth from 7 to 20 metres ; and we anchor over 10.

We can have our supper in peace, and our cardboard Christmas tree, which has been in its box since last year, is brought out again and decorated with all its little knick-knacks, to the delight of the men.

December 25.—Christmas-Day, the season of memories, of thoughts which go afar and strive to imagine what is happening beyond the seas. Here the north-easter has started again, and the weather is grey and cloudy. We all of us land at places which interest us, to go on with our usual work.

There is a curious sound to be heard, which is singularly like the siren of a distant ship. We had already heard it at Pendulum Cove, but although I am convinced that it is produced on board, we cannot discover its origin. So strong is the illusion that the crew several times come to insist that there is a ship in distress and ask me to go to her assistance. No amount of reasoning can convince them of their error, and in the end I send some of them on shore, and these, hearing nothing, while the sound persists on board, finally return converted.

December 26.—The weather has become fine again, and while Bongrain and Boland go from point to point in a Norwegian boat surveying, I start out in the ship for the Bay, properly so-called.

Gourdon and Senouque have landed on a beach on the east coast, and Gain on the west coast, close to a rookery where he found more than 20,000 *Papua* Penguins. We in the *Pourquoi-*

Pas ? make a series of soundings and a good dredge at a depth of 400 metres. At the end of the day we take on board all our comrades and return to our anchorage, after leaving the Christmas tree on a point where it stands up proudly—waiting for the wind to knock it over.

We have left the north-eastern cul-de-sac to go into the north-western. The wind is at first very strong from the north-west, but soon veers to the east-north-east, blowing in very big gusts. This portion of Admiralty Bay is especially picturesque, with lofty black-hued mountains, bare of snow and standing between majestic glaciers. A big high island, also almost totally devoid of snow, occupies as I have said the centre of this branch of the bay, the bottom of which ends in two rounded coves, bordered by high glaciers and separated by a tall rocky promontory. The beaches are fairly numerous, and the corpses of whales in large numbers bear witness that whalers formerly worked there. We make a dredge over about 60 metres and the dynamometer shows from the start either that the trawl-net is caught or that it contains a heavy weight. Almost the whole day is spent in bringing it up. As soon as it begins to come out of the water we see that the netting is full, not only of animals, but of mud, gravel and rock. At all costs, we wish to save the contents and, if it is possible, the net itself.

We hoist it with difficulty, taking infinite precautions. To diminish the enormous weight, we water it with the hose, thus washing away a lot of the mud, and when with the help of a series of slings we have got it a little way out of the sea, I send under it the big canoe, into which the trawl-net is allowed to fall. The boat almost sinks under the weight, but our fine harvest is saved, and promises work for the laboratory.

We anchor 300 metres from the island in 25 metres of water, and Gourdon, going out in the Norwegian boat, comes back loaded with interesting mineralogical specimens and some fine crystals.

December 30.—We have just had here a formidable gale
from the east-north-east. The water of the channel, uplifted
in powdery spray by the gusts, covered the ship. We dragged a
little, but the anchor held in the end, when the ship was overlapping the end of the island. Here the gusts attacked us
from both sides at once and the unfortunate ship could not tell
which shore to avoid. However, we could not complain much,
for the spot where we were was the best sheltered in this part
of Admiralty Bay, and moreover our chain seemed somewhat
eased by the current, which ran against the wind. We barely
managed, during the lulls, to save the precious contents of the
dredger, entrusted to the big canoe ; and we also made some
very fruitful trips, our geologist in particular being enchanted
with his sojourn.

At 1.30, as the weather had a better appearance, we got
under way, and at 2 o'clock we were en route for the sea,
making surveys and taking soundings as we steamed along.
At 5.30 we were outside the bay, feeling after we had turned
the rocks on which the *Telefon* was wrecked, a fairly strong
swell from the east, but no wind. During the evening, however,
the wind began to blow from the north-west, bringing a thick
fog. Still, we were able to ascertain, by passing very close
to its supposed site, that ' Middle Island ' no longer exists.
Already as we made our way toward Joinville Land, it seemed to
us that what might have been taken for an island was nothing
else than a promontory of Greenwich Island. Now we have
certain corroboration of the assertions of the Nordenskjöld
Expedition that this island must be finally erased from the
map. I do not know who was the first to mark it, but it is to
be found notably on George Powell's map, dated 1882,[1] while
Bellingshausen in 1821 did not put it on his.[2] Dumont
d'Urville, Nordenskjöld also, and finally the whalers asserted
that it has no existence. In spite of these assertions, however,
it continued for some unknown reason to figure enormously

[1] *Antarctica*, loc. cit. p. 96.　　[2] *Atlas de Bellingshausen.*

large on the most recent edition of the English Admiralty Chart.

December 31.—North-east wind, fog and rain, which do not prevent us from sounding. At length there is a slight break which allows us to make the land at Deception Island and in the evening to take up our anchorage at Pendulum Cove.

January 6, 1910.—Before our departure to the South Shetlands M. Andresen led me to hope that he could give us, if we called again, another 30 tons of coal. Unfortunately, in taking stock of his bunkers, he found that he could not spare them. This is rather a blow, but I cannot regret the expenditure of these last few days, so fruitful have the results of our last trip been.

The 1st of January has been celebrated in our various ways, and the Norwegians, after having taken 24 hours of complete rest, have never ceased firing their guns, whose sound has echoed all over the island. We have been detained here afresh by frightfully bad weather. This time the wind has blown a little from all directions, varying from the south-west, to the north-west, then to the north-east, to settle down at last in the north-west. In spite of our two anchors we have been blown outside Pendulum Cove, and we found ourselves therefore dangerously near to the shore in a rather heavy sea. We could only keep our place by having the engine at work.

This morning it was calm and in spite of the fog and an abundant snowfall, we got under way. After giving a few casks of spirit in passing to the *Gobernador Bories*, and embarking ourselves a hogshead of oil, I shake hands for the last time with these amiable people and at 10.30 we leave Deception Island.

I consider that the possibility of taking a fresh stock of coal at Deception Island was one of the principal causes of the success of the expedition. We owe it to the extreme kindness of Andresen and the great generosity of the Magellan Whaling Company. Our fellow countrymen MM. Blanchard and Detaille, who live at Punta Arenas, and who are important shareholders in this Company, managed to interest their colleagues in our work. Let me assure them once more of my sincere and profound gratitude.

The south-wester has arisen and blows pretty hard, rather stopping our way, but it scatters the fog and snow, and we see all the neighbouring islands at once, Smith, Low, Hoseason, Brabant, Gand, etc. We eat our 'Twelfth Night' cake, in which for the bean we substitute a pebble picked up on Alexander I Land.

January 7.—The wind continues to blow strongly from the south-west, that is to say, straight ahead, but the weather is clear, there being mist only on land. It has been a hard night, not so much on account of the strength of the wind, but because the choppy sea tosses the ship a lot. We scarcely make 9 knots. In the afternoon, to save coal, and spare the engine, which is working hard without much profit, I set the sails and lay the ship to. Gourdon and I were the only ones at lunch.

January 8.—About 11 o'clock last night, the wind fell completely and then, after a little fog, the north-easter began to blow, while the barometer went down. Snow fell, the weather was thick and the thermometer marked $+1°$. The sea rapidly became rough, the wind was behind us, and we stood for the south-west with all the sail we could carry and the engine at rest. By chance we found ourselves almost at the same spot where the *Français* was the same day five years ago, but the gale from the north-east was then much stronger, and instead of flying before it we were struggling hard against it.

At 9 o'clock the wind calmed down, and I stood in a little more for the south and set the engine to work.

The sufferers are still rather numerous in the ward-room, but nevertheless, after dinner, I had a game of dominoes with Godfroy, Gain and Liouville. We had to go in for regular gymnastics in order not to lose our dominoes.

January 9.—Fog and calm during the night, compelling us to go slow. In the morning the north-easter begins to blow again with its usual accompaniment of mist and soon turns to a gale. Rouch has nevertheless succeeded in taking good soundings, but in bringing up the wire again in the very heavy sea, we lost 1,200 metres of it, and we have also lost, on the same day, two registering-logs.

We intentionally keep out well from the coast in order not to travel over ground already covered. Around us are flying numerous albatrosses, admiral-birds, mollymauks and Cape-pigeons. We are again using sail alone, and the ship, with a good list on, is rolling less.

January 10.—The north-easter still blows as hard, with snow, fog, and drizzle. If one could see a little further in front of one, I should consider the weather fine, since we are making good progress, but we have to keep a most careful look-out. At 3.30, I see to port through the fog, the bluish shape of an iceberg against the grey sky, and then we meet a whole quantity of brash-ice, and lastly, abundant drift-ice, followed by apparently very dense pack. Unfortunately, we can see so little in front of us that it is difficult to know what to do about this ice, and for the present we must content ourselves with skirting it. At 4 o'clock, finding ourselves in a kind of porridge of ice, we stop and, taking a sounding, we find 455 metres. We should be in 69° S. Lat. ; another ten miles and we shall have beaten Evensen's furthest latitude. In clear weather we ought to have had an interesting view of Alexander I Land.

January 11.—I am unwilling to leave this neighbourhood without taking advantage of a break in the weather to have a look about us, and I heave to the ship under light canvas. I am expecting, indeed, after this north-east gale at least a few hours of clear weather and I have told my colleagues, who nevertheless look sceptical. We remain thus gently balanced in the midst of the mass of small ice, under a never ceasing snow-fall, which covers the ship with a pretty white mantle but makes the deck dangerously slippery. Quite close at hand, through the imposing silence of the night, I hear the crashing collisions of the ice tossed by the swell, producing a sound like the distant murmur of a great city at the bottom of a valley. It is the voice of the Antarctic, which, too, can be sweet.

In the morning a few brief rifts which I was expecting appear. From the height of the crow's-nest, I seem to see something strange in the south-east. Is it an iceberg, or is it something else which I cannot venture to describe? I say nothing about it to any one, so afraid am I of being mistaken, and once again the horizon is hidden. Taking advantage of the calm and to disguise my impatience, which is getting actually painful, I have the dinghy manned and in several trips she brings back about a ton of iceberg-débris, which we turn into the boiler for making water. At last, at noon, the weather completely clears up, and I examine the horizon anxiously. Far off in the pack-ice there appears Alexander I Land at a new angle, which allows Bongrain to complete his map ; but nearer at hand, I find again what I saw in the morning, and my conviction is complete. Nevertheless, I will speak of it to no one before acquiring absolute and indisputable certainty. I restart the engine and to every one's great astonishment, contrary to previous orders, I steer for the east. I overhear even a few small criticisms, which might have been well founded, though now they only make me smile. I hurry over lunch in order not to excite any one's attention, and I climb up into the crow's-nest again with my field-glasses. All doubts are gone. Those are not icebergs which lift their pointed summits to the sky ; it is a land, a new land, a land to be seen clearly with the naked eye, a land which belongs to us ! It is necessary to have lived through these months of waiting and anxiety, of fear of failure, of desire to do something, of eagerness to take back to one's country something important, to understand all that is conveyed by these two words, which I repeat to myself under my breath, a *New Land!* I call up Bongrain to the topgallant mast and hand him my glasses, asking him not to say aloud what he is going to see. He utters but one word, ' Oh ! '

We go ahead and now I can announce my discovery, which brings almost everybody with a bound on deck. We make out two high mountainous masses, from which emerge the black rocks and between them a smaller mass, just like Adelaide Island or Alexander I Land, springing from a large cap of ice, which seems to extend very far east and west, though sharply separated from Alexander I Land, south of which it lies. It appears to me that there are some high peaks on the horizon, passing behind Alexander I Land in the direction of Fallières Land ; but not being absolutely certain, I prefer not to have them marked on the map.

My conviction therefore is that Fallières Land continues westward, either in the shape of land or at least as an archipelago, and our soundings in addition to those of De Gerlache (who did not see these lands, since he entered into the ice field further west) might have caused this to be suspected. The fine weather allows us to take observations and to place our discovery in Long. 77° W. and Lat. 70° S.

We have little chance of being able to reach these lands, but I cannot resist the desire of approaching them, and we hurl ourselves into the pack-ice, once more forgetting the injury to our bows. The pack is composed of such big and thick floes, soldered together by an icy mixture, that we cannot even shift them, and in spite of sail and steam combined, we only make 20 metres in the hour. After four hours of this disheartening progress, which wears the boat enormously, we sight a Ross's Seal on the ice. This is a variety lacking in our collection ; at all costs we must have it. Liouville, Godfroy and Jabet, armed with guns, post themselves on the bow and pour a volley at the poor beast at 30 metres. We go to fetch it with a Norwegian boat, hauled over the ice to bring it in,

but we are obliged to abandon another seal of the same kind
which is so far off that the ship, already solidly wedged in the
ice, cannot approach it.

It is useless to persist in our attempt to push forward. With
the greatest difficulty, still under sail and steam, while the
crew push with all their united strength to part the ice with
poles, we seek to regain the edge of the pack. At one moment,
while the ship is among huge icebergs, which roll in the swell,
she grounds on the base of a berg. We dare not use our
engine for fear of smashing our screw, and it is only after
an hour's work with our poles that we rescue ourselves from
our dangerous position.

At last we get into more open sea, and we follow westward
the edge of the pack-ice, while the mist again hides our
discovery from us.[1]

[1] On my return to France, in perusing an interesting work published during
my absence by the learned American geographer, Edwin Swift Balch, I was dis-
agreeably surprised, I must confess, to find on the map of the Antarctic, to the
south-west of Alexander Land, a little island marked Smiley. Although this island
was notably further south than the land which we discovered, and although the
name Smiley was accompanied by a ?, I was justified in fearing that Mr. E. S.
Balch had, during our expedition, found a document bearing witness to this discovery by the American whale-man, of which I was consequently ignorant. I
was quite ready to bow to facts, without a struggle, and I should have been con-
soled by confirming Smiley's discovery. I wrote to this effect to Mr. E. S. Balch,
who, with his accustomed kindness and perfect impartiality answered in a letter
from which I think I should, in view of the undisputed authority of the signatory,
quote the following passage, which sets things out clearly, and caused me to give
a sigh of relief :—

' There is not the smallest doubt that all your discoveries are yours and yours
alone. We know next to nothing of Smiley, simply what is quoted by Wilkes
and Maurey, which I mentioned in my *Antarctica*. I found Smiley Island on a
globe " made " by Gilman Joslin at Boston and " edited " by Charles Copley at
Washington in 1852. I marked this name on my map, because this part of the
Antarctic was then unknown to us. There might have been an island there. It
is clear that this is a mistake. If Smiley had been where you have been, there
would have been a coast marked, not an island. This mistake probably arose in
the following fashion. The cartographer must have had some vague information ;
he must have heard something about Smiley, and must have put down this island
somewhat at haphazard. Very possibly Smiley saw Alexander Land. The old
sealers sometimes went very far afield in pursuit of their accursed work of destruction of the poor fur-seals. Therefore you certainly have the right to say that
you are the first to see Charcot Land. I should like this land to be called thus, and
I hope that your companions have so christened the new discovery. In any case,

On the Edge of the Pack.

January 12.—We have followed the edge of the pack-ice all night, bringing us south of the 70th degree, which is a little record in latitude, in view of the longitude in which we are. What is most interesting is that our route, while a little more to the south, runs almost parallel to that of De Gerlache, so that our soundings thus add their value to his. We are also south of the course sailed by Bellingshausen. The pack-ice, at least in this particular region, stretches less further north than during the years 1821 and 1898.

The edge of the pack has some profound indentations, making the whole look like an enormous saw, but its general direction at the present moment is west. Its configuration makes it identically like what we found to seaward of Alexander I Land, and of our new land, and it is strewn with icebergs and ice-blocks which are also identical in number and character. I am persuaded that if we had been favoured by clear weather we should have seen still more lands. Unfortunately this is far from being the case. The north-easter has been blowing since morning, accompanied by snow squalls and fog, which oblige us to go as slowly as possible. In the afternoon the wind changes to north, moderate. Hoping for a rift, I stop, but in vain. We take the opportunity, however, to sound and to make two dredges, in which we succeed in bringing up, amongst other things, a few specimens of rock.

Wind north-east in the morning, with fog and very violent squalls of snow. We continue on our course, still following the pack-ice, of which we distinguish the edge standing out beneath the grey wall of fog like a vast kerb of white marble, marked out by icebergs rising up like superb pillars of the same

I shall write Charcot Land in all I may publish hereafter, and I have noticed that when a geographer has right in his favour, in the end he prevails.'

Others having supported Mr. E. S. Balch, I thought fit to yield to their amiable insistence, and it is under the name of Charcot Land that this region figures on the map accompanying this book ; but I wish it to be understood that it is the name of my father, Professor Charcot, who has done so much for French science, that is thus honoured, and not mine.

material. One or two detached bergs are floating out at sea. We cross as rapidly as our means allow, this region where the *Belgica* was a long time at sea, frozen up in the ice for the winter. The great indentations still persist, but the general direction is now north-west.

In the afternoon the wind blows feebly from the north-north-east, the sun shows himself for a while, and the horizon clears up in the offing, but the pack still remains enveloped in fog. About 2 o'clock we stop and begin a sweep of the horizon to adjust our compasses, but the sun hides himself again and stops us from finishing the operation. In the evening, the north-easter begins to blow again hard, and the sky grows heavy. Up to now we have been sheltered from the sea by the pack ; in fact we have hardly felt the swell, but now once more we begin to roll.

January 14.—The north-east wind is fairly strong all the morning and all day, accompanied by squalls of snow. It is a worthy sequel to the detestable winter which has caused us so much suffering. If it were not for the continuous daylight we should certainly not be able to guess in what month we are. We go on sounding as regularly as the circumstances of our navigation permit, and to-night about 9 o'clock, in spite of the swell and the wind, we have been able to pursue this operation successfully by putting ourselves to windward of two big ice-bergs. We found a depth of 3,030 metres, and in spite of the bad conditions, we have only lost 15 metres of our wire, which has, as unfortunately often happens, caught in the splintered wood of our damaged bows.

This navigation through the fog along the pack-ice is dreadfully monotonous. Birds, however, are fairly numerous, and a few whales are plunging around us, but we do not see a single Emperor Penguin, which is missing in our collection, though the *Belgica* found it in abundance. The pack seems to lead us now directly to the point where Bellingshausen placed Peter I Island. We are between the route of this navigator, which was considerably more to the north than ours, and the drift of the *Belgica*, which brought her about 1½° to the south of this island.

The icebergs are becoming more and more numerous. There are some superb ones, and as, in spite of the great quantity we have been permitted to see since our arrival in the Antarctic, we are not altogether *blasé* by their marvellous architecture, I pass quite close to a few to enable us to photograph them. The sea breaks on their bases with a dull roar, sometimes sending up its spray to a prodigious height, at other times invading their grottoes which re-echo and then empty themselves with a rumble like a torrent.

The mighty sea and the monstrous icebergs are playing their giant's games under the grey and lowering sky, caressing or fighting, and in the midst of these marvellous manifestations of nature, which are not made for man, we feel that we are merely tolerated, although a kind of intimacy may be created between us and our magnificent hosts.

About 5 p.m. there comes in sight an indescribable welter of these monsters of ice, some recumbent, others broken off as though after a great battle ; and to seaward, on all sides, others are grouped like spectators, or as though waiting their turn to enter the lists. As we climb higher in the mast to enlarge our view others and still others appear, surrounding us with a barrier which seems impassable.

In the fog which melts away two or three miles from us there appears suddenly an enormous black mass enveloped in clouds. It is Peter I Island, which was discovered by Bellingshausen and which we are the first to see since this great navigator. It was on January 11, 1821, that this island was discovered and for a number of years it and Alexander I Land remained the most southerly lands known in the Southern Hemisphere. Bellingshausen, who sighted it when coming from the south-west, and could not get near owing to the ice, assigned to it about nine miles in length, four miles in breadth, and 4,000 'feet' in height. The deplorable circumstances in which we found ourselves at the end of the day did not allow us to add anything to Bellingshausen's description. We can only, while confirming his discovery, admire the accuracy of the observations of this Russian Admiral at a period when navigating instruments were still so inaccurate.

The distance which separates us from Peter I Island is very slight and the drift ice very loose, but the icebergs on the other hand are numerous and closely packed. We attempt, nevertheless, to get nearer and push through the ice. Rouch tries to take a sounding, but the pieces of ice, swept about by the swell, cut his thread. Other soundings, taken later, at a distance of about six miles, give 1,400 metres without touching bottom, so that one can say, without exaggeration, that the island rises up out of the ocean-bed, especially as De Gerlache, $1\frac{1}{2}°$ south of it, found a depth of 1,148 metres.

The weather has become extremely threatening, the wind blowing in a tempest from the south-east, accompanied by fog and a storm of snow which hides everything. Our situation is getting dangerous, and we are menaced on all sides by the icebergs about us. We have not even the resource of lying to, we must try to get away at all costs and to escape from the ring which is closing in upon us.

We leave with heavy hearts, but in the imminent danger we have not time to give way to regrets. To-night has been frightful through the violence of the wind, the seas are gigantic, the rollers are beaten back by the icebergs, and the thick fog is made still worse by heavy squalls of snow.

We stand away from the land at first, taking the wind on the beam, and then as the sea becomes too heavy we let her go before the wind.

Under bare poles, with full steam up, so as to be able to steer quickly, we fly without even knowing where we are going and with no thought but how to avoid collision.

At first things go fairly well, the icebergs which we come across being large and far enough apart to give us time to manœuvre, but at the end of four hours icebergs and ice-blocks stud the boiling sea on every side. The men have to take the helm in turn at short intervals, so wearying is the constant manœuvring. I feel as if I was being hurried by an invisible torrent into a black gulf of which I cannot see the end. Without leaving the speaking-tube I shout out contradictory orders. We are steaming through a winding passage sown with huge blocks, which we must avoid at all costs. Out of the fog, as we gradually advance, there rise up icebergs and still more icebergs, and all idea of a plan vanishes in this heavy atmosphere, for we do not know even whether there will be a way open before us. Our anxiety gives place to a kind of intoxication ; we take no further heed of danger and our course, which the slightest shock or the slightest error of judgment might bring to ruin, becomes a game. Shall we get through or shall we not ? Ever the torrent leads us on. The high icebergs, whose walls our yards seem to touch, tower over us and the smaller ones dance in front of the ship. Like us and with us, the hours fly on and our mad course through the unknown continues. At this moment had the strangest of sights risen up before my eyes it would not have astonished me, but there is never anything except the white masses and walls emerging from the black background, growing larger, hurling the sea off in great waves, whose spray dashes over the ship, and then vanishing behind us.

All of a sudden before me the black gulf turns brilliant and golden, dazzling with light, adding to the fantastic strangeness of the scene, but giving the impression of an entry into paradise after leaving hell. This brightness is merely produced by the iceblink from a large sheet of drift-ice, and as soon as we penetrate amid the small ice the sea calms down, and the dull roar of the ice is like a restful silence after the crash of the waves breaking on the base of the icebergs.

We quickly get through this drift ice, and the storm still rages ; but the weather is brightening and the icebergs become fewer. I throw myself for a couple of hours on my berth, and when I awake I ask myself whether this strange voyage was not a dream.

January 15.—The wind still continues very strong and the temperature is at zero. The seas are tremendous, and the icebergs are still rather numerous but easy to avoid now the weather is clear. The engine is stopped and we go ahead with our sails only. In the evening we set the engine going and forge ahead with wind and sail to the west-south-west and then to the south-west.

January 16.—From midnight onward the wind has been blowing moderately from the south-east and soon the weather is radiantly clear. There are still a lot of icebergs, some of them very fine and large, but they are comparatively far apart and do not trouble us. We enjoy all these hours of sunshine the first for a long time, and we feel as if we had come out of a vault.

At noon the pack-ice lies before us, sprinkled with a large number of bergs. We are in Lat. 69° 12′.

We swing ship to adjust our compasses and take a sounding, which gives us a depth of 4,000 metres. The pack-ice runs in a huge point towards the north, continued by a collection of icebergs, and prolonged still further north by the iceblink, which we now know so well and which augurs nothing good.

At 4 p.m. a moderate wind rises from the north-east then veers to the north-west, bringing a fog which thickens until it prevents us from seeing further than 30 metres ahead. I limit the number of revolutions of the engine in such a way as to keep the ship stationary in the wind, merely steering her

The *Pourquoi-Pas?* charging a big Floe.

straight, and it is thus that we pass with the protection of Providence through the midst of dangers. From time to time a small block of ice appears suddenly before us, passes alongside, and as rapidly disappears. Occasionally it is a huge mass, one end of which is already hidden in the fog before we can see the other, and the silence is so impressive in the midst of this damp pall that we ourselves speak low. At last at 3 a.m. the curtain rises, and we discover that as we drifted we passed the icebergs at the northern end of the pack. All the rigging of the ship is encased in a shell of ice one or two centimetres thick, and it is absolutely impossible to make the ropes run.

Libois is tired out, and we are obliged to order him to sleep. Frachat very courageously offers to take his place in the stokehole, but as he is little accustomed to this work he will not be able to keep it up for long. Many of the crew are pale, for the severe winter has rather damaged all our healths. Godfroy especially begins to cause me anxiety again ; he looks dreadfully bad and drags himself along rather than walks. He will not complain but I know full well that he is attacked by scurvy again. As far as I am concerned, since we left Petermann my condition is always the same. I cannot make an effort without suffering from a stifling feeling and palpitation, and in climbing the mast, which I have to do more than twenty times a day, I have to take frequent rests ; but things have gone on like this up to now and since they are getting no worse, there is no reason for me to feel anxious about them.

January 17.—Moderate wind from the north-east to north-west, often very light. The thermometer at zero.

We are still skirting the edge of the pack-ice, which is very compact, and through which it would be practically impossible to navigate. Its contour causes several changes of route, but keeps us several miles south of the 69th degree.

Banks of fog are very frequent and prevent us from seeing the indentations in the pack, which is generally composed of small loose blocks of ice which we could easily get through and which would offer us some short cuts. The iceblink, however, despite the fog, gives us useful warnings. Like last night, for some hours we are enveloped in a thick fog, which is increased by an abundant fall of snow in thick white flakes. We are steaming through a fairly dense pack, without knowing much where we are going.

January 18.—The weather is foggy this morning and the winds light, between north and north-west ; but soon the sun shines out and the sky becomes very fine and clear to the south.

Our course has turned during the last few hours to the south-west. In the same latitude of 70° we have passed the longitude where Knox, captain of one of the ships in the Wilkes Expedition, was stopped by the ice on March 22, 1839. He narrated that he had seen, at this spot, a high impassable barrier, which impression I suppose must be attributed to a mirage. It was in the same longitude, but 50 miles further south, that the *Belgica* escaped from the pack after her long winter in 1899.

Frequently we have to navigate amid ice, violently cutting our way through. We are now in the longitude which the great English navigator, Cook, reached on January 30, 1774, 106° 54′ West of Greenwich, 71° 10′ South latitude, which remained the record for a long time. At the same place, we are stopped by the pack-ice in 70° 30′ South latitude. I think I may say that it would have been easy for us, pushing straight forward into the ice, to make some 60 miles, which would have allowed us to say that we had beaten Cook's latitude, but this small satisfaction would have cost us a lot of time and still more coal, and just as Bellingshausen voluntarily took Cook's course, judging it to be more profitable to science to continue eastward, so we in our turn voluntarily continued westward. It is interesting, nevertheless, to note that we found at the same spot as Cook a deep notch in the pack[r]; it was certainly not an ordinary indentation caused by the prevailing wind such as one meets on all the edges of these fields. My impression that land is not far off still continues, and I see another proof of this in the accumulation of icebergs and ice-blocks.

We stop to go alongside a huge fragment of iceberg, which I have moored to the ship. Some of the men get in the dinghy to break off pieces, which we take on board, and put into the pipe of the boiler for making fresh water. Finally, we let down the Prince of Monaco's vertical net to a depth of 1,000 metres, with one of the best results of our whole campaign. The table-bergs in the pack-ice are of colossal size, one of them in particular being certainly the biggest I have ever seen. This agrees well with Cook's description, for he was astonished at the size of the icebergs which he came across at this spot.

January 19.—This night the barometer went down a lot, the appearance of the weather grew bad, and the ship was tossed by a great swell. The gale thus heralded was not slow in making itself felt and began to blow immediately very strongly from the north-east. We were in a bad plight, for besides the very numerous icebergs to be looked out for, the pack-ice lay to leeward, sloping toward the north-east, far into the distance, as the iceblink only too plainly showed us. In the prevailing state of the sea it would have been disastrous to be driven into this moving pack-ice, composed of big thick floes and the remains of icebergs, so, cost what it might, we had to haul up. We succeeded in beating to windward under steam, but we were obliged to force our way through the heavy drift-ice and thus to encounter some big shocks, which made me tremble for our badly damaged bows, of which we are taking so little care. The presence of drift-ice, even in small quantity, always stops the sea from breaking, even during most violent storms, and makes big zones of calm, but it does not in any way check the swell, and the fragments which crash against one another are terrible foes for the ship that finds itself amongst them.

It seems that the pack-ice is in process of closing up at the entrance to the bay into which we succeed in penetrating, and when we get through the narrow channel, we find ourselves in free water but in the midst of a heavy and agitated sea. Happily the ship is behaving admirably, though it is evident that we cannot congratulate ourselves on being in a safe haven.

January 20.—The gale has gradually diminished in strength during the night, veering to the south-east after a succession of very short squalls of sleet. The barometer has gone up immediately, the thermometer falling to $-2°$. At 4 a.m. I set all sail and steer for the west. We are in 68° 32′ South lattitude, and we are thus crossing, at a speed of 8 knots, a region never yet explored. Cook indeed, to reach his high latitude, starting from the 64th degree, followed a course due south and then turned again straight north. Bellingshausen, and then Biscoe, coming from the west, stopped by the ice, were sailing, the first in 63° and 64° south latitude, the second in 65°. We are therefore more than 3° farther south than our predecessors, and soon we shall be able to go beyond the 69th degree.

The sea is good, but the icebergs are innumerable and increase in number as we gradually advance. For some days I have tried, merely when on the watch, to count them, but I have had to give it up after reaching, in 48 hours, the respectable figure of 5,000.

The coal question is beginning to worry me again. It is impossible to dream for a moment of navigation by sail alone in the midst of these icebergs, which are so thick that we are obliged every minute to alter our course to avoid them, and our stock is gradually giving out. We must keep a little, in view of the very long passage we have before us to return to civilization, and there is no possibility in this neighbourhood of taking in ballast to replace the weight gradually growing less as we burn the coal. I have put into the bottom of the hold all that I can, but I see nothing more to be moved. The general health also worries me, Godfroy looking worse and worse, though he persistently refrains from complaint and continues to discharge his duties, and many others having long faces. We ought to have some fresh meat, but in spite of all our efforts, we have not succeeded in capturing any of the seals which we see on the ice. We ought to have rest also for the invalids, and even among those who are in the best health there are only too evident symptoms of weariness. Nevertheless, I wish to push on, for we are in a totally unknown region of the greatest interest.

January 21.—Light winds from the south-south-east with a fine morning, a smooth sea, and a clear sky except on the horizon. At noon foggy and overcast, and then again up to 6 o'clock, fairly clear weather with a moderate wind from the south-south-east. The thermometer fell to $-3°$ at night, to rise to $+3°$ during the day.

During the whole of the night we steered south-west, and this morning from the crow's-nest, I see the pack-ice to starboard stretching as far as N. 10° E. Soon after it appears in front of us. We steer south and pass the 70th degree, being stopped again this time by the ice. We have therefore penetrated into a huge bay formed by the pack-ice. We have reached an unhoped-for latitude in this region and we push on. At last in the afternoon, in 118° 50′ West longitude, blocked by the ice, we stop and moor ourselves to a huge ice-block to get some fresh water in the usual way.

Meanwhile, Rouch sounds and finds only 1,040 metres, with a rocky bottom. There is, therefore, a big chance of land being not far from us, and perhaps in clearer weather we should see it! In any case, the pack-ice and icebergs are of the same character throughout, and the water is of the same colour. I have no doubt in my mind that land must be near, and this sounding, confirming those of De Gerlache further east and the discovery of our new land, seems to prove the junction of Fallières and Edward VII Lands. What would I not give to be here with my bunkers full of coal, an undamaged boat, and a healthy crew, at the beginning of a campaign!

At 6.15 we get under way, and not without some difficulty and a few heavy shocks, succeed in extricating ourselves from the ice which shuts us in the bay full of pack-ice.

January 22.—The weather is still fine and the wind constantly in the south. At midnight the sky was super band the sun set with half its disc above the horizon ; this is the half-sun of midnight.

With all sail set, making 8 knots, we steer west and then a little northward, following the general line of the pack. The icebergs, so far from diminishing in number, seem on the contrary as if they were increasing. At 2 o'clock I see from the masthead, which I scarcely ever leave, a long strip of drift-ice composed of extremely thick blocks and the pack-ice on the horizon running north-west.

We wish to stop and heave to to leeward of the strip of drift-ice, but the engine does not answer in time and the ship plunges into the big floes, some of which rise 5 metres above the level of the water, overhanging the sides of the ship. Fortunately they are composed of soft ice and we get free with ease. While Rouch takes a sounding of 2,310 metres without finding bottom, we try to kill some seals which are asleep on the ice, but our boats cannot push through the thick ice, and if we shot them from on board it would be useless slaughter.

To my great regret we must turn north ; there are too many arguments in favour of return. I had made up my mind to continue westward until we met the ice, and now it bars my way. I have long thought that if Bellingshausen and Biscoe were stopped so much farther north than we, it was by a floating ice-pack like that which must be crossed to reach Victoria Land ; but the very great quantity of icebergs we are meeting would argue in favour of one or two rather exceptional winters in this neighbourhood, of which we have been able to take advantage, and which, by dispersing a great portion of the pack, have thus set at liberty the icebergs it imprisoned. Nevertheless, if the first hypothesis were the true one, we should have still to struggle with the ice and the small amount of coal remaining to us would be indispensable for making our way through it.

It would be no use, however, giving way to barren regrets. During this second summer campaign, whose discoveries and observations have supplemented those of the first campaign and the winter season, we have reached 124° West longitude, navigating nearly all the time between the 69th and 70th degrees of latitude, sometimes even further south. In spite of the very bad conditions under which we have done this, there has been no accident, we have accomplished our programme, and we have done our best.

January 25.—We are making a good trip to Terra de Fuego. Since the 22nd we have been favoured by light winds, veering from the south-west to the east-south-east, bringing with them very fine clear weather, while the temperature remains between zero and 2°. In Lat. 67° we have to cut through a strip of rather thick pack-ice, extending east and west. Is this the pack-ice coming still further north, which must have stopped Bellingshausen ? The very closely crowded icebergs to the south are now scattered. There is a very distinct dividing line here, beyond which they gradually grow fewer and fewer. Since this morning we have not even seen one. We are making 8 knots with our sails. The swell is fairly strong, but the sun is shining and the whole crew is busy making the ship's toilet. Our stout ship is surely in a condition which may be called glorious, since it is the result of the fights she has been through ; but when we get back to civilization, I want her to be clean, so that it may be seen that, so far from wishing to pose as people who have been through much, we are striving to hide the traces of our struggles. All the paint is off the hull and the wood is bare, but in this respect we can do nothing for the moment. Within, the paint on the bulwarks and roofs is in a sad state, and we begin to scrape and clean it. Lastly we start to polish the little brasswork we have on board and soon our panel 'Honour and Country' blazes under the rays of the sun.

In 66° 15′ South latitude, and 118° West longitude, we hove to and sounded, finding a depth of 5,100 metres. There is, therefore, a profound depression here.

Now that we have definitely stood in for the north, Godfroy confesses to me what I suspected, that his legs have been very swollen for some ten days.

January 26.—Gale between west-south-west and west-north-west, with a sky now clear, now overcast, the temperature being + 5°. To tell the truth, it is the wind-gauge which enables me to say that we are going through a gale, for the ship carries herself so well that navigation is pleasant. We are making our 9 knots with sails alone. We leave on our starboard side an iceberg and some débris of ice. This is the first berg we have seen since yesterday, and perhaps it is our last. It is night now, 11 o'clock. The moon, which we have not been able to see for so long in the twenty-four hours of daylight, is now at her full and rises brilliant and superb, as though to wish us a safe return to the inhabited world.

January 29.—Since the 26th, we have certainly returned to the zone of west winds. We have had a strong gale from the west-south-west, with overcast weather and drizzle, which drove us ahead rapidly. The wind then veered to south-west by west, with some short clear-ups. To-day again the weather is very fine, with a moderate west-south-west wind. The sea is extremely heavy, but the *Pourquoi-Pas ?* troubles herself little about it, lifting herself admirably on the swell and making good progress. She seems to smell the stable !

Yesterday a shoal of dolphins accompanied the boat. Liouville recognized them as belonging to a species up to now not systematically described, but noticed, and very accurately drawn, by Dr. Wilson, the *Discovery's* zoologist, who also came across them in these southern seas.

The cleaning-up on board continues.

January 31.—The wind has calmed down for three days, veering to the north-west, and we have had to turn somewhat eastward, still making good progress under sail and steam.

The thermometer has gradually gone up to 8°. The barometer followed by going down, and we have come in for a strong gale between north-north-west and north-west, accompanied by rain and fog. There is a heavy sea abeam, but the ship still carries herself admirably, not taking on board a single drop of water and beating 9 knots with all her sails set except her topgallant. At this rate, we ought to enter Magellan Straits to-morrow.

February 1.—During the night, in a full gale, with all our sails set, we made our 10 knots, but unfortunately the wind increases in violence, and rain is reinforced by fog. We can no longer see further than 200 metres ahead. We reckon that we ought at 11 a.m. to be on the Evangelists, a rocky islet at the entrance to Magellan Straits, with a lighthouse on it. But at 10.30, the fog becomes so thick that it would be a folly to push on, and we needs must put about and try to keep away from the shore. The sea is tremendous, and our plight is very bad, for if the wind veers to the west, we are in danger of being hurled on to the coast. At 1 o'clock there is a break, and Bongrain is able to take a position-line. Almost at the same moment there appears through the fog the outline of a cliff, which ought to be Cape Pillar, and the wind veers to the west-north-west. Land is quite close and the current is rapidly driving us on to it. At all costs we must double Cape Pillar, and that is not easy in the sea and wind prevailing. I give orders for full steam ahead and to prepare to chock the valves. At the same time we set all possible sail, but a staysail is torn away as it is being hoisted. The coast emerges from the mantle of fog which envelops it and reveals itself close at hand, threatening and terrible, with the sea breaking on the Apostle Rocks. But the *Pourquoi-Pas ?* is a stout boat and little by little she gains on the wind, and at 4.30, with a sigh of relief, I head her for

301

Magellan Straits. At 7 o'clock we enter them and anchor
in Tuesday Bay. As a matter of fact, to-day is Tuesday.

We have made a superb passage, taking ten days to come
from the ice-pack to here. To-night I at last undress and go
to bed. The second French Antarctic Expedition is at an end.
If we have invalids on board, still, thank Heaven, no one is
absent at the muster.

And now, in a few days time, what shall we hear at Punta
Arenas, where our letters are awaiting us ? At the other end
of the telegraph, which will put us in a few hours in communication with our families, what will be the answer to my despatch ?
I left my home and happiness of my own free will to do what I
considered my duty. What shall I find on my return ?

What I feel for myself, I feel also for the twenty-nine others
with me. And now that the great effort has been made I
ask myself if it was worth all the sorrow which accompanied
our absence, and if I had really a right and a call to cause such
sorrows. But my eyes turn to the motto on the poop-
deck which, although false shame would not let us confess it,
has spurred on and supported us all through this expedition,
and up to where, standing out against the sky and flapping
in the wind, our ship's ensign answers me, *Pourquoi-Pas ?*
(Why not ?).

I decided, for the sake of the men's health, not to go to
Punta Arenas until we had rested and recovered ourselves a little
in Magellan Straits, where we could find a sufficiency of game and
fresh fish. Tuesday Bay seemed an excellent spot to me, but
the violence of the gusts, the great depth, and the bad holding
necessitated so many moves that I was obliged to go and moor
in the excellent little roadstead of Puerto Gallante. We found
there an Austrian and a Chilian, who barter goods with the
Fuegians and who were able to give us fresh meat, eggs and
salad.

On February 11 we reached Punta Arenas. The steam
launch *Laurita* was awaiting us in the roadstead, bringing on

board all our friends who came, 14 months ago, to wish us good voyage ; but one, alas ! was lacking, Père Poivre, whose brave life, so full of smiles and kindness, had come to an end.

In this Chilian town we had a charming welcome. Our consul, M. Blanchard, whose friendship is a pleasure and an honour, threw open his house to us and gave us a foretaste of home life, justifying once more his reputation for kindness and generosity. The Governor, M. Chaigneau, proved to us that a high Chilian official's protestations of friendship are no mere words. We spent some charming days there with our good friends, MM. Detaille, Adriasola, Rocca, Beaulier, Bonvalot, Grossi, Baylac and so many others. The little French colony fêted us as on our way out, vieing with the rest of the town to make us feel at home. Punta Arenas will remain unforgettable in all our hearts.

Telegrams of congratulation from all quarters of the world showed us that our labours were appreciated and known. Although I had thought that I had done no more than my best, I had now to persuade myself that we had done well ; but once more I refer the credit to my companions.

A few weeks later we reached Montevideo, where we were obliged to make a long stay. We got such a welcome there that we did not regret it. As we entered the harbour, the English cruiser *Amethyst*, Captain Webb, signalled to us ' Congratulations and welcome,' and the compatriots of Captain Scott and Sir E. Shackleton proved to us that the *entente cordiale* had lost nothing in our absence. Antonio Lussich and his cousin, the directors of the great Lifeboat Society, to whom humanity and the mercantile marine owe so much, and whose acquaintance I had the pleasure of making seven years ago, when the *Français* was here, with Dr. Visca, a pupil of my father's, received us with such generosity and cordiality that an indissoluble tie of friendship and gratitude was formed. The condition of the *Pourquoi-Pas ?* called for immediate repairs, about which I worried myself needlessly ; for I had a

visit from M. A. Amiot, engineering director of the French
Montevideo Company, who put at our disposal the great
resources of his company—a company whose admirable work
does the greatest honour to our country, and especially to the
Director M. Sillard (since become a friend whom I cannot forget) and to the engineers, MM. Caubois, Plazonich, and Muller.
A few months later M. Amiot succumbed in the middle of his
work. His memory is ineffaceable ; well placed with his
colleagues in charge of this great French enterprise, he was a
type of intelligent energy, one who knew how to hide under an
affectation of brusqueness his enthusiasm and good heart.
He has gone, but his memory will remain with us.

Thanks to the generosity and activity of our fellow-countrymen of the French Montevideo Company, and of A. Lussich,
the *Pourquoi-Pas ?* left the harbour in good repair and as
smart as a yacht and made her way to Rio de Janeiro.

Already in Montevideo the reception we got from M. de
Lisboa, Brazilian Minister to Uruguay, gave us a foretaste of
the welcome awaiting us in the great South American republic,
but it surpassed all our expectations. Our friend, M. Boudet,
French Consul, and all the kindly French colony in Brazil,
received us with open arms. Captain Barros Cobra, from the
first an enthusiastic supporter of the Expedition, did his best,
together with the inhabitants and the government of this great
and generous country, to make us forget that we were being
awaited with impatience in France. At Pernambuco, the
authorities, our friend Sanpiao Feraz, and the port engineers,
MM. Barbière, Beraud, Rouberol and Baudin took care that
our last stop in South America should not leave us with the
least pleasant memory.

Our trip from this port to the Azores, along the sailing
vessels' route to Europe, was long and tedious, but at Punta
Deldada the reception prepared for us by the Governor, M.
Luis Bettencourt de Medeiros e Comara, Commandant Alfonso
Chaves, and our Vice-consul, M. A. Ferin, quickly made us

forget it. Portugal, who reckons among her glories the greatest explorers in the world, kindly welcomed, at their first stop in an European port, the humble French explorers.

I could not forget the little port of St. Pierre, Guernsey, that refuge which we had had no cause to regret during the tempest which assailed us as we left France. So at this island, where we were sure to find a hearty welcome, I wished to have the *Pourquoi-Pas ?* cleaned and re-painted, that she might reach France after her arduous labours, trim and neat. After about two years' absence, I met my family again and in a few minutes the toils and anxieties were effaced as though by magic.

June 4, 1910.—At 10 o'clock yesterday evening in Havre roadstead, we exchanged the ordinary signals with the pilot, who came on board at once, and at 11 we were anchored, awaiting the tide. Our anchor, for the first time for two years, was fixed in French soil. At 4 a.m. we get under way. Chance has it that I am on the last sea watch of the Expedition. It is grey weather and a small fine rain is falling. I see Trouville, the charming coast of Vilerville, and then Honfleur, the picturesque little old town with its grey houses where the presence of a steamer seems an anachronism. The great grass meadows over which the cattle are grazing spread themselves out before me, and then the wooded hillsides with their restful verdure, the chateaux, the villas, the coquettish farms. The sun now drives away the rain and the bright patches of field flowers and clumps of fruit-trees enamel the green plain, through which the waters of the river cut a channel. We are penetrating into the heart of France. Nature herself is elegant, and man's work in the erection of the humblest buildings has but given an additional touch of charm to her grace. A bend of the Seine hides from us the sea, our home for so many long months. We push further and further through this ideal countryside, the most beautiful in the world. It sets the heart beating, not with that violence of anguish which extorts a cry, but with a sigh of pure enjoyment of perfection.

My eyes have just ceased contemplating the noble and unforgettable spectacle of the Antarctic's dreaded pack-ice, the cliffs and magnificently savage mountains of Magellan Straits, the wonderful scenery of Rio Bay, the splendours of tropical vegetation, the smiling Azores, but now it is really *La doulce France*, our beautiful country ; and we are entering her by the road which should naturally lead to great cities, the homes of art and science, where courage is gay and labour smiles.

On this morning of our return, in my solitary watch on the bridge of the *Pourquoi-Pas ?*, which has just crossed the whole breadth of the world, I felt more than ever how beautiful is our France, how she deserves to be loved and to be served at the price even of the greatest sacrifices. With a smile she has amply repaid me for all my toil.

8 o'clock.—The ensign rises slowly to the gaff. The sailor who hoists it must feel like myself. The blue, white and red unfold themselves and flap in the breeze, giving a finishing touch to the wonderful scenery, which seems to light up with a new gleam. Mechanically, standing all alone, I uncover my head in honour of this emblem. To the devil with reasoning and researches into the why of our feelings, and with the excuses which false shame makes for our actions ! It is our country, and that is enough !

We anchor at Duclair. Only the families of my companions have been apprised of this stoppage, which I do not wish public, so that, away from the crowd and official receptions, amid the peace of this charming little corner of the world, they may take to their arms those who have passed so many months of anxiety and fear.

At last, on June 5, at 2 o'clock precisely, the *Pourquoi-Pas ?* escorted by two torpedo boats sent to meet her by Admiral Boué de la Peyrère, Minister of Marine [1] (whom I can never thank sufficiently for his benevolent interest), by numerous

---

[1] Admiral Boué de la Peyrère, then in command of the Atlantic Fleet, had been the first to welcome the *Français* on her return to Buenos Aires in 1905.

yachts and excursion-steamers, reached Rouen. In our journey up the Seine every village, and every gaily decorated house echoed with cries of welcome, but the magnificent reception which Rouen reserved for us was unexpected, and will never be forgotten by us. We felt the movement of the hearts of the whole population of this beautiful and famous town, which by its enthusiastic emotion proved that it knew how to appreciate disinterested scientific work and to reward the efforts of those engaged in it.

This fête, which touched us deeply, was organized by the Norman Geographical Society. Let me here express my profound gratitude to MM. Leblond and Monflier, President and General Secretary of the Society.

The Government was represented by Admiral Fournier, the Minister of Foreign Affairs by M. Pavie, the Minister of Public Instruction by M. Rabot, the Minister of Marine by Lieutenant Dumesnil, the Museum by Professor Joubin, H.S.H. the Prince of Monaco by Lieutenant Bourrée, the Paris Geographical Society by M. Margerie, and the Oceanographical Institute by M. Meyer, who handed us a magnificent medal in the name of the Institute. The very choice of these representatives, teachers, savants and friends who worked so hard for the organization of the expedition, proved to us once more the sympathy which it was desired to show us.[1]

M. Paul Doumer, the father of the Expedition, President of its Committee of Organization, who was the last to wish me a safe voyage as we left Havre, was the first to welcome me at Rouen, and as he shook my hand he assured me that he did not regret the interest that he had never ceased to take in us all through. Admiral Fournier presented to the whole crew, on

[1] I cannot bring this book to an end without giving an assurance of my affectionate gratitude to my masters and friends, MM. Joubin and Rabot, who, near and far alike, were, with M. G. Deschamps and C. Boyn, the illustrious supporters of the Expedition and its leader, and who watched over its interests in a spirit of that precious friendship which I have put to the test for so many years.

behalf of the Government, medals of honour, which deservedly adorned the brave fellows' breasts.

The mission was received by M. Leblond, Deputy and Mayor of Rouen, supported by the whole Municipality, at the Hôtel de Ville, and then at the Geographical Society, and lastly, at a magnificent banquet in the Chamber of Commerce by Senator Waddington, President of the Chamber, who presented to me a magnificent medal in memory of the day.

Next day, on its arrival in Paris, the mission was received afresh at the station by M. Bayet, Superintendent of Higher Education, representing the Minister of Public Instruction, Professor Edmond Perrier, Member of the Institute and Governor of the Museum, and H.I.H. Prince Roland Bonaparte, Member of the Institute and President of the Geographical Society.

And now the *Pourquoi-Pas ?* is resting at Rouen amid the greenery of the pretty yacht-harbour, whose constructor, M. Depeaux has kindly given her hospitality. Her hull is still all covered with the glorious scars of the fight she carried through to victory, but she is ready to take again her mark of interrogation into the region of the unknown and to face fatigues and dangers for the honour of French Science.

INDEX

INDEX

INDEX

INDEX

INDEX

INDEX

RABOT, Ch., 6, 10, 171, 307
Rabot Island, 84
Rallier-du-Baty Channel, 251, 252
Rats, 128, 180
Raun, 31–33, 46
Rey, 61
Reynolds, J. N., 85
Rio Branco, Baron, 26
Rio de Janeiro, 25, 304
Riou, Monseigneur, 10
Robert, 216
Rocca, 29, 303
Roosen Channel, 44, 53–55, 252
Rosetti, Chief Engineer Sumblad, 26
Ross Barrier, 17, 113, 214
Ross, James, 1, 3, 41, 54
Ross Land, 2
Ross Sea, 2
Ross's Seal, 156, 285
Rosselin, F., 23, 169, 183, 187, 195, 201, 202, 205, 214, 238, 246, 257, 274
Rouch, J., 22, 43, 48, 55, 58, 59, 77, 78, 116, 142, 145, 153, 159, 161, 184, 188, 191, 194, 215, 216, 238, 273, 274, 283, 290, 297, 298
Rouen, 307
Rouvre, Captain, 272, 273

SAIL Rock, 265
St. George Channel, 277
Salpetrière Bay, 65, 240, 251
Scholaert Channel, 53–55
Scotia, 2
Scott, Captain, 2, 3, 8, 17, 212, 303
Sea Gull, 38
Sea-leopards, 124, 154, 155, 178
Seals, 124, 155
Senouque, A., 22, 43, 56, 59, 78, 102, 110, 113, 153, 159, 165, 169, 181, 206, 212, 215, 222, 224–227, 229, 232, 234, 265, 273, 278
Shackleton, Sir Ernest, 2–4, 8, 254, 303
Sheffield, Captain James P., 34, 35
Sillard, M., 304
Skelton, 17
Smiley, Captain W. H., 39, 52, 286
Smith Island, 31, 53, 282
Smith, W., 34, 37

Snow Hill, 275
Sobroan Harbour, 43
Sögen Island, 60, 64
Sola, Father, 26
Somerville, Crichton, 17, 50
South Orkney Islands, 3, 8, 46, 96, 252, 276
South Shetland Islands, 31, 34–37, 42, 46, 156, 236, 259, 281
Stolhani, Captain, 45, 261, 272
Svip, 273
Sydney Harbour, 37

Tegethoff expedition, 131
Telefon, 45, 253, 255–257, 259, 263, 265, 270, 274, 280
Terra de Fuego, 299
Thays, 26
'Thermos' bottles, 17
Thiébault, 26
Thomas, 23, 159, 188, 211, 221
Thomson, G., 6
Thrashers, 124
Toby, 64
Trinity Island, 35, 52, 91
Tuesday Bay, 302
Tula, 87
Two Hummocks Island, 55, 91, 252

Uruguay, 34, 38, 39, 43, 44, 54, 274
Ushaia, 30, 44

Valdivia, 54
Van Acken, 23
Van Drygalski, 2, 8
Vélain Peak, 92
'Venesta' cases, 20, 143
Victor Hugo Island, 82–84, 137, 138, 169
Victoria Land, 2–4, 298
Vimont, 16
Visca, Doctor, 303

WANDEL Island, 8, 42, 47, 51, 53, 54, 56, 57, 60, 61, 63, 67, 112, 123, 137, 140, 142, 148–150, 153, 154, 160, 169, 180, 189, 209, 220, 225, 236, 238, 239, 241, 247, 250–252, 257
Webb, Captain, 303
Webster, Doctor, 37, 38, 40
Weddell, 1

INDEX